LATIN AND GREEK TEXTS 6

M000306772

TIBULLUS: ELEGIES

TIBULLUS: ELEGIES

Introduction, Text, Translation and Notes

GUY LEE

THIRD EDITION
(including Book 3, Text and Translation)
revised in collaboration with
ROBERT MALTBY

FRANCIS CAIRNS

Published by Francis Cairns (Publications) Ltd
c/o The University, LEEDS, LS2 9JT, Great Britain

1st edition 1975, published by Guy Lee, St John's College, Cambridge
2nd edition, revised and expanded, 1982, published by Francis Cairns
Third edition, revised and expanded, 1990

Reprinted 1995

British Library Cataloguing in Publication Data

Tibullus, Albius
    Tibullus : elegies – (Latin and Greek texts ISSN
    0951-751) 3rd ed
    I. Title   II. Lee, Guy   III. Maltby, Robert
    871.01

    ISBN 0-905205-82-0

Printed in Great Britain by
Redwood Books, Trowbridge, Wiltshire

CONTENTS

Acknowledgements   vii
Introduction   ix

TEXT AND TRANSLATION

Book I   2
Book II   48
Book III   72
Epitaphium Tibulli and *Vita Tibulli*   106

Textual Note   109
Explanatory Notes   113
Chronological Guide   164
Select Bibliography   165

NOTE TO SECOND EDITION (1982)

For this second edition, undertaken at the kind request of Professor Francis Cairns, I have added notes to the Introduction; returned to the reading of the Ambrosian at 1.5.35; 8.53; 9.75; 10.64; 2.2.8; 3.5; 3.51; 5.36; altered the translation in some two dozen places (listed below); and much enlarged the Explanatory Notes and the Bibliography.

St John's College, Cambridge *A.G.L.*

Alterations to translation at:
Book I: 1.2; 5.35-36; 6.23 and 32-34; 8.15, 27 and 53; 9.40-44; 10.46-47
Book II: 2.13; 3.30, 35-38, 51-53, 58-59, 63-64, 67-68, 80; 4.28, 31-34, 36, 40-42; 5.34-36, 114-15; 6.37 and 44

NOTE TO THIRD EDITION

Copies of the second edition having run out while strong demand continued, a third edition has proved necessary. To produce it in time for the coming academical year we have jointly revised the second edition.

The reading has been altered at the following places:
Book One: 3.12 and 81-2; 5.30 and 47; 6.21 and 55; 7.14 and 27; 8.36; 9.40 and 48
Book Two: 2.17 and 21; 3.37 and 63; 5.35, 110 and 122.

The translation has been altered at:
Book One: 2.48 and 89-90; 3.11-12; 5.30 and 47-8; 6.39, 55-6 and 79; 8.35-6; 9.47-8
Book Two: 1.19; 2.17-18 and 21; 3.63 and 71.

Notes have been added, deleted, altered, or replaced at:
Book One: 2.48; 3.11-12 and 81-2; 5.30 and 47; 6.39-42 and 55-6; 7.27; 8.15 and 36
Book Two: 1.19-20; 2.17 and 21-2; 5.121-2.

In addition text and translation of Book 3 have been provided and the Bibliography enlarged.

A.G.L., St John's College, Cambridge
R.M., University of Leeds
May 1990

ACKNOWLEDGEMENTS

My thanks are due to Dr A. Paredi of the Biblioteca Ambrosiana for kind permission to base my text on the Ambrosian MS, and to Mr W.A. Camps for generously allowing me to make use of his unpublished commentary on Tibullus.

I also wish to thank the following, who have helped me in various ways: Mr J.A. Crook, Miss J.M. Gilmartin, Dr N.F.M. Henry, Miss P.D. Huskinson, Sir Joseph Hutchinson, Prof. H.H. Huxley, Prof. G. Luck, Mr R.E. Thoday, Prof. K.D. White, and above all Helen Lee.

St John's College, Cambridge

INTRODUCTION

The reader who comes to Tibullus from the love poetry of Ovid will be surprised to discover in parts of his work a distinctly Ovidian tone. The *Consultation with Priapus* (1.4) in which the grotesque fertility god treats the poet to a brief lecture on the art of pederasty in elegantly balanced couplets is evidently intended to shock and to amuse and its unexpected conclusion to raise a laugh or at any rate a smile. On the formal side also the fact that no fewer than forty of the poem's forty-two pentameters end in a word of two syllables, a proportion unparalleled in the first book of Propertius, the immediate predecessor of Tibullus's first collection — this fact only serves to strengthen the Ovidian impression made by the tone of the poem as a whole. Further, of the two exceptions to the disyllabic majority both in their different ways are justified by point. What is more, one of the two couplets concerned displays a feature without parallel in the whole of the output of Propertius, anticipating a device which is particularly associated with Ovid:

> Pieridas, pueri, doctos et amate poetas,
> aurea nec superent munera Pieridas.

> Love the Muses, O ye striplings, and the scholar poets,
> nor value gifts of gold above the Muses.

The structure of this couplet, with the Greek name of the Muses beginning the hexameter and ending the pentameter like an echo, is clearly meant to exemplify the poetic *doctrina* which the couplet itself explicitly recommends. Ovid in the *Amores* pushes this Tibullan idea[1] a stage further when he mints the analogous couplet:

> Militat omnis amans et habet sua castra Cupido:
> Attice, crede mihi, militat omnis amans.

> Lovers are soldiers all — in Cupid's private army.
> Atticus, take it from me — lovers are soldiers all.

But when Tibullus published his first collection in 27 or 26 BC, Ovid was a youth of sixteen, still attending the lectures of Porcius Latro and Arellius Fuscus in the school of rhetoric. It follows therefore that what we have called the Ovidian tone originates in

Latin poetry with Tibullus. The wit, the grace, the easy and natural flow, the subdivision of the elegiac couplet into smaller self-contained units, sometimes as many as four, the predominance of the disyllabic ending to the pentameter, the relatively frequent enjambment or running on of the hexameter into the first or second foot of the pentameter — all these Ovidian features are already present in the elegiacs of Tibullus, who should accordingly be regarded as an important metrical innovator.[2] Ovid was aware of his debt and repaid it at the age of twenty-four by writing a fine funeral elegy on the death of his master.

But the Ovidian tone, in the sense of light wit and elegance of manner, is only a part of what this nowadays much underrated poet has to offer. Though always 'polished and discriminating', *tersus atque elegans* (the words of Quintilian, who regards him as the best of the Latin elegists), Tibullus is more often serious than the Ovid of the amatory poems. He expresses, I believe, a wider range of feeling: humour and high spirits on occasion, as we have seen, but nostalgia too and melancholy, tenderness (his favourite adjective is *tener*) and compassion, fear, hatred, admiration, reverence —the list is incomplete; enough to say that if Propertius is the poet of passion and Ovid of wit, Tibullus is the poet of feeling. Granted that such labels are over-simplifications likely to mislead, that it is impossible to pin down any poet with a single blunt word, still they may serve perhaps as provisional pointers, aids to the sorting out of inarticulate impressions.

Three examples may help to make clearer something of the quality I am trying to express. First, Tibullan melancholy:

> Ibitis Aegaeas sine me, Messalla, per undas,
> o utinam memores ipse cohorsque mei!
> me tenet ignotis aegrum Phaeacia terris,
> abstineas auidas Mors modo nigra manus.

> Alas, Messalla, you will sail Aegean seas without me,
> you and the company, but not, please God, forgetting
> the sick man, captive in Phaeacia, land of the unknown —
> if only the Black Goddess withholds her grasping hand.

The poet appeals directly for our sympathy. His situation in real life, ill in bed somewhere in Corfu (for which the accepted name was then Corcyra), is transposed into the world of mythology, for Phaeacia was the mysterious island where the shipwrecked Odysseus swam ashore on the last stage of his long journey home to Ithaca. The Alexandrian poet Callimachus had identified it with Corcyra, but this identification was not accepted by the geographers and the island's real position (if it ever had one) unknown: hence one of the shades of meaning in *ignotis* here, a touch of subdued wit which helps to avoid self-pity. In each couplet grave slower-moving statement is followed by emotive dactylic exclamation; there is also contrast between *me tenet* and *ibitis*, *terris* and *undas*, compound *abstineas* and simple *tenet*. The lines are noticeably musical, have an almost hypnotic quality, largely owing perhaps to the diphthong *ae* and the long vowels *a* and *i*, which combined together in this context are suggestive of sorrow. I do not think these two couplets could be mistaken for the work of the younger Ovid or Propertius, though they anticipate the tone of Ovid's *Tristia*.

Secondly, a fine expression of that feeling of elation and invulnerability experienced at times by the young lover when Nature has played her age-old trick upon him and he 'walks on air', convinced that he bears a charmed life and that all is for the best in the best of all possible worlds:

> quisquis amore tenetur eat tutusque sacerque
> qualibet; insidias non timuisse decet.
> non mihi pigra nocent hibernae frigora noctis,
> non mihi cum multa decidit imber aqua.
> non labor hic laedit, reseret modo Delia postes
> et uocet ad digiti me taciturna sonum.

> The love-possessed are sacred, safe to wander where they
> to fear no ambush is their privilege.   [will;
> In the freezing winter night no frost can bite me;
> no rain can damp me though it falls in floods.
> No harm in present hardship if my Delia turns the lock
> and calls me silently — with one click of her finger.

The Latin lines have a lift about them that is partly the result of the predominantly dactylic movement, a sense of special individual magic that is partly due to the repetition, or anaphora (to use the technical term), of *non mihi ... non mihi ... non ...*, and at the same time a gaiety that betrays itself in the word-play of *nocent ... noctis* and the paradox of *uocet ... taciturna*. Though the passage is closer to Ovid than to Propertius, it is still, I believe, unmistakably Tibullan.

The third example brings alive for the reader the feeling of tension followed by relief at two characteristic moments in the course of a clandestine affair:

> haec mihi te adducit tenebris multoque timore
> coniungit nostras clam taciturna manus.

> haec foribusque manet noctu me affixa, proculque
> cognoscit strepitus me ueniente pedum.
>
> In the dark she leads you to me and though terrified
> stealthily with no word spoken joins our hands.
> Pressed to the door at night, she listens, waiting for me,
> can recognise, far off, approaching steps as mine.

The first couplet conveys excitement, a sense of difficulty perhaps in the doubled consonants of *adducit tenebris* and of groping danger in the separation of *nostras* from *manus* by the monosyllabic adverb and the longer adjective. In the second hexameter the feeling of expectation is heightened by the pause after *affixa*, a word which pictures her as not only glued to the door but also intent on listening. The listening is further emphasised by the slight pause after *proculque*; then she recognises one sound in particular: he's coming — that's his footstep.

As regards the structure of a Tibullan poem, here again feeling is the deciding factor. Ovid, as is well known, constructs his elegies in a linear fashion, giving them an argumentative or narrative thread on which he keeps a pretty firm grip throughout. For example, the poem which starts with the echo couplet quoted above goes on to develop a point by point comparison of the lover and the soldier designed to prove that love has the highest military authority, for the greatest heroes of the *Iliad* and even the War-god himself were lovers; then maintains that love has toughened the poet, raised his morale and kept him busy; and finally advises all who want an active life to take up love. Tibullus on the other hand is more devious. The very transpositions that scholars from the time of Scaliger until late in the nineteenth century introduced into his text are themselves evidence that poetic structure with him is not a logical thing, not perhaps even a rational thing (though there is always a good reason behind it), but rather an intentional avoidance of the obvious and the straightforward in favour of something more subtle and supple. His poems tend to grow rather than move forward — to grow by a proliferation of short sections expressing various related and contrasted moods. These sections quite often take the form of wishes or prayers, and the connexions between them, though discoverable on reflexion, are not always explicit. The whole poem is often held together by the repetition of certain key words and phrases that embody the main ideas with which the poem is concerned. To make this last point clear I must ask the reader to turn to the tenth poem of the first book and examine the following repetitions there: 2 *ferreus* and 59 *ferrum*; 4 *dirae mortis* and 33 *atram* ... *Mortem*; 7 *bella*, 33 *bellis* and 53 *Veneris bella*; 11-12 *tristia* ... *arma* and 49-50 *tristia* ... *arma*; 15 *aluistis*, 47 *aluit* and 67 *alma*; 22 *spicea* and 67 *spicam*; 45 *Pax candida* and 67-8 *Pax* ... *candidus*. These seven seem to me the most important repetitions, but there are at least a dozen more that any interested reader can discover for himself, not counting such related words as 8 *faginus* and 20 *ligneus*, which also play their part in building up the Tibullan unity.[3] Here too, in structure, as also in metre, we find that Tibullus shows marked originality.

If however the individual poem seems to grow to its completion, the relative placing of the ten poems that make up Book One is clearly the result of careful calculation. The first and the tenth go together as giving the poet's philosophy of life, if that is not too grand a phrase to use of such an unsystematic thinker as Tibullus. In between these two, which serve as introduction and conclusion to the collection, are placed three pairs of poems, each pair separated from the next by a single contrasting poem on a different theme. Thus, the second and third poems, about Delia, are separated from the fifth and sixth on the same subject, by the consultation with Priapus on homosexual love, a poem contrasting in treatment, tone and theme with the heterosexual pair on either side of it. Similarly the fifth and sixth, about Delia, are separated from the eighth and ninth, about Marathus, by the birthday poem for Messalla, which in its turn makes a complete contrast in tone and theme with its surroundings. Again, the two members of each of the three pairs, though all alike in being about love unfulfilled, nevertheless contrast with one another: for example, in the second poem the lovers are separated by the guard set on Delia by her absent husband; in the third they are separated by war, the poet being on his way to the Near East on the staff of Messalla and taken ill, as we have seen above.[4]

The second book is roughly half the length of the first and consists of only six poems. These, though contrasted with one another in a similar way, taken together leave an impression of incompletion. This book lacks the evident unity of the first; it has not been fully achieved and at the same time is unusually short for a collection of elegies. We are therefore probably right to infer that it was unfinished when Tibullus died and published posthumously by his executor. He died young in 19 or 18 BC, shortly after Virgil, as we gather from a contemporary epigram by the poet Domitius Marsus, which will be found on p.106. Precisely how young we can only guess, but according to Varro a man could be called *iuuenis* from the age of thirty to the age of forty-five.[5]

Of his life we know little more than can be gleaned from these two books of elegies. Admittedly there is a *Vita* or brief biography (printed on p.106) which appears in some of his manuscripts and which on linguistic evidence can be said to derive from the work of Suetonius, *De Poetis*, written considerably more than a century after the poet's death. But this as it stands contains nothing that could not have been gathered by inference from the elegies themselves, from the epigram of Domitius Marsus, which it quotes, and, finally, from the verse epistle of Horace (*Epist.* 1.4) to the elegiac poet Albius, who in antiquity, as today, was taken to be one and the same as Albius Tibullus. His *praenomen* or first name is not recorded.

He was a Roman knight and owned a small estate in Latium, on which he was born — a fact which makes him one of the very few truly Latin poets, as opposed to Italians like Horace and Ovid, or provincials like Catullus and Virgil. His patron was the soldier, statesman and orator Marcus Valerius Messalla Corvinus (64 BC to AD 8), distinguished member of an ancient patrician family, famous too as a literary purist. In the troubled times of the Civil Wars Messalla steered a prudential course, first supporting Brutus and Cassius, then after the defeat at Philippi (where he commanded the victorious right wing of their army) transferring his support to Antony, later still attaching himself to Octavian, with whom he was Consul in 31 BC and took part in the battle of Actium. It is remarkable, by the way, that Tibullus, Messalla's protégé, unlike the other Augustan poets nowhere in his elegies refers to the Caesar. The omission must be intentional; whether it implies a slight is open to argument, but certainly it indicates a conservative loyalty, in the tradition of the old Republic, to his own aristocratic patron.

He fought under Messalla's command as a military tribune in Gaul and was awarded, so the *Vita* informs us, military decorations, *militaria dona* (but this *may* be an inference extorted from 1.7.9 *non sine me tibi partus honos* 'not without me was your glory gained'). He accompanied Messalla on his expedition to the Levant, but fell ill on the way; whether he rejoined the expeditionary force on his recovery is uncertain, though he writes in 1.7 with some knowledge of Cilicia, Syro-Palestine and Egypt.

The Delia celebrated in his first collection, blonde and blue-eyed, as we gather from 1.5.43-6, is said by Apuleius, almost two centuries later, to have been in real life named Plania. If this is true two consequences follow: her Greek pseudonym is a translation of her Latin gentile name, for the Latin adjective *planus* is equivalent to the Greek *dēlos*; and secondly, she was a *ciuis Romana*, for only Roman citizens bore gentile names. In 1.6 she has a 'husband' (*coniunx*), to whom she is not in the full Roman sense married, because she does not wear the traditional dress of a Roman *matrona*; there she is the man's concubine and probably also a freedwoman, or *libertina*, manumitted by (and perhaps the concubine of) her former master, for it is rather improbable that a free-born *ciuis Romana* in Equestrian Society would consent to concubinage.

The poet's liaison with Delia ended at some date after the publication of Book One. In Book Two he is in love with a woman called Nemesis, but as we have no word about her from Apuleius or any other source we are left to speculate on his reason for choosing this ill-omened name for Delia's successor. Nemesis is the Greek goddess of Retribution; Catullus calls her *uemens dea* 'a passionate goddess' and perhaps Tibullus has this description in mind. She is thought of as ready to pounce on anyone who 'talks big' and in particular as the avenger of slighted lovers. In the Greek Anthology there is an epigram (12.140) describing how Nemesis punished the anonymous author for decrying the good looks of a certain boy by making him fall madly in love with the boy; this epigram is imitated by Meleager (12.141), the anthologist of the famous *Garland*, which was available in Italy early in the first century BC. It is an epigram that may well have been known to Tibullus, who elsewhere shows a good knowledge of Greek poetry and very likely of the *Garland* itself (see note on 1.2.29-30). So we may perhaps guess that he had at one time thought poorly of the girl he calls Nemesis and later found himself infatuated by her. Some scholars, it is true, have regarded her as a literary figure merely, with no real existence; but this means that we must also regard as pure fiction the extraordinary passage in 2.6 about her little sister, who fell to her death from an upper window. The incredulity of some modern literati is itself a phenomenon beyond belief.

And belief is Tibullus's most endearing characteristic. He believes in the gods; he half believes in magic;[6] he believes in an idealized past and a happy future; he believes in Delia, Marathus, Nemesis; but above all he believes in the traditional religious rituals:

> Nam ueneror seu stipes habet desertus in agris
> seu uetus in triuio florida serta lapis.

> For I pray at every solitary tree-stump in the fields
> or old stone at the crossways that is garlanded with
>   [flowers.

One is surprised to meet this couplet at the start of a collection of love elegies. It reminds one of Virgil's admonition at *Georgics* 1.338 *in primis uenerare deos* 'first and foremost worship the Gods' and can at the same time be regarded as a deliberate contradiction of Lucretius 5.1198-9

> Nec pietas ullast uelatum saepe uideri
> uertier ad lapidem

> And there is no piety in being often seen
> with head covered turning towards a stone.

Again, a little later in the same elegy one meets the following couplet:

> Adsitis, diui, neu uos a paupere mensa
> dona nec e puris spernite fictilibus.

> O Gods, vouchsafe your presence and do not scorn the gifts
> from a poor man's table and spotless earthenware.

The reader of Propertius and Ovid is unprepared for this simple and direct expression of religious feeling. Critics can talk of literary *topoi*, the poet's *persona*, the intentional or the documentary fallacy, but all the same the common reader senses at these points, as he senses when reading Wordsworth, that the poet is telling the truth about himself, that his feeling for religion is genuine and indeed basic to his character.

At the centre of this religion stand the homely Lares, guardian spirits of hearth and farm, depicted in art as young men dressed in short tunics, holding above their heads a wine-bowl or a drinking-horn, and very often dancing. Their images were placed beside the hearth and worshipped with offerings of food and wine, incense and flowers. These are the gods addressed in the quotation above and requested not to despise the gifts from the poet's simple table. They are never mentioned in the first book of Propertius, never mentioned in the three books of Ovid's *Amores*, but their name occurs five times in Book One and four times in Book Two of Tibullus. Altogether he devotes some thirty lines to them, promising them sacrifices and offerings of incense, undertaking to wear the myrtle in their honour, mentioning their ancient images of wood inherited from his ancestors, and praying for their protection on the field of battle:

> Sed patrii seruate Lares: aluistis et idem
> cursarem uestros cum tener ante pedes.

> Save me, Lares of my fathers, as you nurtured me
> when I ran around in childhood at your feet.

This simple but vivid reminiscence of his childhood, employing incidentally a verb (*cursare*) which occurs nowhere else in the whole of Latin elegy, is typical of his backward-looking cast of mind and very appealing.[7] We suspect that there is a similar autobiographical touch in his finest poem of all, the first of the second book, when he tells us that it was a country child who first made a garland of spring flowers as a chaplet for the Lares; he himself in childhood had probably done the same. Certainly from his earliest years he will have witnessed or taken part in the ancient annual ceremony with which that poem opens — the ceremony of the purification of the fields and crops by 'going about' them in solemn white-robed procession, and he will have heard his father speaking the traditional form of prayer whose distant echo still lingers in the couplet

> Di patrii, purgamus agros, purgamus agrestes:
> uos mala de nostris pellite liminibus.

> Gods of our fathers, we purge the fields and the field-
> drive away all evil from our boundaries.[8]   [workers:

And, as the commentators tell us, among the *di patrii* the Lares would hold an important place as guardians of the family estate and its bounds.

Tibullus' evident respect for the ancestors, his nostalgia for an idealized past when life was simple, gods wooden and men honest, his love of the country and its seasonal ritual round of labour and religious observance, these habitual attitudes owe at least as much to the Lares as they do to his military experience under Messalla in the civil war or to the worst excesses of the economic boom that began with the return of peace to the Roman world. Even Catullus, the 'urbane' provincial for whom urban Rome had been home and life, who regarded the country as crude and witless (*rus inficetum*), fit stamping-ground for goat-milkers and clodhoppers — even Catullus could appreciate the beauty of his estate at Sirmione when he returned to his *Lar Familiaris* from foreign service in Bithynia. But Tibullus was no provincial. Born in Latium, near enough to Rome not to want to live there, with no desire to shine in the smart set of the capital, he had served in Gaul and perhaps in the Near East: to such a man his family home in the country, seen in imagination from a legionary tent among the Aquitani or from distant and mountainous Cilicia, must have appeared a small earthly paradise, under the protection of the familiar Lares.

Propertius in a mood of lovelorn gloom retires to a lonely grove, the property of Zephyrus, to carve the name of Cynthia on the bark of beeches, and of pines too (perhaps a more difficult operation this), to pour out his complaint to the woods and rocks and hear them echo her name as Virgil's bucolic woods had echoed the name of Amaryllis.[9] But the country celebrated by Tibullus in a number of his poems is no Arcadian landscape. It is the countryside of Latium, of the *regio Pedana*, a few miles east of Rome, where cereals and wine are the chief crops, pigs and sheep the chief livestock, where at vintage-time the grapes are trodden in portable boat-shaped vats (*lintres*), where the daily work is hard and where festivals are looked forward to as days of well-earned rest from labour. Of course the picture is somewhat idealized, as it also is in the *Georgics* of Virgil, but it is firmly based on the realities of the way of life into which he was born and for which he retained a lifelong affection, nourished by that deeper affection for the gods who presided over it.

To these gods he attributes the origin of civilisation and the arts. House-building, the domestication of animals, the invention of the wheel, agriculture, spinning and weaving were their gifts to man; the arts of music, song, dance and poetry originated in their worship, invented by country people as expressions of individual and communal supplication and thanksgiving. He is pleased to call himself *rusticus*, giving the word (which carries strong overtones of boorishness) a positive value lacking in its use by Ovid and Propertius. He regards the small sheep-farmer as a greater hero than the valiant soldier: the sheep-farmer too fights for a living, but constructively; he represents stability, continuity, the simple, useful life. Peace is the natural human condition. Peace, one might say, is the greatest of the country gods, for the civilisation that they gave the human race depends on her.

> Ipse quoque inter agros interque armenta Cupido
> natus et indomitas dicitur inter equas . . .
> a miseri quos hic grauiter deus urget; at ille
> felix cui placidus leniter afflat Amor.
> sancte, ueni dapibus festis, sed pone sagittas
> et procul ardentes hinc, precor, abde faces.

> Cupid himself, in fable, was born among the fields,
>   among the cattle and the wild mares . . .
> Wretched are they, alas, on whom this god bears hard,
>   but happy he who feels Love's breath serene.
> Come, Holy One, attend our feast, but lay aside your arrows
>   and far away, I pray you, hide your blazing torch.

Again the religious tone is very marked. True, Catullus had called Cupid *sancte puer*, but the emphasis on the god's boyhood detracts a little, perhaps, from the force of the adjective and conjures up a mental picture of the putti of the Pompeian frescoes.[10] In the Tibullan context, however, despite the conventional arrows and torches, the impression made is that of a more powerful and elemental figure than the Alexandrian boy-god, a force ambivalent and irresistible, ruling the world of beasts and men. Only once does Tibullus directly call Cupid *puer* — in the last poem of Book Two. In fact it is not until Book Two that he uses the name Cupid at all — and then only three times; in Book One, and elsewhere in Book Two, he refers to the god as Amor.

Book One indeed is remarkable for the general picture it presents of love as a positive moral force, a force contrasting strongly with the destructive passion attacked in the fourth book of Lucretius and of Cicero's *Tusculans* and realised so vividly in the first elegy of Propertius. The majestic figure of Venus predominates. She rules from high Olympus. Though merciful to her servants yet as the daughter of blood and raging sea she takes vengeance on those who sin against her in word or deed. She teaches her worshippers through suffering and rewards them with an after-life in Elysium. She helps the brave but demands of them reverence, secrecy and kindness. She punishes the mockers, the tale-bearers, the hard-hearted, above all those who break faith for mercenary reasons:

> Si quis diuitiis captus uiolauit amorem,
>   asperaque est illi difficilisque Venus.

> If anyone for money does violence to love,
>   Venus is hard on him and difficult.

Clearly the pentameter has a double meaning: Venus is at the same time the goddess of love and the sex-life over which she rules; the Latin *asperaque est illi* means 'rough *for* him' as well as 'rough *on* him'. But more interesting here is the concept of the violation of love. *Violare* is a strong word with implications not only of physical violence but of religious desecration and spiritual defilement.

Tibullus is unique in his application of this word to love; he uses it five times in Book One, always in an erotic context — clear evidence of his religious attitude towards love at this stage in his poetic career. This attitude is very different from the down-to-earth view of love presented by Ovid in his celebration of *Love's Triumph* (*Amores* 1.2):

> Mens Bona ducetur manibus post terga retortis
> et Pudor et castris quidquid Amoris obest ...
> Blanditiae comites tibi erunt Errorque Furorque,
> adsidue partes turba secuta tuas.
> his tu militibus superas hominesque deosque;
> haec tibi si demas commoda, nudus eris.
> laeta triumphanti de summo mater Olympo
> plaudet et adpositas sparget in ora rosas.

> Conscience and Common Sense and all Love's enemies
> will be dragged along with hands tied behind their backs...
> Your loyal irregulars Flattery Passion and Illusion
> will act as bodyguard,
> the forces that bring you victory over gods and men,
> providing cover for your nakedness.
> Your laughing mother will watch the Triumph from Olympus
> and clap her hands and shower you with roses.

Ovid the reductionist here strips off love's mystery, leaving the god denuded and open to epicurean management by the clear-sighted reason. His more maternal and decorative Venus, though she too watches the scene from the summit of Olympus, is content to scatter roses and forget about revenge.

In the first two poems of Book Two love still retains a religious aura, but thereafter the point of view changes completely. Like Catullus in the final stage of his affair with Lesbia, Tibullus now looks on love as a disease, but (here, though, unlike Catullus) a disease whose pain can actually be enjoyable:

> Et faueo morbo, cum iuuat ipse dolor

> Clinging to my sickness, finding pleasure in the pain.

Alternatively he describes love as a form of slavery, using for once a long mythological example to illustrate the point, the story of how Apollo, god of poetry, prophecy and medicine, fell in love with the young Admetus and served as herdsman on his farm, living in a shack, his passion unrequited. But just as Tibullus accepts the disease, so he accepts love's slavery, though not of course without complaint. He is prepared to put up with the avarice of Nemesis as a

fact inevitable in an avaricious society. He is even prepared to turn
the tables on Venus herself, by robbing her temples to get the means
to buy gifts for his mistress:

> Aut rapiam suspensa sacris insignia fanis:
> sed Venus ante alios est uiolanda mihi.
> illa malum facinus suadet dominamque rapacem
> dat mihi: sacrilegas sentiat illa manus.

> Or I'll steal the sacred offerings hung up on temple walls:
> and Venus shall be first to be profaned.
> She tempts me to do evil and devotes me to a grasping
> mistress: she deserves to suffer sacrilege.

The situation is paradoxical: he himself is now willing to desecrate
true love (the very thing he maintained in Book One that Venus
would inevitably punish) by buying Nemesis' affection. Venus has
been demythologised and the sinister figure of Nemesis deified in her
place; the worship of Amor is now subjected to her conditions. Yes,
for her the poet would even sell his estate and part with the ancestral
Lares (another complete reversal of his attitude in Book One):

> illius est nobis lege colendus Amor.
> quin etiam sedes iubeat si uendere auitas,
> ite sub imperium sub titulumque, Lares.

> Love's worship means obedience to her laws.
> Why, even if she bade me sell my ancestral home,
> I'd pack the Lares off under a bill of sale.

But nevertheless in this cycle of poems to Nemesis the attitude to love
is still positive; the suffering is still worthwhile. What makes it
worthwhile is Hope. The poet signs off suddenly, leaving the reader
with Love (unfulfilled) and Hope, and with the strong impression
that in the long run Hope is the higher value.[11]

NOTES

1. It was new to Latin but taken over from Greek; see Callimachus *Epigram* 22 (Pfeiffer) where the first couplet begins *Astakiden* and ends *Astakides.*

2. For disyllabic endings see Postgate (1922) p. lii and Barsby. For subdivision of the couplet see in 1.4 lines 3-4, 27-28, 35-36, 53-54, 55-56, 77-78, 81-82. For enjambment see in 1.4 lines 16, 26, 28, 40, 54, 78.

3. Kurt Witte was the first to draw attention to such repetition of words in Tibullus: see his *Die Geschichte der römischen Elegie I. Tibull* (Erlangen 1924). P. Troll rejected the idea in his Bursian review (*Jahresbericht* 208 (1926) 78), and so did M. Schuster 11-12.

4. These points are made by Littlewood. —In this connexion I can record a curious discovery. Take Postgate's Oxford Text, add up the number of lines in *Elegies* 1 and 9, 2 and 7, 3 and 10, 4 and 8, 5 and 6 of the first book, and you will find that the total for each pair is 162. When I mentioned this to Dr J.A. Richmond of University College, Dublin, he immediately pointed out that in Book 2 the pairs 1 and 6, 2 and 5, 3 (counting 14a, 14b, 14c and the missing pentameter there) and 4 make 144. Is not this more remarkable than the number-magic of the *Eclogues*, and from the poetical point of view quite as irrelevant?

5. Varro's five stages of life are recorded at Censorinus *De Die Natali* 14.2.

6. W.B. Yeats's interest, and indeed belief, in magic is well known.

7. To be honest, Catullus uses the compound *circumcursans* at 68.133, in another memorable autobiographical passage.

8. See Walter Pater *Marius the Epicurean* chapter 1, from where 'going about' is quoted (an etymological reference to the Ambarvalia).

9. Propertius 1.18 and Virgil *Eclogue* 1.5.

10. Catullus 64.95.

11. I acknowledge a debt to W. Heilmann's unpublished dissertation. See now R.B. Palmer.

TEXT

TRANSLATION

LIBER PRIMVS

I

Diuitias alius fuluo sibi congerat auro
    et teneat culti iugera magna soli,
quem labor assiduus uicino terreat hoste,
    Martia cui somnos classica pulsa fugent:
me mea paupertas uitae traducat inerti   5
    dum meus assiduo luceat igne focus.

Ipse seram teneras maturo tempore uites
    rusticus et facili grandia poma manu,
nec Spes destituat, sed frugum semper aceruos
    praebeat et pleno pinguia musta lacu: 10
nam ueneror seu stipes habet desertus in agris
    seu uetus in triuio florida serta lapis,
et quodcumque mihi pomum nouus educat annus
    libatum agricolam ponitur ante deum.

Flaua Ceres, tibi sit nostro de rure corona   15
    spicea quae templi pendeat ante fores,
pomosisque ruber custos ponatur in hortis
    terreat ut saeua falce Priapus aues.
uos quoque, felicis quondam, nunc pauperis agri
    custodes, fertis munera uestra, Lares;   20
tunc uitula innumeros lustrabat caesa iuuencos,
    nunc agna exigui est hostia parua soli:
agna cadet uobis, quam circum rustica pubes
    clamet 'io, messes et bona uina date'.

Iam modo, iam possim contentus uiuere paruo   25
    nec semper longae deditus esse uiae,
sed Canis aestiuos ortus uitare sub umbra
    arboris ad riuos praetereuntis aquae.
nec tamen interdum pudeat tenuisse bidentem
    aut stimulo tardos increpuisse boues;   30
non agnamue sinu pigeat fetumue capellae
    desertum oblita matre referre domum.

2

BOOK ONE

1

Wealth let others gather for themselves in yellow gold
and occupy great acres of cultivated land —
scared on active service, in contact with the enemy,
their sleep put to flight by the blare of trumpet-calls.
But let my general poverty transfer me to inaction,
so long as fire glows always in my hearth.

Early in the season I should set the tender vines
and the tall maidens with a peasant's practised hand.
Hope would never fail me, but deliver an abundance
of produce, brimming over the vat at vintage time.
For I pray at every solitary tree-stump in the fields
or old stone at the cross-roads that is garlanded with flowers;
and the first of every fruit the new season raises for me
is offered at the feet of the farmer God.

For you, O golden Ceres, my land would bear a crown
of wheaten spikes to hang on your temple door.
I'd place a red Priapus to stand sentry in the orchard
and scare away the birds with his reaping-hook.
You, O Lares, also receive your gifts as guardians
of a property once prosperous, now poor:
once a slaughtered heifer purified uncounted steers;
now my little acres offer a ewe-lamb.
The ewe-lamb shall be yours and at her sacrifice the peasants
can shout 'O Lares, grant us good harvest and good wine'.

If only, now at last, I can live content with little
and not be handed over to the never-ending road,
but avoid the summer rising of the Dog-star, in the shadow
of a tree, beside the waters of a running stream!
Not that I would be ashamed to wield a mattock sometimes
or reprimand the slow oxen with a goad,
nor would I be too civilised to bring home in my arms
a lamb or kid abandoned by a careless mother.

At uos exiguo pecori, furesque lupique,
    parcite: de magno est praeda petenda grege.
hic ego pastoremque meum lustrare quotannis   35
    et placidam soleo spargere lacte Palem.
adsitis, diui, neu uos e paupere mensa
    dona nec e puris spernite fictilibus:
fictilia antiquus primum sibi fecit agrestis,
    pocula de facili composuitque luto.   40

Non ego diuitias patrum fructusque requiro
    quos tulit antiquo condita messis auo:
parua seges satis est, satis est requiescere lecto
    si licet et solito membra leuare toro.
quam iuuat immites uentos audire cubantem   45
    et dominam tenero continuisse sinu!
aut gelidas hibernus aquas cum fuderit Auster,
    securum somnos igne iuuante sequi!
hoc mihi contingat: sit diues iure furorem
    qui maris et tristes ferre potest pluuias.   50

O quantum est auri pereat potiusque smaragdi
    quam fleat ob nostras ulla puella uias!
te bellare decet terra, Messalla, marique
    ut domus hostiles praeferat exuuias:
me retinent uinctum formosae uincla puellae,   55
    et sedeo duras ianitor ante fores.

Non ego laudari curo, mea Delia; tecum
    dum modo sim, quaeso segnis inersque uocer.
te spectem suprema mihi cum uenerit hora;
    te teneam moriens deficiente manu.   60
flebis et arsuro positum me, Delia, lecto,
    tristibus et lacrimis oscula mixta dabis.
flebis: non tua sunt duro praecordia ferro
    uincta, nec in tenero stat tibi corde silex.
illo non iuuenis poterit de funere quisquam   65
    lumina non uirgo sicca referre domum.
tu manes ne laede meos, sed parce solutis
    crinibus et teneris, Delia, parce genis.

Interea, dum Fata sinunt, iungamus amores:
    iam ueniet tenebris Mors adoperta caput;   70

But let the robber and the wolf spare my little flock
and plunder the big folds,
for here I never fail to purify my shepherd
and sprinkle kindly Pales every year with milk.
O Gods, vouchsafe your presence, and do not scorn the gifts
from a poor man's table and spotless earthenware:
earthenware was the invention of a countryman
long ago, who shaped cups from pliant clay.

I do not miss the fortune or the profit
that garnered harvest brought my grandfather of old.
Enough is a small crop, enough is sleeping in a bed
and lightening the limbs on the familiar couch.
How pleasant lying there at night to listen to wild winds
and contain a mistress in tender embrace!
Or when the wintry southern gale slings down the freezing sleet,
to pursue sleep in safety, aided by a fire:
Let this be my good fortune: I resign the right to wealth
to those who can endure sad rain and raging sea.

O perish all the gold and every emerald in the world
sooner than any girl weep as we march away!
It is right that you, Messalla, campaign by land and sea
to adorn your town-house with the spoils of war.
But I am held a pris'ner, fettered by a lovely girl,
and take my post as keeper at her cruel door.

Glory has no charms for me, my Delia. They can call me
slack and ineffective, if only I'm with you.
O let me gaze at you, when my last hour comes —
hold you, as I die, in my failing grasp!
Delia, you will weep for me laid on the bed of burning
and you will give me kisses mixed with bitter tears.
Yes, you will weep: your heart is not encased in iron
nor is there flint in your tender breast.
There will be no young man and no unmarried girl
going home dry-eyed from my funeral.
But do no violence, Delia, to my departed spirit:
spare your flowing tresses and spare your tender cheeks.

Meanwhile, with Fate's permission, let us unite and love.
Tomorrow Death will come, head hooded — in the dark,

iam subrepet iners aetas, neque amare decebit,
    dicere nec cano blanditias capite.
nunc leuis est tractanda Venus, dum frangere postes
    non pudet et rixas inseruisse iuuat.
hic ego dux milesque bonus. uos, signa tubaeque,   75
    ite procul; cupidis uulnera ferte uiris,
ferte et opes: ego composito securus aceruo
    dites despiciam despiciamque famem.

II

Adde merum uinoque nouos compesce dolores,
    occupet ut fessi lumina uicta sopor;
neu quisquam multo percussum tempora Baccho
    excitet, infelix dum requiescit amor:
nam posita est nostrae custodia saeua puellae,   5
    clauditur et dura ianua firma sera.

Ianua difficilis domini, te uerberet imber,
    te Iouis imperio fulmina missa petant.
ianua, iam pateas uni mihi, uicta querelis,
    neu furtim uerso cardine aperta sones;   10
et mala siqua tibi dixit dementia nostra,
    ignoscas: capiti sint precor illa meo.
te meminisse decet quae plurima uoce peregi
    supplice, cum posti florida serta darem.

Tu quoque, ne timide custodes, Delia, falle;   15
    audendum est: fortes adiuuat ipsa Venus.
illa fauet seu quis iuuenis noua limina temptat
    seu reserat fixo dente puella fores.
illa docet furtim molli decedere lecto,
    illa pedem nullo ponere posse sono,   20
illa uiro coram nutus conferre loquaces
    blandaque compositis abdere uerba notis;
nec docet hoc omnes sed quos nec inertia tardat
    nec uetat obscura surgere nocte timor.

En ego cum tenebris tota uagor anxius urbe   25
    . . . .

or useless Age creep up, and it will not be seemly
to make white-headed love or pretty speeches.
Light Venus is our duty now, while there is no disgrace
in breaking down a door, while brawling brings delight.
Here I can lead and soldier well. Eagles and trumpets, dismiss!
Bring wounds to greedy husbands, and bring them money too.
But let me live at peace myself, with produce heaped in store,
looking down on hunger as I look down on the rich.

2

Pour it neat, boy. Discipline fresh misery with drink,
letting sleep invade these tired defeated eyes,
and when the Wine-God in his strength has hit me on the temples
see that no one wakes me while unhappy love's at rest.
For now a cruel sentinel stands watch upon my girl
and her heavy door is shut and firmly barred.

O door, stubborn as your master, may the rainstorm lash you
and launched at Jove's command may flash of lightning blast you!
Please, door — open just for me, moved by my complaining.
But silence, as you swing on slowly turning hinge!
Forgive me if I cursed you in my infatuation.
Let the curses light on my own head.
It's right you should remember all my prayers and promises
when I hung those garlands of flowers on your post.

You too, Delia: be bold and trick the guard.
You must do and dare, for Venus helps the brave.
She favours the young man who reconnoitres a new threshold,
and the girl who opens a door with home-made key.
She teaches the withdrawal by stealth from the soft bed,
the inaudible positioning of feet,
the conference by nod in the presence of a husband,
concealment of sweet words in signals pre-arranged.
Her teaching's not for everyone but only those with courage
and capacity to rise in the shadow of the night.

Look, when in the dark I wander through the city streets distraught

. . . .

nec sinit occurrat quisquam qui corpora ferro
    uulneret aut rapta praemia ueste petat.
quisquis amore tenetur eat tutusque sacerque
    qualibet; insidias non timuisse decet.   30
non mihi pigra nocent hibernae frigora noctis,
    non mihi cum multa decidit imber aqua;
non labor hic laedit, reseret modo Delia postes
    et uocet ad digiti me taciturna sonum.

Parcite luminibus, seu uir seu femina fiat   35
    obuia; celari uult sua furta Venus.
ne strepitu terrete pedum neu quaerite nomen
    neu prope fulgenti lumina ferte face.
siquis et imprudens aspexerit, occulat ille
    perque deos omnes se meminisse neget;   40
nam fuerit quicumque loquax, is sanguine natam,
    is Venerem e rabido sentiet esse mari.

Nec tamen huic credet coniunx tuus, ut mihi uerax
    pollicita est magico saga ministerio.
hanc ego de caelo ducentem sidera uidi;   45
    fluminis haec rapidi carmine uertit iter;
haec cantu finditque solum manesque sepulcris
    elicit et tepido deuocat ossa rogo.
iam tenet infernas magico stridore cateruas;
    iam iubet aspersas lacte referre pedem.   50
cum libet, haec tristi depellit nubila caelo;
    cum libet, aestiuo conuocat orbe niues.
sola tenere malas Medeae dicitur herbas,
    sola feros Hecatae perdomuisse canes.

Haec mihi composuit cantus quis fallere posses;   55
  · ter cane, ter dictis despue carminibus:
ille nihil poterit de nobis credere cuiquam,
    non sibi, si in molli uiderit ipse toro.
tu tamen abstineas aliis, nam cetera cernet
    omnia, de me uno sentiet ille nihil.   60
quid credam? nempe haec eadem se dixit amores
    cantibus aut herbis soluere posse meos,
et me lustrauit taedis, et nocte serena
    concidit ad magicos hostia pulla deos.

and stops me meeting anyone who stabs you in the back
or steals clothes for a living.
The love-possessed are sacred, safe to wander where they will;
to fear no ambush is their privilege.
In the freezing winter's night no frost can bite me;
no rain can damp me though it falls in floods.
No harm in present hardships, if my Delia turns the lock
and calls me silently — with one click of her finger.

Male or female, should you meet me, look the other way:
the thefts of Love are secret — that is Venus' will.
Do not scare me with your footstep, do not ask my name
or shine your torches near me.
Any accidental witness is to hide the truth
and by all the gods deny his memory.
For every tell-tale shall be taught that Venus is the daughter
of blood and raging sea.

In any case your husband won't believe him, Delia;
for so an honest witch assured me by her magic.
I have seen her drawing down the stars from heaven.
Her chanting can reverse the river's flow.
Her spells can split the ground, lure ghosts from graves
and call down bones from smouldering pyres.
Now with magic wailing she holds the infernal troop;
now with sprinkled milk orders their return.
When she pleases she can drive the clouds from sullen skies;
when she pleases muster snow in summer's dome.
Only she, I'm told, knows all Medea's evil herbs;
only she can tame Hecate's fierce hounds.

She has written me a spell to enable you to trick him.
Speak it thrice and spit thrice when you have spoken.
He'll then believe no story anyone may tell of us —
not even his own eyes if he catches us in bed.
But keep away from other men. He'll see everything else.
I'm the only one he will never notice.
The same witch even promised, though it passes my belief,
by her spells or herbs to free me of my love.
She fumigated me with pitch-pine on a moonlit night
and slaughtered a black victim to the gods below.

non ego totus abesset amor sed mutuus esset   65
   orabam, nec te posse carere uelim.

Ferreus ille fuit qui, te cum posset habere,
   maluerit praedas stultus et arma sequi.
ille licet Cilicum uictas agat ante cateruas,
   ponat et in capto Martia castra solo,   70
totus et argento contectus, totus et auro,
   insideat celeri conspiciendus equo:
ipse boues — mea si tecum modo Delia — possim
   iungere et in solito pascere monte pecus;
et te dum liceat teneris retinere lacertis,   75
   mollis et inculta sit mihi somnus humo.
quid Tyrio recubare toro sine amore secundo
   prodest, cum fletu nox uigilanda uenit?
nam neque tunc plumae nec stragula picta soporem
   nec sonitus placidae ducere possit aquae.   80

Num Veneris magnae uiolaui numina uerbo
   et mea nunc poenas impia lingua luit?
num feror incestus sedes adiisse deorum
   sertaque de sanctis deripuisse focis?
non ego, si merui, dubitem procumbere templis   85
   et dare sacratis oscula liminibus;
non ego tellurem genibus perrepere supplex
   et miserum sancto tundere poste caput.

At tu qui lentus rides mala nostra caueto.
   mox tibi, non uni saeuiet usque deus.   90
uidi ego qui iuuenum miseros lusisset amores
   post Veneris uinclis subdere colla senem,
et sibi blanditias tremula componere uoce,
   et manibus canas fingere uelle comas;
stare nec ante fores puduit caraeue puellae   95
   ancillam medio detinuisse foro.
hunc puer, hunc iuuenis turba circumterit arta,
   despuit in molles et sibi quisque sinus.

At mihi parce, Venus. semper tibi dedita seruit
   mens mea. quid messes uris acerba tuas?   100

I prayed that love be mutual, not absent altogether.
How could I ever wish to live without you?

Steel-hearted was the man who had you for the asking
but chose, the fool, to follow arms and plunder.
Let him drive Cilician prisoners in their crowds before him
and pitch his camp in captured territory
and cased from head to foot in gold and silver armour
parade before the public on his charger.
Myself, if I could only be with you, my Delia,
I'd yoke the oxen, feed the flock on the familiar hill.
So long as I could hold you prisoner in tender arms
my sleep would be soft on the natural ground.
What's the good of lying love-lorn on a purple couch
when night arrives with wakefulness and weeping?
For neither feathers then nor painted coverlets
nor sound of quiet water can bring sleep.

Has word of mine profaned the majesty of Venus
and is my tongue now paying the price of blasphemy?
Can I be accused of defiling the gods' temples
or of stealing garlands from their holy hearths?
If guilty I'd not hesitate to fall down on my face
in the porch and kiss the consecrated threshold,
to crawl in penance on my knees and beat my wretched head
against the holy door.

But you who heartlessly deride my sufferings beware.
Your turn will come; the God won't punish me for ever.
I have seen the mocker of youth's unhappy love
as an old man yield his neck to Venus' chain,
practise pretty speeches in a quavering voice
and try with trembling hand to set his grizzled hair.
Nor was he ashamed to serenade his precious girl
and accost her maid in public in the Forum.
The young men and the children throng and thrust around him,
spitting in their tunics to avoid bad luck.

But, Venus, my devoted heart is ever at your service.
Have mercy. Why in rancour burn the harvest that is yours?

III

Ibitis Aegaeas sine me, Messalla, per undas,
  o utinam memores, ipse cohorsque, mei!
me tenet ignotis aegrum Phaeacia terris,
  abstineas auidas Mors modo nigra manus.
abstineas, Mors atra, precor: non hic mihi mater,   5
  quae legat in maestos ossa perusta sinus;
non soror, Assyrios cineri quae dedat odores
  et fleat effusis ante sepulcra comis;
Delia non usquam, quae me quam mitteret urbe
  dicitur ante omnes consuluisse deos.   10

Illa sacras pueri sortes ter sustulit: illi
  rettulit e triviis omina certa puer.
cuncta dabant reditus, tamen est deterrita nusquam
  quin fleret nostras respiceretque uias.
ipse ego, solator, cum iam mandata dedissem,   15
  quaerebam tardas anxius usque moras:
aut ego sum causatus aues aut omina dira
  Saturniue sacram me tenuisse diem.
o quotiens ingressus iter mihi tristia dixi
  offensum in porta signa dedisse pedem!   20
audeat inuito ne quis discedere amore
  aut sciet egressum se prohibente deo.

Quid tua nunc Isis mihi, Delia, quid mihi prosunt
  illa tua totiens aera repulsa manu,
quidue, pie dum sacra colis, pureque lauari   25
  te (memini) et puro secubuisse toro?
nunc, dea, nunc succurre mihi — nam posse mederi
  picta docet templis multa tabella tuis —
ut mea uotiuas persoluens Delia uoces
  ante sacras lino tecta fores sedeat   30
bisque die resoluta comas tibi dicere laudes
  insignis turba debeat in Pharia.
at mihi contingat patrios celebrare Penates
  reddereque antiquo menstrua tura Lari.

Quam bene Saturno uiuebant rege, priusquam   35
  tellus in longas est patefacta uias!

3

Alas, Messalla, you will sail Aegean seas without me —
you and the company — but not, please God, forgetting
the sick man, captive in Phaeacia, land of the unknown,
if only the Black Goddess withholds her grasping hand.
Dark Death, withhold, I pray you. I have no mother here
to gather up the calcined bones to her sad breast;
no sister to bestow Assyrian perfumes on the ashes
and weep beside the grave with streaming hair;
no Delia — and yet, before she let me leave the city,
she sought at every temple counsel of the gods.

Three times she drew the boy's sacred lots; for her
the boy reported sure signs from the crossroads:
all promised safe return. But nothing could dissuade her
from weeping for regret of our long journey.
I too, her comforter, after the last farewell,
looked for postponement in despair
and made excuses, claiming that unlucky birds or omens
or Saturn's sacred day compelled my staying.
How often I convinced myself, after the march began,
that my stumble in the gateway promised ill!
Let no man dare depart from a reluctant love
or he shall know that God forbade his going.

What help, O Delia, your Queen of Heaven now —
devout percussions of the bronze rattle,
observance of the ritual ablutions,
nights apart so memorably pure?
Haste, Goddess, to my aid, for many a painted tablet
on temple walls proclaims your saving power;
and then my Delia, in payment of her vow,
linen-clad shall sit before your holy door
and twice a day with loosened hair duly tell your praises,
conspicuous among the Egyptian congregation.
But grant that I may worship the Penates of my fathers
and offer incense every month to the ancient Lar.

How good the life in Saturn's reign, before
the world was opened into long roads!

nondum caeruleas pinus contempserat undas,
    effusum uentis praebueratque sinum;
nec uagus ignotis repetens compendia terris
    presserat externa nauita merce ratem.   40
illo non ualidus subiit iuga tempore taurus,
    non domito frenos ore momordit equus;
non domus ulla fores habuit, non fixus in agris
    qui regeret certis finibus arua lapis;
ipsae mella dabant quercus, ultroque ferebant   45
    obuia securis ubera lactis oues;
non acies, non ira fuit, non bella, nec ensem
    immiti saeuus duxerat arte faber.

Nunc Ioue sub domino caedes et uulnera semper,
    nunc mare, nunc leti mille repente uiae.   50
parce, Pater: timidum non me periuria terrent,
    non dicta in sanctos impia uerba deos.
quod si fatales iam nunc expleuimus annos,
    fac lapis inscriptis stet super ossa notis:
HIC IACET IMMITI CONSVMPTVS MORTE TIBVLLVS   55
    MESSALLAM TERRA DVM SEQVITVRQVE MARI.

Sed me, quod facilis tenero sum semper amori,
    ipsa Venus campos ducet in Elysios.
hic choreae cantusque uigent, passimque uagantes
    dulce sonant tenui gutture carmen aues;   60
fert casiam non culta seges totosque per agros
    floret odoratis terra benigna rosis:
ac iuuenum series teneris immixta puellis
    ludit, et assidue proelia miscet Amor.
illic est cuicumque rapax Mors uenit amanti,   65
    et gerit insigni myrtea serta coma.

At scelerata iacet sedes in nocte profunda
    abdita, quam circum flumina nigra sonant:
Tisiphoneque impexa feros pro crinibus angues
    saeuit et huc illuc impia turba fugit;   70
tunc niger in porta serpentum Cerberus ore
    stridet et aeratas excubat ante fores.
illic Iunonem temptare Ixionis ausi
    uersantur celeri noxia membra rota,

Pine timbers then had not defied blue waves
or spread billowing canvas to the winds.
No roving sailor seeking profit from strange lands
had freighted ship with foreign merchandise.
No mighty bull in those days bore the yoke
or stallion tamely chawed the bit.
Houses had no doors. No stone stood in the fields
to rule the arable with straight edge.
There was honey from the oak, and heavy-uddered ewes
offered milk on meeting carefree countryfolk.
Anger and armies and war were not yet known:
no blacksmith's cruel craft had forged the sword.

But now, in Jove's dominion, it is always wounds and slaughter;
now there is the sea and sudden Death's one thousand roads.
Have mercy on me, Father, for although I am afraid
no perjury or blasphemy justifies the fear.
But if today I have completed my predestined years
let my bones be laid beneath a stone inscribed
HERE LIES TIBULLUS WASTED BY UNTIMELY DEATH
WHILE SERVING WITH MESSALLA ON LAND AND SEA.

My spirit, though, as I have always welcomed tender love,
Venus herself will lead to the Elysian fields.
There songs and dances flourish, and flitting everywhere
sweetly sing the birds their slender-throated tune.
Untilled the land bears cassia and over whole acres
heavy-scented roses bloom from the rich loam.
Young men and tender girls make sport, lined up together,
continually engaging in the battles of Love.
There are all those whom Death raped while they were lovers
and they wear the myrtle in token on their hair.

But the place of wickedness lies hidden deep in night
and all around it black rivers roar.
Tisiphone, the Fury with snakes for hair uncombed,
whips in all directions the godless multitude.
Then, black in the gateway, Cerberus serpent-mouthed
hisses, lying guard before the brazen door.
There the guilty limbs of Juno's would-be ravisher,
the bold Ixion, twist on the whirling wheel.

porrectusque nouem Tityos per iugera terrae 75
    assiduas atro uiscere pascit aues.
Tantalus est illic, et circum stagna, sed acrem
    iam iam poturi deserit unda sitim;
et Danai proles, Veneris quod numina laesit,
    in caua Lethaeas dolia portat aquas. 80
illic sit quicumque meos uiolauit amores,
    optauit lentas et mihi militias.

At tu casta, precor, maneas sanctique pudoris
    assideat custos sedula semper anus.
haec tibi fabellas referat positaque lucerna 85
    deducat plena stamina longa colu,
ac circa, grauibus pensis affixa, puella
    paulatim somno fessa remittat opus.
tunc ueniam subito nec quisquam nuntiet ante
    sed uidear caelo missus adesse tibi. 90
tunc mihi, qualis eris, longos turbata capillos,
    obuia nudato, Delia, curre pede.
hoc precor; hunc illum nobis Aurora nitentem
    Luciferum roseis candida portet equis.

IV

'Sic umbrosa tibi contingant tecta, Priape,
    ne capiti soles ne noceantque niues:
quae tua formosos cepit sollertia? certe
    non tibi barba nitet, non tibi culta coma est;
nudus et hibernae producis frigora brumae, 5
    nudus et aestiui tempora sicca Canis.'

Sic ego. tum Bacchi respondit rustica proles,
    armatus curua, sic mihi, falce deus:
'O fuge te tenerae puerorum credere turbae,
    nam causam iusti semper amoris habent. 10
hic placet angustis quod equum compescit habenis;
    hic placidam niueo pectore pellit aquam.
hic quia fortis adest audacia cepit; at illi
    uirgineus teneras stat pudor ante genas.

And Tityos, spreadeagled over nine terrestrial acres,
feeds with bleeding flesh the indefatigable birds.
There in the pool is Tantalus, but when he stoops to drink
the water slides away from his raging thirst.
And the Danaids, who violated Venus' majesty,
are heaving Lethe water into leaking vats.
Let any man lie there who desecrates my love
and prays for my long service in the army.

But, Delia, please be true to me, and let the old duenna
be there to guard your honour with her continual care.
She shall tell you stories and when the lamp is lit
draw the lengthening thread from her laden distaff,
while the girls around her, intent on heavy stints,
gradually for weariness nod off at their work.
Then suddenly I shall arrive and no one give you warning
but your first thought will be that I have dropped from heaven.
Then, simply as you are, in long-haired confusion,
run to greet me, Delia, with naked feet.
That is my desire: let bright Aurora bring me
on her rose-red steeds that shining Morning Star.

4

'So may a shady roof be given you, Priapus,
to protect your person from the sun and snow,
if you tell me your technique for catching handsome boys.
Not yours, I see, the wavy hair, not yours the glossy beard,
and naked you prolong the cold of winter solstice,
naked too the drought of summer Sirius.'

Thus I. Whereat the God armed with a reaping-hook,
Bacchus' yokel son, thus to me replied:
'O flee and never trust thee to the troop of tender boys,
for cause of true love evermore is theirs.
Here is one who pleases by his skill in horsemanship;
there another who can part the pool with pale white breast.
This one's impudence is charming, while on that one's tender cheek
innocence mounts blushing guard.

Sed ne te capiant, primo si forte negabit,   15
  taedia: paulatim sub iuga colla dabit.
longa dies homini docuit parere leones;
  longa dies molli saxa peredit aqua.
annus in apricis maturat collibus uuas;
  annus agit certa lucida signa uice.   20

Nec iurare time: Veneris periuria uenti
  irrita per terras et freta summa ferunt.
gratia magna Ioui: uetuit pater ipse ualere
  iurasset cupide quicquid ineptus amor;
perque suas impune sinit Dictynna sagittas   25
  affirmes, crines perque Minerua suos.

At si tardus eris errabis. transiet aetas
  quam cito! non segnis stat remeatue dies.
quam cito purpureos deperdit terra colores!
  quam cito formosas populus alta comas!   30
quam iacet, infirmae uenere ubi fata senectae,
  qui prior Eleo est carcere missus equus!
uidi iam iuuenem premeret cum serior aetas
  maerentem stultos praeteriisse dies.
crudeles diui. serpens nouus exuit annos;   35
  formae non ullam Fata dedere moram.
solis aeterna est Baccho Phoeboque iuuentas,
  nam decet intonsus crinis utrumque deum.

Tu puero quodcumque tuo temptare libebit
  cedas: obsequio plurima uincet amor.   40
neu comes ire neges quamuis uia longa paretur
  et Canis arenti torreat arua siti,
quamuis praetexens picta ferrugine caelum
  uenturam †amiciat† imbrifer arcus aquam.
uel si caeruleas puppi uolet ire per undas,   45
  ipse leuem remo per freta pelle ratem.
nec te paeniteat duros subiisse labores
  aut opera insuetas atteruisse manus.
nec, uelit insidiis altas si claudere ualles,
  dum placeas, umeri retia ferre negent.   50
si uolet arma, leui temptabis ludere dextra;
  saepe dabis nudum, uincat ut ille, latus.

Yet be thou of good courage if at first he should refuse.
Slowly will he bring his neck beneath the yoke.
Time can teach the lion obedience to man;
gentle water bites through the rock in time.
A year revolves the shining signs in regular succession;
grapes on sunny slopes ripen in a year.

And fear thou not to swear. The perjuries of Venus
are blown invalid over land and sea.
All thanks be to the Father. For Jove himself forbade
the longing oaths of lovers to have weight.
A promise by Diana's arrows or Minerva's hair
may be broken without fear of punishment.

But wait too long and thou'lt be wrong. How swiftly prime is flying!
Time is never idle, never turns again.
How swiftly disappear earth's lively colours!
How swiftly the tall poplar's lovely locks!
How fall'n, when Fate brings on old age and weakness,
the horse that was Olympic winner once!
A young man have I seen with middle age upon him
lament the foolish passing of his days.
Ah, cruel Gods! The snake re-born sloughs off its years
but Fate has granted Beauty no delaying.
Bacchus and Apollo have sole right to eternal youth,
for long hair suits their twin divinity.

Then humour thou the boy in all he has a mind to:
Love will conquer most by giving in.
Deny him not thy company upon the longest journey,
though the thirsty Dog-star parches the ground,
though bordering the sky with dim and dusky colours
the rainbow warns of an approaching storm.
If he should wish to sail across the billows blue
row the dinghy o'er the main thyself.
And let it not repent thee of thy labour and distress
or of blisters on thine unaccustomed hands.
Should he then desire to set a snare in some high valley
shoulder thou the nets, if haply thou canst please.
Or if he fancy fencing fence thou not with heavy hand;
oft expose thy flank and suffer him to win.

tunc tibi mitis erit, rapias tum cara licebit
  oscula: pugnabit sed tibi rapta dabit.
rapta dabit primo, post afferet ipse roganti,   55
  post etiam collo se implicuisse uelit.

Heu male nunc artes miseras haec saecula tractant!
  iam tener assueuit munera uelle puer.
at tu qui Venerem docuisti uendere primus,
  quisquis es, infelix urgeat ossa lapis.   60
Pieridas, pueri, doctos et amate poetas,
  aurea nec superent munera Pieridas.
carmine purpurea est Nisi coma; carmina ni sint,
  ex umero Pelopis non nituisset ebur.
quem referent Musae uiuet dum robora tellus,   65
  dum caelum stellas, dum uehet amnis aquas.
at qui non audit Musas, qui uendit amorem,
  Idaeae currus ille sequatur Opis
et ter centenas erroribus expleat urbes
  et secet ad Phrygios uilia membra modos.   70
blanditiis uult esse locum Venus: illa querelis
  supplicibus, miseris fletibus illa fauet.'

Haec mihi quae canerem Titio deus edidit ore,
  sed Titium coniunx haec meminisse uetat.
pareat ille suae: uos me celebrate magistrum   75
  quos male habet multa callidus arte puer.
gloria cuique sua est: me qui spernentur amantes
  consultent; cunctis ianua nostra patet.
tempus erit cum me Veneris praecepta ferentem
  deducat iuuenum sedula turba senem.   80

Eheu, quam Marathus lento me torquet amore!
  deficiunt artes deficiuntque doli.
parce, puer, quaeso — ne turpis fabula fiam
  cum mea ridebunt uana magisteria.

V

Asper eram et bene discidium me ferre loquebar,
  at mihi nunc longe gloria fortis abest;

Then will he be kind to thee — thou'lt steal a precious kiss.
He will surely struggle, but grant thee kisses stolen.
Stolen kisses first, thereafter kisses for the asking,
then will he peradventure embrace thee on his own.

Alas, an evil generation treateth not the Arts aright:
tender boys are now accustomed to seek gifts.
Woe to him who first taught the marketing of Venus!
Let the stone of stumbling lie upon his bones.
Love the Muses, O ye striplings, and the scholar poets,
nor above the Muses value gifts of gold.
Nisus' lock in song is purple; were it not for song
never had the ivory shone from Pelops' shoulder.
He of whom the Muses tell shall live while earth bears oak-trees
and the heaven stars and the rivers water.
But he who hears the Muses not, who makes of love a market,
shall follow the Idaean chariot of Ops
and traversing three hundred cities in his wanderings
cut off his vile members to the Phrygian mode.
Venus wills a place for loving-kindness and she hears
the suppliant's complaint and the tears of the afflicted.'

To this, my song for Titius, the God gave utterance,
but Titius' wife commands him to forget it.
Let him obey his own. But let all you who suffer
the wiles of crafty boys hail me as Master.
To each his own ambition. Mine is counselling rejected
lovers. Yes, my door stands open to them all.
The time will come when I as bearer of Love's message
am attended in old age by troops of studious youth.

Alas, how Marathus in love's slow fire torments me!
Science profits nothing — neither do arts.
Have pity, boy, I beg you, or my reputation's gone
and all will ridicule the magisterial fool.

5

I was angry and proclaimed that separation did not hurt,
but such heroics now are far beyond me.

namque agor, ut per plana citus sola uerbere turben
    quem celer assueta uersat ab arte puer.
ure ferum et torque, libeat ne dicere quicquam   5
    magnificum posthac: horrida uerba doma.
parce tamen, per te furtiui foedera lecti,
    per Venerem quaeso compositumque caput.

Ille ego, cum tristi morbo defessa iaceres,
    te dicor uotis eripuisse meis.   10
ipseque te circum lustraui sulpure puro,
    carmine cum magico praecinuisset anus.
ipse procuraui ne possent saeua nocere
    somnia ter sancta deueneranda mola.
ipse ego, uelatus filo tunicisque solutis,   15
    uota nouem Triuiae nocte silente dedi.
omnia persolui: fruitur nunc alter amore,
    et precibus felix utitur ille meis.

At mihi felicem uitam, si salua fuisses,
    fingebam demens, sed renuente deo: 20
'rura colam, frugumque aderit mea Delia custos,
    area dum messes sole calente teret;
aut mihi seruabit plenis in lintribus uuas
    pressaque ueloci candida musta pede.
consuescet numerare pecus; consuescet amantis   25
    garrulus in dominae ludere uerna sinu.
illa deo sciet agricolae pro uitibus uuam,
    pro segete spicas, pro grege ferre dapem.
illa regat cunctos, illi sint omnia curae,
    at iuuet in tota me nihil esse domo.   30
huc ueniet Messalla meus, cui dulcia poma
    Delia selectis detrahat arboribus,
et tantum uenerata uirum, hunc sedula curet,
    huic paret atque epulas ipsa ministra gerat.'

Haec mihi fingebam, quae nunc Eurusque Notusque   35
    iactat odoratos uota per Armenios.
saepe ego temptaui curas depellere uino:
    at dolor in lacrimas uerterat omne merum.
saepe aliam tenui: sed iam cum gaudia adirem
    admonuit dominae deseruitque Venus.   40

I am driven, like a top spinning on a flat surface,
whipped by an agile boy who knows his business.
Twist and sear my pride with torture till I never fancy
grandiloquence again. Tame my ranting speech.
But forgive me, I beseech you, by the bond of stolen love,
by Venus and the heads of our agreement.

When you lay exhausted on the bed of fever,
mine, I am assured, were the prayers that saved you.
It was I who purified your room with burning sulphur
after the wise woman had chanted her spells;
I who counteracted the menace of your nightmares,
offering holy meal thrice in expiation;
I who wearing woollen fillet and unbelted tunic
in the silent night made nine vows to Diana.
I paid them all, and now someone else enjoys my love
and profits from my prayers, the lucky man.

In my folly I had dreamed that the lucky life was mine
if you recovered, but the God willed otherwise.
'I'll farm' I thought 'and Delia will be there to guard the grain
while the sun-baked floor threshes harvest in the heat.
Or she will watch the grapes for me in the laden troughs
and the white new wine pressed by trampling feet.
She will learn to count the sheep. The children of the house-slaves
will learn to play and prattle on a loving mistress' lap.
She will offer to the farmer God grapes for the vines,
ears for the standing corn, a victim for the flock.
She can rule us all, take charge of everything,
but I'll enjoy non-entity at home.
When my Messalla comes to see us, Delia will pick him
delicious apples from our choicest trees,
and in the great man's honour attend to all his needs,
prepare a dinner for him and wait on him herself.'

These were my dreams, but now from East and South the breezes
toss them unfulfilled beyond perfumed Armenia.
Often have I tried to drink away my troubles,
but the sorrow turned every wine to tears;
often embraced another, but Venus on joy's brink
reminding me of Delia forsook me.

tunc me, discedens, deuotum femina dixit —
   a pudet! — et narrat scire nefanda meam.
non facit hoc uerbis; facie tenerisque lacertis
   deuouet et flauis nostra puella comis.
talis ad Haemonium Nereis Pelea quondam   45
   uecta est frenato caerula pisce Thetis.

Haec nocuere mihi; quod adest huic dives amator,
   uenit in exitium callida lena meum.
sanguineas edat illa dapes atque ore cruento
   tristia cum multo pocula felle bibat.   50
hanc uolitent animae circum sua fata querentes
   semper et e tectis strix uiolenta canat.
ipsa fame stimulante furens herbasque sepulcris
   quaerat et a saeuis ossa relicta lupis;
currat et inguinibus nudis ululetque per urbem,   55
   post agat e triuiis aspera turba canum.
eueniet: dat signa deus. sunt numina amanti,
   saeuit et iniusta lege relicta Venus.

At tu quam primum sagae praecepta rapacis
   desere. num donis uincitur omnis amor?   60
pauper erit praesto semper tibi, pauper adibit
   primus et in tenero fixus erit latere.
pauper in angusto fidus comes agmine turbae
   subicietque manus efficietque uiam.
pauper ad occultos furtim deducet amicos   65
   uinclaque de niueo detrahet ipse pede.

Heu, canimus frustra, nec uerbis uicta patescit
   ianua, sed plena est percutienda manu.
at tu, qui potior nunc es, mea fata timeto:
   uersatur celeri fors leuis orbe rotae.   70
non frustra quidam iam nunc in limine perstat
   sedulus, ac crebro prospicit, ac refugit,
et simulat transire domum, mox deinde recurrit
   solus, et ante ipsas exscreat usque fores.
nescioquid furtiuus Amor parat. utere, quaeso,   75
   dum licet: in liquida nat tibi linter aqua.

Then calling me bewitched the woman left and to my shame
spread rumours that my girl uses the black arts.
What need has she of spells, with that bewitching face,
soft arms and yellow hair
like the Nereid of old who rode a bridled dolphin
to Thessalian Peleus — Thetis the blue-eyed?

Such my downfall. That a rich lover's at her side
means a crafty bawd has come to ruin me.
Let her eat raw meat and her lips drip blood
as she drinks full cups of bitter gall.
Let the ghosts flap round her bewailing their fate
and the vampire-owl screech from her eaves.
Let her go hunger-mad and search for herbs on graves,
for any bone left over by ravening wolves.
Let her run with naked crotch, howling through the city,
hunted by a savage pack of crossroad curs.
So be it. God has given the sign. A power stands over lovers
and Venus takes revenge when unlawfully abandoned.

O Delia reject forthwith that grasping witch's guidance.
Must every love surrender to a bribe?
Your poor man is prepared to offer service always,
the first to come at need, inseparate from your side.
Your poor man, trusty comrade in the pressure of a crowd,
will use his hands to good effect and find a way.
Your poor man will escort you unobserved to secret friends,
slipping the sandal from your snow-white foot himself.

Alas I sing in vain. Her door unmoved by words
is waiting for the knock of a money-laden hand.
But you, her darling of today, take warning from my fate.
Fortune's fickle wheel quickly turns.
Not for nothing even now someone stands upon her threshold —
first he looks about him, then he backs away,
and pretends to pass the house, then returns without his slave
and coughs persistently right by the door.
Love the thief has plans. Take your pleasure while you may.
Water is unstable and your ship is still at sea.

VI

Semper, ut inducar, blandos offers mihi uultus,
  post tamen es misero tristis et asper, Amor.
quid tibi saeuitiae mecum est! an gloria magna est
  insidias homini composuisse deum?

Nam mihi tenduntur casses. iam Delia furtim   5
  nescioquem tacita callida nocte fouet.
illa quidem tam multa negat, sed credere durum est;
  sic etiam de me pernegat usque uiro.
ipse miser docui quo posset ludere pacto
  custodes: eheu, nunc premor arte mea.   10
fingere tunc didicit causas ut sola cubaret,
  cardine tunc tacito uertere posse fores.
tunc sucos herbasque dedi quis liuor abiret
  quem facit impresso mutua dente Venus.

At tu, fallacis coniunx incaute puellae,   15
  me quoque seruato peccet ut illa nihil.
neu iuuenes celebret multo sermone caueto,
  neue cubet laxo pectus aperta sinu,
neu te decipiat nutu, digitoque liquorem
  ne trahat et mensae ducat in orbe notas.   20
exibit quam saepe, time, seu uisere dicet
  sacra Bonae maribus non adeunda Deae.
at mihi si credas, illam sequar unus ad aras;
  tunc mihi non oculis sit timuisse meis.

Saepe, uelut gemmas eius signumque probarem,   25
  per causam memini me tetigisse manum.
saepe mero somnum peperi tibi, at ipse bibebam
  sobria supposita pocula uictor aqua.
non ego te laesi prudens; ignosce fatenti.
  iussit Amor; contra quis ferat arma deos?   30
ille ego sum (nec me iam dicere uera pudebit)
  instabat tota cui tua nocte canis.
quid tenera tibi coniuge opus, tua si bona nescis
  seruare? frustra clauis inest foribus.
te tenet, absentes alios suspirat amores   35
  et simulat subito condoluisse caput.

6

Always, to entice me, Love, you wear a smiling face,
but later to my sorrow assume an angry frown.
How hard on me you are! Is it so glorious
for an immortal God to set a man-trap?

Your nets are spread against me, now that devious Delia
in the secrecy of night hugs another man.
True, she denies it strongly, but belief is difficult;
she makes the same denials to her husband about me.
It was I, alas, who taught her how to fool the guard,
and now I am the victim of my own device.
She learnt to find excuses then for sleeping on her own,
to open creaking doors without a sound
and use the herbs and simples that I gave her to remove
the marks imprinted by the teeth of passion.

But you, sir, careless husband of a deceitful girl,
keep watch on both of us to stop her playing false.
Take care she does not talk too much with young admirers
or at a dinner wear a dress that shows her breast
or fool you with a nod or dip her finger in the wine
and trace a secret message on the table-top.
Worry when she's often out or tells you she'll attend
the rites of the Good Goddess, where men are not allowed.
If you trusted her to me, I'd attend her to the altar
and as the one man present I'd not fear for my eyes.

Often I remember how I touched her hand
on pretext of appraising her signet cameo,
and how my wine sent you to sleep while I drank sober cups
victoriously substituting water.
The sin was not cold-blooded and confession earns forgiveness.
It was Love that gave the order. Who can fight against a God?
I was the man — no longer shall I blush to tell the truth —
the man your dog was barking at all night.
What good's a tender wife to you if you don't guard
your treasure? Doors have keys in them for nothing.
Her sighs while she embraces you are for an absent lover
and the sudden head-ache is a subterfuge.

At mihi seruandam credas: non saeua recuso
  uerbera, detrecto non ego uincla pedum.
tunc procul absitis, quisquis colit arte capillos,
  et fluit effuso cui toga laxa sinu;   40
quisquis et occurret, ne possit crimen habere
  stet procul aut alia transeat ille uia.

Sic fieri iubet ipse deus, sic magna sacerdos
  est mihi diuino uaticinata sono.
haec, ubi Bellonae motu est agitata, nec acrem   45
  flammam, non amens uerbera torta timet.
ipsa bipenne suos caedit uiolenta lacertos
  sanguineque effuso spargit inulta deam,
statque latus praefixa ueru, stat saucia pectus,
  et canit euentus quos dea magna monet: 50
'parcite quam custodit Amor uiolare puellam,
  ne pigeat magno post tetigisse malo.
attigerit, labentur opes, ut uulnere nostro
  sanguis, ut hic uentis diripiturque cinis.'

Et tibi nescioquas dixit, mea Delia, poenas;   55
  si tamen admittas, sit precor illa leuis.
non ego te propter parco tibi, sed tua mater
  me mouet atque iras aurea uincit anus.
haec mihi te adducit tenebris multoque timore
  coniungit nostras clam taciturna manus.   60
haec foribusque manet noctu me affixa proculque
  cognoscit strepitus me ueniente pedum.

Viue diu mihi, dulcis anus: proprios ego tecum,
  sit modo fas, annos contribuisse uelim.
te semper natamque tuam te propter amabo: 65
  quicquid agit, sanguis est tamen illa tuus.
sit modo casta doce, quamuis non uitta ligatos
  impediat crines nec stola longa pedes.
et mihi sint durae leges, laudare nec ullam
  possim ego quin oculos appetat illa meos;   70
et, siquid peccasse putet, ducarque capillis
  immerito pronas proripiarque uias.

Non ego te pulsare uelim, sed uenerit iste
  si furor, optarim non habuisse manus.

But let me be her keeper. You could flog me when you liked
or fling me into fetters and I'd take my punishment.
Then you'd have to clear off, all you fops with curly hair
and expansive togas falling in loose folds.
Anyone who met us would be halted at a distance
or pass us by another road to prove his innocence.

Thus runs the God's commandment, this Bellona's high-priestess
with utterance inspired prophesied to me.
When in trance, possessed and shaken by the goddess,
she fears no roaring flame or flailing scourge,
slashes her own arms in frenzy with a double axe,
unscathed soaks the image in a stream of blood,
and standing there with wounded breast and skewered flank
chants Bellona's warning oracles:
'See ye do no violence to the girl whom Love protects,
lest ye repent of touching her to your great evil after.
If any man should touch her his wealth shall flow away
as blood flows from my wounds and wind scatters this ash.'

She also spoke of punishments for you, my Delia,
but if you should transgress I pray that she be lenient.
I spare you for your mother's sake and not your own deserving;
old and golden-hearted she disarms my wrath.
In the dark she leads you to me and though terrified
stealthily with no word spoken joins our hands.
Pressed to the door at night, she listens, waiting for me —
can recognise, far off, approaching steps as mine.

Long life to you, sweet lady. If it were possible
I'd give you part of mine.
You I shall always love and thanks to you your daughter;
she is still your blood however she behaves.
But teach her to be faithful though her braided hair is free
and no Roman wife's long robe confines her feet.
I too can take harsh terms: if I praise another woman
Delia is welcome to attack my eyes;
and if she thinks me false she can pull me by the hair
and drag me in my innocence along the street face down.

I'd never strike you, Delia, but should the mad fit come
I'd pray to lose my hands.

nec saeuo sis casta metu sed mente fideli;   75
   mutuus absenti te mihi seruet amor.
at quae fida fuit nulli, post uicta senecta
   ducit inops tremula stamina torta manu,
firmaque conductis adnectit licia telis,
   tractaque de niueo uellere ducta putat.   80
hanc animo gaudente uident iuuenumque cateruae
   commemorant merito tot mala ferre senem.
hanc Venus ex alto flentem sublimis Olympo
   spectat et infidis quam sit acerba monet.

Haec aliis maledicta cadant. nos, Delia, amoris   85
   exemplum cana simus uterque coma.

VII

Hunc cecinere diem Parcae, fatalia nentes
   stamina non ulli dissoluenda deo:
hunc fore Aquitanas posset qui fundere gentes,
   quem tremeret forti milite uictus Atur.
euenere: nouos pubes Romana triumphos   5
   uidit et euinctos bracchia capta duces;
at te uictrices lauros, Messalla, gerentem
   portabat nitidis currus eburnus equis.

Non sine me est tibi partus honos: Tarbella Pyrene
   testis et Oceani litora Santonici,   10
testis Arar Rhodanusque celer magnusque Garunna,
   Carnutis et flaui caerula lympha Liger.

An te, Cydne, canam, tacitis qui leniter undis
   caeruleus placidis per uada serpis aquis?
quantus et aetherio contingens uertice nubes   15
   frigidus intonsos Taurus alat Cilicas?
quid referam ut uolitet crebras intacta per urbes
   alba Palaestino sancta columba Syro?
utque maris uastum prospectet turribus aequor
   prima ratem uentis credere docta Tyros?   20
qualis et, arentes cum findit Sirius agros,
   fertilis aestiua Nilus abundet aqua?

Be true then not from fear but faithfulness of heart.
Let mutual love for me in absence guard you.
The woman true to no one, when overcome by age
must pull the yarn with shaking hand, a pauper,
and tie the leashes firm to the loom for hire and clean
the locks of wool pulled out from snow-white fleeces.
Her plight gives hearty pleasure to all the young men watching,
who declare it serves her right to suffer in old age.
Aloof on high Olympus Venus sees her tears and warns us
how merciless she is to infidelity.

But these ill wishes are for others. Delia, you and I
must be Love's paradigm when we are both white-haired.

7

Of this day sang the Fates, as they spun the threads of doom
that no God can unwind:
this would be the day of rout for tribes of Aquitaine,
of dread for the Adour, conquered by brave cohorts.
And so it came to pass. Our Roman race has seen
new Triumphs, chiefs with captive wrists in chains,
and you, Messalla, wearing the victorious laurel,
drawn by shining steeds in the ivory chariot.

Not without me was your glory gained: witness the Tarbellian
Pyrenees and shores of the Santonic Ocean;
witness Saône and rapid Rhone and great Garonne
and Loire, blue stream of flaxen-haired Carnutes.

Or shall I sing of Cydnus, whose quiet waters glide
softly through smooth blue shallows?
Of Taurus, cold and huge, with airy summit cloudcapped,
unshorn Cilicia's livelihood?
Why tell of white doves flying, safe through crowded towns,
sacrosanct in Syropalestine?
How the tall towers of Tyre, the mother of sailing ships,
survey the sea's expanse?
How fertile Nile floods in summer
when Sirius cracks the thirsty fields?

Nile pater, quanam possim te dicere causa
    aut quibus in terris occuluisse caput?
te propter nullos tellus tua postulat imbres,   25
    arida nec pluuio supplicat herba Ioui.
te canit atque suum pubes miratur Osirim
    barbara, Memphitem plangere docta bouem.

Primus aratra manu sollerti fecit Osiris
    et teneram ferro sollicitauit humum.   30
primus inexpertae commisit semina terrae
    pomaque non notis legit ab arboribus.
hic docuit teneram palis adiungere uitem,
    hic uiridem dura caedere falce comam.
illi iucundos primum matura sapores   35
    expressa incultis uua dedit pedibus.
ille liquor docuit uoces inflectere cantu,
    mouit et ad certos nescia membra modos.
Bacchus et agricolae magno confecta labore
    pectora laetitiae dissoluenda dedit.   40
Bacchus et afflictis requiem mortalibus affert,
    crura licet dura compede pulsa sonent.
non tibi sunt tristes curae nec luctus, Osiri,
    sed chorus et cantus et leuis aptus amor,
sed uarii flores et frons redimita corymbis,   45
    fusa sed ad teneros lutea palla pedes,
et Tyriae uestes et dulcis tibia cantu
    et leuis occultis conscia cista sacris.

Huc ades et Genium ludis Geniumque choreis
    concelebra et multo tempora funde mero.   50
illius et nitido stillent unguenta capillo,
    et capite et collo mollia serta gerat.
sic uenias, hodierne: tibi dem turis honores,
    liba et Mopsopio dulcia melle feram.

At tibi succrescat proles quae facta parentis   55
    augeat et circa stet ueneranda senem.
nec taceat monumenta uiae quem Tuscula tellus
    candidaque antiquo detinet Alba Lare.
namque opibus congesta tuis, hic glarea dura
    sternitur, hic apta iungitur arte silex.   60

Where or wherefore, Father Nile,
can I say you hide your head?
Thanks to you your country never prays for rain;
no withered grass petitions pluvial Jupiter.
Your folk in barbarous lamentation for the Memphian bull
praise and worship you as their Osiris.

The skilled hands of Osiris constructed the first plough,
solicited the virgin soil with iron,
committed the first seed to inexperienced earth
and gathered fruit from unfamiliar trees.
Osiris taught the tying of the tender vine to poles,
the lopping of green hair with pruning-hooks.
To him the ripe grapes trodden by uncultivated feet
first gave delicious savours.
That liquor taught the modulations of the voice in song,
moving ignorant limbs to sure rhythms.
To farmers' hearts exhausted by long labour
Bacchus brings deliverance and joy.
Bacchus offers respite to mortals in affliction,
though chains clank on their ankles.
Not sorrow or dull care, but song and dance, Osiris,
and fickle love suit you,
and flowers of every colour, brows with ivy-berries bound,
robes of saffron flowing down to tender feet,
Tyrian fabrics, dulcet melodies upon the pipe,
and the wicker casket for your holy mysteries.

O hither come and join us in the games and in the dances
to celebrate the Genius and drench his brow with wine.
Let perfumes of anointing drip from his gleaming locks
and garlands soft adorn his head and neck.
So come you, hodiernal: I will honour you with incense
and bring you meal-cake sweetened with the honey of Hymettus.

Messalla, may your family grow up to increase your glory
and stand about you in old age with honour.
May visitors to Tusculum and white Alba's ancient Lar
talk of your memorial, the road —
for here is hard-packed gravel laid at your expense
and here are stone blocks fitted skilfully together.

te canat agricola a magna cum uenerit Vrbe
    serus inoffensum rettuleritque pedem.

At tu, Natalis, multos celebrande per annos,
    candidior semper candidiorque ueni.

VIII

Non ego celari possum quid nutus amantis
    quidue ferant miti lenia uerba sono,
nec mihi sunt sortes nec conscia fibra deorum,
    praecinit euentus nec mihi cantus auis:
ipsa Venus magico religatum bracchia nodo   5
    perdocuit, multis non sine uerberibus.
desine dissimulare: deus crudelius urit
    quos uidet inuitos succubuisse sibi.

Quid tibi nunc molles prodest coluisse capillos
    saepeque mutatas disposuisse comas?   10
quid fuco splendente genas ornare? quid ungues
    artificis docta subsecuisse manu?
frustra iam uestes, frustra mutantur amictus
    ansaque compressos colligat arta pedes.
illa placet, quamuis inculto uenerit ore   15
    nec nitidum tarda compserit arte caput.

Num te carminibus, num te pallentibus herbis
    deuouit tacito tempore noctis anus?
cantus uicinis fruges traducit ab agris,
    cantus et iratae detinet anguis iter,   20
cantus et e curru Lunam deducere temptat,
    et faceret si non aera repulsa sonent.

Quid queror, heu, misero carmen nocuisse? quid herbas?
    forma nihil magicis utitur auxiliis,
sed corpus tetigisse nocet, sed longa dedisse   25
    oscula, sed femori conseruisse femur.

Nec tu difficilis puero tamen esse memento;
    persequitur poenis tristia facta Venus.

May farmers sing of you, as they come from the great city,
returning in the dark without a stumble.

And may your Birthday Spirit attend his celebration
bright and ever brighter for many years to come.

8

I cannot miss the augury of a lover's nod
or gently whispered words,
and yet I use no lots or divinatory lobes
and hear no prophecy in bird-song.
Venus herself, tying my arms with magic knot,
has flogged me to full knowledge.
Be honest, then. The God has fiercer fires
for those unwilling to submit to him.

It does you no good now to cultivate those curls
and try out various hair-styles,
no good to paint your cheeks with bright orchella
and have your nails professionally trimmed.
It's useless to keep changing your tunic and your cloak
and cramp your feet in tight-laced shoes.
That girl can please, although she wears no make-up
and takes no pains to sleek her hair.

Maybe some beldame in the silent night
with spells or pallid herbs bewitched you?
Spells can lift the crops from neighbours' fields,
can halt the hissing snake,
would draw the Moon down from her chariot
if brasses were not clashed.

Alas why blame the poor boy's hurt on spells or herbs?
Beauty needs no magic aids.
What hurts is body's touch, and giving long kisses,
and pressing thigh to thigh.

But you are to remember to take him seriously,
albeit but a boy. Venus punishes unkindness.

munera nec poscas; det munera canus amator
    ut foueat molli frigida membra sinu.   30
carior est auro iuuenis cui leuia fulgent
    ora nec amplexus aspera barba terit.
huic tu candentes umero suppone lacertos
    et regum magnae despiciantur opes.

At Venus inuenit puero concumbere furtim,   35
    dum timet et teneros conserit usque sinus,
et dare anhelanti pugnantibus umida linguis
    oscula et in collo figere dente notas.

Non lapis hanc gemmaeque iuuant quae frigore sola
    dormiat et nulli sit cupienda uiro.   40
heu sero reuocatur amor seroque iuuentas
    cum uetus infecit cana senecta caput.
tum studium formae est; coma tum mutatur ut annos
    dissimulet uiridi cortice tincta nucis;
tollere tum cura est albos a stirpe capillos   45
    et faciem dempta pelle referre nouam.

At tu, dum primi floret tibi temporis aetas,
    utere: non tardo labitur illa pede.
neu Marathum torque. puero quae gloria uicto est?
    in ueteres esto dura, puella, senes.   50
parce, precor, tenero. non illi sontica causa est,
    sed nimius luto corpora tingit amor.

Vel miser absenti maestas quam saepe querelas
    conicit, et lacrimis omnia plena madent.
'quid me spernis?' ait. 'poterat custodia uinci;   55
    ipse dedit cupidis fallere posse deus.
nota Venus furtiua mihi est — ut lenis agatur
    spiritus, ut nec dent oscula rapta sonum.
et possum media quauis obrepere nocte
    et strepitu nullo clam reserare fores.   60
quid prosunt artes, miserum si spernit amantem
    et fugit ex ipso saeua puella toro?
uel cum promittit subito sed perfida fallit
    et mihi nox multis est uigilanda malis?
dum mihi uenturam fingo, quodcumque mouetur   65
    illius credo tunc sonuisse pedes.'

Demand no gifts, but make your grizzled gallant give
to warm his chilly limbs in soft embrace.
Dearer than gold the youth with smooth and shining face
whose kiss no stubble rasps.
Under this one's shoulder lay your dazzling arms
and look down on the wealth of kings.

Venus has found the way to lie with a lad by stealth,
while he's afraid and keeps clinging in tender embrace,
and to give moist kisses, breathless in the duel of tongues,
and bite her cipher on his neck.

No pearl or precious stone can pleasure her who sleeps
in the cold alone, no man's desire.
Too late alas is love and too late youth recalled
when white-haired age has stained the head.
Beauty then is studied. Hair is changed to hide
the years with dye from a nut's green rind.
Solicitude then turns to rooting out white hairs
and recovers face by slack skin's removal.

Therefore while there flowers for you the season of the prime
use it, for it slips away fleet-footed.
And do not torture Marathus. What glory in a boy's defeat?
Be hard in girlhood on your veterans
but spare the innocent. No need to isolate his sickness.
That pallor is a symptom of immoderate love.

Yes, poor lad, how often he reproaches you in absence
and floods the place with tears!
'Why do you scorn me?' he asks. 'The guard could be won over.
God himself gives lovers licence to deceive.
I know clandestine Venus — how to draw breath gently
and steal a silent kiss.
I too can creep at midnight anywhere you please
and open doors without a sound.
But what's the good of arts if the cruel girl disdains
her wretched lover, runs away from bed,
and without warning treacherously breaks her word
and I must wake in night-long misery,
imagining that she will come at last
and thinking every movement is her footfall?'

Desistas lacrimare, puer. non frangitur illa,
    et tua iam fletu lumina fessa tument.
oderunt, Pholoe, moneo, fastidia diui,
    nec prodest sanctis tura dedisse focis.   70
hic Marathus quondam miseros ludebat amantes,
    nescius ultorem post caput esse deum.
saepe etiam lacrimas fertur risisse dolentis
    et cupidum ficta detinuisse mora.
nunc omnes odit fastus, nunc displicet illi   75
    quaecumque opposita est ianua dura sera.
et te poena manet, ni desinis esse superba.
    quam cupies uotis hunc reuocare diem!

IX

Quid mihi, si fueras miseros laesurus amores,
    foedera per diuos clam uiolanda dabas?
a miser, etsi quis primo periuria celat,
    sera tamen tacitis Poena uenit pedibus.

Parcite, caelestes: aequum est impune licere   5
    numina formosis laedere uestra semel.
lucra petens habili tauros adiungit aratro
    et durum terrae rusticus urget opus.
lucra petituras freta per parentia uentis
    ducunt instabiles sidera certa rates.   10
muneribus meus est captus puer: at deus illa
    in cinerem et liquidas munera uertat aquas.
iam mihi persoluet poenas, puluisque decorem
    detrahet et uentis horrida facta coma.
uretur facies, urentur sole capilli,   15
    deteret inualidos et uia longa pedes.

Admonui quotiens 'auro ne pollue formam:
    saepe solent auro multa subesse mala.
diuitiis captus si quis uiolauit amorem,
    asperaque est illi difficilisque Venus.   20
ure meum potius flamma caput et pete ferro
    corpus et intorto uerbere terga seca.
nec tibi celandi spes sit peccare paranti:
    scit deus occultos qui uetat esse dolos.

Stop crying, lad. The girl is unrelenting,
and now your tired eyes are swollen with tears.
I warn you, Pholoe: the Gods hate arrogance.
You waste your incense on their altars.
Our Marathus made fools of his poor lovers once,
blind to the avenging God behind him.
They even say he ridiculed their tears of anguish
and kept desire on edge with false excuses.
But now he hates all pride and fails to appreciate
the opposition of a bolted door.
You too will pay the price unless you stop being proud —
with prayers of yearning for today's return.

9

Why give me solemn promises if you intended wronging
my wretched love by breaking them in secret?
Unhappy boy! Though perjury can be hidden for a time,
punishment is bound to catch you in the end.

Forgive him, Heavenly Powers. Beauty has a right
to wrong your godheads once and go unpunished.
For profit peasants yoke their bulls to the wieldy plough
and press their hard work forward on the land.
For profit, over waters obedient to the winds,
unstable ships are drawn by fixed stars.
My boy was caught by bribery. May God convert those bribes
to ash and running water.
Later he will pay me the punishment in full:
dust and wind-blown hair will slight his charm;
the sun will burn his beauty, bleach his locks;
the long road chafe those vulnerable feet.

'Don't' I often warned him 'don't pollute your bloom with gold.
Behind the gold are sufferings in plenty.
If anyone for money does violence to love,
Venus is hard on him, and difficult.
I'd sooner have my hair burnt off, my body stabbed.
my shoulders lashed with knotted thongs.
But if you plan deception, never hope to hide it;
the God who brings deceit to light — he knows.

ipse deus tacito permisit saepe ministro   25
    ederet ut multo libera uerba mero.
ipse deus somno domitos emittere uocem
    iussit et inuitos facta tegenda loqui.'

Haec ego dicebam: nunc me fleuisse loquentem,
    nunc pudet ad teneros procubuisse pedes.   30
tunc mihi iurabas nullo te diuitis auri
    pondere, non gemmis uendere uelle fidem,
non tibi si pretium Campania terra daretur,
    non tibi si Bacchi cura Falernus ager.
illis eriperes uerbis mihi sidera caeli   35
    lucere et pronas fluminis esse uias.
quin etiam flebas, at non ego fallere doctus
    tergebam umentes credulus usque genas.
quid faciam, nisi et ipse fores in amore puellae?
    sic precor, exemplo sit leuis illa tuo.   40

O quotiens, uerbis ne quisquam conscius esset
    ipse comes multa lumina nocte tuli!
saepe insperanti uenit tibi munere nostro
    et latuit clausas post adoperta fores.
tum miser interii, stulte confisus amari;   45
    nam poteram ad laqueos cautior esse tuos.
quin etiam attonita laudes tibi mente canebam,
    et me nunc nostri Pieridumque pudet.
illa uelim rapida Vulcanus carmina flamma
    torreat et liquida deleat amnis aqua.   50
tu procul hinc absis, cui formam uendere cura est
    et pretium plena grande referre manu.

At te, qui puerum donis corrumpere es ausus,
    rideat assiduis uxor inulta dolis,
et cum furtiuo iuuenem lassauerit usu,   55
    tecum interposita languida ueste cubet.
semper sint externa tuo uestigia lecto
    et pateat cupidis semper aperta domus.
nec lasciua soror dicatur plura bibisse
    pocula uel plures emeruisse uiros.   60
illam saepe ferunt conuiuia ducere Baccho
    dum rota Luciferi prouocet orta diem.

The God himself has often authorised free speech
for silent servants in their cups,
has bidden sleepers talk and tell unconsciously
of their most secret deeds.'

Such my advice, but now it shames me to remember
that as I spoke I wept and fell down at your feet.
Then you'd swear to me once more that you'd never sell your promise,
not for pearls and not for pounds of gold,
not for an estate in rich Campania,
not for the Falernian acres Bacchus loves.
Those words could well have robbed me of my certainty
that rivers run downhill and stars shine in the sky.
Yes, you even wept, and I, unschooled in guile,
trusted you and wiped away the tears.
What should I do if you were not in love yourself?
I pray the girl be faithless — in your fashion.

O how many times, lest any overhear you,
I as your servant carried the light at midnight!
Often by my gift she came to you unhoped for
and hid with covered head behind closed doors.
That was my undoing. Poor fool, I thought you loved me.
I should have been more wary of your snares.
I even versified your praises, moonstruck as I was,
and now I am ashamed of us and the Pierians.
Let Vulcan roast those eulogies in roaring flame
and the running river liquidate them.
Out of my sight! You only love to sell your looks
and carry home, full-fisted, a fat fee.

But as for you who dared corrupt my boy with bribes,
may your own wife gull you with her cuckoldry
and when her furtive needs have tired out a young lover,
limply lie with you, tunic interposed.
Ever may your bed bear the marks of strangers
and your door be open to the lecherous.
Never be it said that even your licentious sister
sank more wine or served more lovers than your wife.
They tell me that the drinking at her parties often lasts
till Lucifer's bright wheel rolls in the day.

illa nulla queat melius consumere noctem
  aut operum uarias disposuisse uices.

At tua perdidicit, nec tu, stultissime, sentis   65
  cum tibi non solita corpus ab arte mouet.
tune putas illam pro te disponere crines
  aut tenues denso pectere dente comas?
istane persuadet facies auroque lacertos
  uinciat et Tyrio prodeat apta sinu?   70
non tibi sed iuueni cuidam uult bella uideri,
  deuoueat pro quo remque domumque tuam.
nec facit hoc uitio, sed corpora foeda podagra
  et senis amplexus culta puella fugit.

Huic tamen accubuit noster puer! hunc ego credam   75
  cum trucibus Venerem iungere posse feris.
blanditiasne meas aliis tu uendere es ausus?
  tune aliis, demens, oscula ferre mea?
tunc flebis cum me uinctum puer alter habebit
  et geret in regno regna superba tuo.   80
at tua tum me poena iuuet, Venerique merenti
  fixa notet casus aurea palma meos:
HANC TIBI FALLACI RESOLVTVS AMORE TIBVLLVS
DEDICAT ET GRATA SIS DEA MENTE ROGAT.

X

Quis fuit horrendos primus qui protulit enses?
  quam ferus, et uere ferreus, ille fuit!
tum caedes hominum generi, tum proelia nata;
  tum breuior dirae mortis aperta uia est.

An nihil ille miser meruit, nos ad mala nostra   5
  uertimus in saeuas quod dedit ille feras?

Diuitis hoc uitium est auri, nec bella fuerunt
  faginus astabat cum scyphus ante dapes.
non arces, non uallus erat, somnumque petebat
  securus uarias dux gregis inter oues.   10

There's no one who can better spend the night than she
or play a more exotic range of parts.

Except your wife — she's learnt it all. But you, big fool, don't notice
when she moves her body for you with a new-found ease.
Do you suppose it is for you she sets those curls
or runs the fine comb through that silky hair?
Is yours the face that tempts her to sport the golden bracelets
and leave the house attired in Tyrian gown?
She wants to look attractive for a young man I could name:
for him she'd blast your home and blue your money.
And nobody can blame her. As a girl of taste she finds
your gout and senile gallantry repulsive.

To think my boy has bedded with this creature!
He's capable of coupling with wild beasts.
How could you sell my tendernesses to another man?
How export my kisses? You must be out of your mind.
Just wait till your replacement takes me prisoner
and proudly rules your kingdom — you'll weep then.
And I'll enjoy your grief and dedicate to Venus
my rescuer a golden leaf of palm inscribed:
TIBULLUS FREED FROM LOVE DECEITFUL, GODDESS,
OFFERS THIS AND ASKS FOR GRATITUDE.

10

Tell me, who invented the terrifying sword?
Hard he must have been, and truly iron-hearted.
War that day and slaughter were born to humanity;
that day there was opened a short cut to grim death.

Or was the poor wretch blameless? Do we turn against ourselves
the blade intended for wild beasts?

Rich gold — the fault lies there. No wars when stoups of beechwood
stood at the sacrificial feast,
no citadels, no palisades. The leader led a flock
and sued for sleep in safety among the speckled ewes.

Tunc mihi uita foret, Valgi, nec tristia nossem
    arma, nec audissem corde micante tubam.
nunc ad bella trahor, et iam quis forsitan hostis
    haesura in nostro tela gerit latere.

Sed patrii seruate Lares: aluistis et idem   15
    cursarem uestros cum tener ante pedes.
neu pudeat prisco uos esse e stipite factos:
    sic ueteris sedes incoluistis aui.
tunc melius tenuere fidem, cum paupere cultu
    stabat in exigua ligneus aede deus.   20
hic placatus erat, seu quis libauerat uuam
    seu dederat sanctae spicea serta comae;
atque aliquis uoti compos liba ipse ferebat
    postque comes purum filia parua fauum.

At nobis aerata, Lares, depellite tela   25
    .   .   .   .
.   .   .   .
    hostiaque e plena rustica porcus hara.
hanc pura cum ueste sequar, myrtoque canistra
    uincta geram, myrto uinctus et ipse caput.
sic placeam uobis. alius sit fortis in armis,
    sternat et aduersos Marte fauente duces,   30
ut mihi potanti possit sua dicere facta
    miles et in mensa pingere castra mero.

Quis furor est atram bellis arcessere Mortem!
    imminet et tacito clam uenit illa pede.
non seges est infra, non uinea culta, sed audax   35
    Cerberus et Stygiae nauita turpis aquae.
illic percussisque genis ustoque capillo
    errat ad obscuros pallida turba lacus.

Quin potius laudandus hic est quem prole parata
    occupat in parua pigra senecta casa?   40
ipse suas sectatur oues, at filius agnos;
    et calidam fesso comparat uxor aquam.
sic ego sim, liceatque caput candescere canis,
    temporis et prisci facta referre senem.

O Valgius, were I living then, never had I known
sad arms or heard the trumpet with a pounding heart.
Now I am dragged to war, and some enemy perhaps
already wears the weapon that will pierce my side.

Save me, Lares of my fathers, as you nurtured me
when I ran around in childhood at your feet.
And do not think it shameful to be shaped from an old log:
in that shape you protected my forefathers' estate.
Men kept better faith in the days when wooden gods
humbly decked and tended stood in tiny shrines,
friendly if one gave them the first of the grapes
or bound their sacred locks with spikes of grain;
& the man whose prayer was answered would bring them cakes of meal,
his little daughter following with honey in the comb.

Then turn aside, O Lares, the bronze missiles from us
.   .   .   .
.   .   .   .
and the country offering, a hog from a full sty.
I shall follow, clad in white, bearing a rush basket
bound with myrtle, wearing a myrtle wreath myself.
So may I find your favour. Others can be brave in arms
and by the grace of Mars cut down the opposing leaders,
to tell me, as I drink, of their exploits in the army
and paint camp on the table-top in wine.

What madness to join forces with sombre Death in war!
Her threat is close, and unperceived her coming.
Below there are no cornfields, no tended vines, but barking
Cerberus and the ugly steersman of the Styx.
There, with cheeks grief-smitten, and with ashen hair,
a pallid multitude drifts by sunless lakes.

But is not the true hero the man slow age surprises
in a little hut with children round him?
He shepherds his own sheep, and his son follows the lambs,
and his wife prepares hot water for the bath.
Such life be mine and with it leave to shine white-haired,
recounting in old age old memories.

Interea Pax arua colat. Pax candida primum   45
   duxit araturos sub iuga curua boues.
Pax aluit uites et sucos condidit uuae,
   funderet ut nato testa paterna merum.
Pace bidens uomerque nitent, at tristia duri
   militis in tenebris occupat arma situs.   50

       .   .   .   .

rusticus e lucoque uehit, male sobrius ipse,
   uxorem plaustro progeniemque domum.
sed Veneris tunc bella calent, scissosque capillos
   femina perfractas conqueriturque fores.
flet teneras subtusa genas, sed uictor et ipse   55
   flet sibi dementes tam ualuisse manus.
at lasciuus Amor rixae mala uerba ministrat,
   inter et iratum lentus utrumque sedet.

A lapis est ferrumque, suam quicumque puellam
   uerberat: e caelo deripit ille deos.   60
sit satis e membris tenuem rescindere uestem,
   sit satis ornatus dissoluisse comae,
sit lacrimas mouisse satis. quater ille beatus
   quo tenera irato flere puella potest.
sed manibus qui saeuus erit, scutumque sudemque   65
   is gerat et miti sit procul a Venere.

At nobis, Pax alma, ueni spicamque teneto,
   profluat et pomis candidus ante sinus.

Meanwhile let Peace attend the fields. White Peace in the beginning
led ploughing oxen under the curved yoke.
Peace fed the vines and stored the juices of the grape
for sons to draw wine from their fathers' casks.
In peacetime hoe & ploughshare shine while rust in the dark attacks
the soldier's cruel weapons.

. . . .

Home from the sacred grove the farmer far from sober
drives wife and children in the wagon.
Then Venus' war flares up. The woman then bewailing
torn hair and broken door
weeps for soft cheeks bruised, and the winner also weeps
for the mad strength in his hands.
But Love, the mischief-maker, feeds the brawling with abuse
and sits there obstinate between the angry pair.

Ah stone is he and steel who strikes his girl:
he drags down Gods from heaven.
It is enough to rip off the thin dress,
enough to disarrange the well-set hair,
enough to draw her tears. O four times happy he
whose anger makes a tender woman weep!
But the cruel-handed should carry shield and stake
and soldier far away from gentle Venus.

Then come, life-giving Peace, to us, holding the spikes of corn,
and from your white-robed lap let the fruit spill over.

LIBER SECVNDVS

I

Quisquis adest, faueat: fruges lustramus et agros,
    ritus ut a prisco traditus exstat auo.
Bacche, ueni dulcisque tuis e cornibus uua
    pendeat, et spicis tempora cinge, Ceres.
luce sacra requiescat humus, requiescat arator,   5
    et graue suspenso uomere cesset opus.
soluite uincla iugis: nunc ad praesepia debent
    plena coronato stare boues capite.
omnia sint operata deo: non audeat ulla
    lanificam pensis imposuisse manum.   10
uos quoque abesse procul iubeo, discedat ab aris
    cui tulit hesterna gaudia nocte Venus.
casta placent superis: pura cum ueste uenite
    et manibus puris sumite fontis aquam.

Cernite fulgentes ut eat sacer agnus ad aras   15
    uinctaque post olea candida turba comas.

Di patrii, purgamus agros, purgamus agrestes:
    uos mala de nostris pellite limitibus.
neu seges eludat messem fallacibus herbis,
    neu timeat celeres tardior agna lupos.   20
tunc nitidus plenis confisus rusticus agris
    ingeret ardenti grandia ligna foco,
turbaque uernarum, saturi bona signa coloni,
    ludet et ex uirgis exstruet ante casas.

Euentura precor. uiden ut felicibus extis   25
    significet placidos nuntia fibra deos?

Nunc mihi fumosos ueteris proferte Falernos
    consulis et Chio soluite uincla cado.
uina diem celebrent: non festa luce madere
    est rubor, errantes et male ferre pedes.   30
sed 'bene Messallam' sua quisque ad pocula dicat,
    nomen et absentis singula uerba sonent.

BOOK TWO

1

Keep silence, all: we purify the fruits and fields
according to the usage of our ancestors.
Come, Bacchus, with the sweet grapes hanging from your horns,
and bind your brow with wheaten garland, Ceres.
Let rest the land in holy daylight, let the ploughman rest,
hard labour over, while the share hangs idle.
Unstrap the yokes. Today the oxen are to stand
at laden mangers, garlanded with flowers.
Serve God in every action. Let no woman dare
to lay hand on the daily weight of wool.
I charge all you whom Venus granted joy last night
to stand apart and not approach the altar.
The Gods love purity. Come wearing clean clothes
and take in clean hands water from the spring.

See, the sacred lamb advances to the shining altar,
leading the white procession wreathed with olive.

Gods of our fathers, we purge the fields and the field-workers.
Drive away all evil from our boundaries.
Let no cornland cheat the harvest with deceptive blades,
no swift wolf terrify the laggard lamb.
Then the cheerful farmer, trusting his full fields,
will pile the fire with large logs, while a troop
of servants' children, token of their master's plenty,
play before it, building houses of sticks.

My prayers are answered: look, the entrails promise well
and the liver's lobe announces Heaven's favour.

Now bring me smoked Falernian, some long-dead consul's vintage.
Unseal a jar of Chian.
Wine to celebrate the day! It is no blushing matter
to drink deep at a feast and walk unsteadily.
But everyone must drink Messalla's health in absence
and every conversation speak his name.

gentis Aquitanae celeber Messalla triumphis
    et magna intonsis gloria uictor auis,
huc ades aspiraque mihi dum carmine nostro   35
    redditur agricolis gratia caelitibus.

Rura cano rurisque deos: his uita magistris
    desueuit querna pellere glande famem;
illi compositis primum docuere tigillis
    exiguam uiridi fronde operire domum;   40
illi etiam tauros primi docuisse feruntur
    seruitium et plaustro supposuisse rotam.
tum uictus abiere feri, tum consita pomus,
    tum bibit irriguas fertilis hortus aquas,
aurea tum pressos pedibus dedit uua liquores   45
    mixtaque securo est sobria lympha mero.
rura ferunt messes, calidi cum sideris aestu
    deponit flauas annua terra comas;
rure leuis uerno flores apis ingerit alueo,
    compleat ut dulci sedula melle fauos.   50
agricola assiduo primum satiatus aratro
    cantauit certo rustica uerba pede,
et satur arenti primum est modulatus auena
    carmen, ut ornatos diceret ante deos;
agricola et minio suffusus, Bacche, rubenti   55
    primus inexperta duxit ab arte choros;
huic datus a pleno memorabile munus ouili
    dux pecoris paruas auxerat hircus opes.
rure puer uerno primum de flore coronam
    fecit et antiquis imposuit Laribus;   60
rure etiam teneris curam exhibitura puellis
    molle gerit tergo lucida uellus ouis;
hinc et femineus labor est, hinc pensa colusque,
    fusus et apposito pollice uersat opus,
atque aliqua assidue textrix operata Mineruae   65
    cantat et a pulso tela sonat latere.

Ipse quoque inter agros interque armenta Cupido
    natus et indomitas dicitur inter equas.
illic indocto primum se exercuit arcu:
    ei mihi, quam doctas nunc habet ille manus!   70
nec pecudes uelut ante petit: fixisse puellas
    gestit et audaces perdomuisse uiros.

Messalla, famed for triumphs over Aquitanian tribes,
conqueror bringing glory to bearded ancestors,
hither come with inspiration while my song returns
thanks to the Gods of farming.

Country I sing and country Gods. Life as their disciple
ceased to drive away hunger with the acorn.
They taught men first to tie rafters together
and roof a little home with green thatch.
They were the first to teach the bull his bondage
and place the wheel beneath the wagon's weight.
Then wild fare was forgotten: fruit-trees then were planted
and kitchen-gardens drank the channeled stream;
then the trampled grapes gave golden liquor;
then sober water mixed with carefree wine.
The country brings us harvest in the shimmering heat
when Earth each year lays down her yellow hair.
In springtime, in the country, light bees are busy bearing
flowers to the hive to fill the combs with honey.
It was a farmer, wearied with continual ploughing,
who first sang country words in fixed metre
and after feasting measured on the first oaten pipe
a tune to play to Gods he had adorned.
A farmer too, O Bacchus, daubed with cinnabar,
improvised your dithyramb, receiving
that memorable trophy from a full fold, the flock's leader,
a he-goat to augment his modest means.
It was a country child first fashioned of spring flowers
a diadem to crown the ancient Lares.
And in the country too, future trouble for tender girls,
soft fleeces line the backs of milk-white sheep.
Hence woman's work, hence woollen stint and distaff,
the spindle twisting yarn beneath the thumb,
the weaver's song, Minerva's constant votary,
and the loom's clatter as the weights collide.

Cupid himself, in fable, was born among the fields,
among the cattle and the wild mares.
There he practised first his unskilled archery.
Alas, how skilful are his hands today!
His aim has shifted from the beasts and now he takes delight
in wounding girls and taming insolent males.

hic iuueni detraxit opes, hic dicere iussit
    limen ad iratae uerba pudenda senem;
hoc duce custodes furtim transgressa iacentes   75
    ad iuuenem tenebris sola puella uenit,
et pedibus praetemptat iter, suspensa timore,
    explorat caecas cui manus ante uias.
a miseri quos hic grauiter deus urget, at ille
    felix cui placidus leniter afflat Amor.   80

Sancte, ueni dapibus festis, sed pone sagittas
    et procul ardentes hinc, precor, abde faces.
uos celebrem cantate deum pecorique uocate:
    uoce palam pecori, clam sibi quisque uocet —
aut etiam sibi quisque palam, nam turba iocosa   85
    obstrepit et Phrygio tibia curua sono.
ludite: iam Nox iungit equos, currumque sequuntur
    matris lasciuo sidera fulua choro,
postque uenit tacitus, furuis circumdatus alis,
    Somnus, et incerto Somnia nigra pede.   90

II

Dicamus bona uerba; uenit Natalis ad aras:
    quisquis ades, lingua, uir mulierque, faue.
urantur pia tura focis, urantur odores
    quos tener e terra diuite mittit Arabs.
ipse suos Genius adsit uisurus honores,   5
    cui decorent sanctas mollia serta comas.
illius puro destillent tempora nardo,
    atque satur libo sit madeatque mero.

Adnuat et, Cornute, tibi quodcumque rogabis.
    en age, quid cessas? adnuit ille — roga.   10
auguror uxoris fidos optabis amores;
    iam reor hoc ipsos edidicisse deos.
nec tibi malueris totum quaecumque per orbem
    fortis arat ualido rusticus arua boue,
nec tibi gemmarum quicquid felicibus Indis   15
    nascitur, Eoi qua maris unda rubet.

He robs the young of riches and commands the middle-aged
to use unseemly language at an angry woman's door.
Guided by him the girl steps over sleeping sentries,
creeping to a lover in the lonely dark,
feeling the way with her feet, pausing on timid tiptoe,
with hand outstretched exploring blind directions.
Wretched they, alas, on whom this God bears hard,
but happy he who feels Love's breath serene.

Come, Holy One, attend our feast, but lay aside your arrows
and far away I pray you hide your blazing torch.
Sing all of you the glorious God and call him to the flock:
call him aloud to the flock, in silence to yourselves —
or even aloud to yourselves, for the din of the merry crowd
and the skirl of the Phrygian pipe will drown the words.
Make sport, for Night already yokes her horses and the yellow
stars in wanton dance attend their mother's car;
and silently behind them, flanked by dusky wings,
comes Sleep — and unsure-footed the black Dreams.

2

Natalis comes to the altar: let us speak no idle word,
but all here present, male and female, guard their tongues.
Burn upon the brazier holy incense, burn the perfumes
which the supple Arab sends from his rich land.
Let the Genius be present to behold the honours paid him
and let soft woollen fillets adorn his hallowed hair.
With oil of spikenard dripping from his temples let him eat
his fill of cake and drink deep of the unmixed wine.

And may he nod assent, Cornutus, to all your requests.
Don't wait, but make them now. Look, he nods assent.
I prophesy that you will pray for a wife's faithful love:
the Gods, I guess, already know that prayer by heart.
Nor would you change that choice for all the cornfields in the world
ploughed by sturdy peasants and the straining ox,
or for all the pearls that grow by India the Blest
where the waves of the Eastern Sea are red as blushes.

Vota cadunt: utinam strepitantibus aduolet alis
    flauaque coniugio uincula portet Amor,
uincula quae maneant semper, dum tarda senectus
    inducat rugas inficiatque comas.   20
hic veniat, Natalis, auis prolemque ministret,
    ludat et ante tuos turba nouella pedes.

III

Rura meam, Cornute, tenent uillaeque puellam:
    ferreus est, eheu, quisquis in urbe manet.
ipsa Venus latos iam nunc migrauit in agros,
    uerbaque aratoris rustica discit Amor.

O ego cum aspicerem dominam, quam fortiter illic   5
    uersarem ualido pingue bidente solum,
agricolaeque modo curuum sectarer aratrum,
    dum subigunt steriles arua serenda boues!
nec quererer quod sol graciles exureret artus,
    laederet et teneras pussula rupta manus.   10

Pauit et Admeti tauros formosus Apollo,
    nec cithara intonsae profueruntue comae.
nec potuit curas sanare salubribus herbis:
    quicquid erat medicae uicerat artis amor.
ipse deus solitus stabulis expellere uaccas   15

    . . . .
et miscere nouo docuisse coagula lacte,
    lacteus et mixtis obriguisse liquor.
tunc fiscella leui detexta est uimine iunci
    raraque per nexus est uia facta sero.   20
o quotiens illo uitulum gestante per agros
    dicitur occurrens erubuisse soror!
o quotiens ausae, caneret dum ualle sub alta,
    rumpere mugitu carmina docta boues!
saepe duces trepidis petiere oracula rebus,   25
    uenit et a templis irrita turba domum.
saepe horrere sacros doluit Latona capillos
    quos admirata est ipsa nouerca prius.
quisquis inornatumque caput crinesque solutos
    aspiceret, Phoebi quaereret ille comam.   30

Prayers befall. May Love fly here on noisy wings
bearing the golden bonds of marriage,
bonds to endure for always, till belatedly
old age applies the wrinkles and bedaubs the hair.
Natalis, may he come and bring grandparents offspring
and a troop of little ones play before your feet.

3

Estates and country-houses intern my girl, Cornutus;
only a man of steel could stay in town.
Venus herself has flitted now to lonely fields
and Love is learning ploughman's dialect.

With what determination, if I could see my mistress,
I'd loosen the rich loam with potent mattock
and follow the curved plough in agricultural fashion
while gelded cattle worked the land for sowing,
with never a complaint when the sun scorched my thin arms
or broken blisters made my soft hands sore!

Even fair Apollo fed the cattle of Admetus,
but cithara and long hair did not help,
nor could he cure his cares with therapeutic herbs,
for Love defeated all his skill in medicine.
Himself, albeit God, he drove cows from a byre.
. . . .
and to have taught the mixing of rennet with fresh milk,
coagulating thus the milky mixture.
Frails were woven then of the light stems of rushes
and space left in the tight weave for the whey.
O how many times his sister blushed to meet him
carrying a bull-calf home through the fields,
or while he sang in some deep valley, cows presumed
to interrupt his music with their moos!
Leaders in time of crisis sought his oracles
and trooped home disappointed from the shrine.
The sacred locks that even Juno used to envy
in disarray dismayed his mother Leto.
Anyone who saw the shaggy head and tousled tresses
must have looked in vain for Phoebus' hair-style.

Delos ubi nunc, Phoebe, tua est? ubi Delphice Pytho?
  nempe Amor in parua te iubet esse casa.
felices olim, Veneri cum fertur aperte
  seruire aeternos non puduisse deos!
fabula nunc ille est, sed cui sua cura puella est   35
  fabula sit mauult quam sine amore deus.

At tu, quisquis is est, cui tristi fronte Cupido
  imperat ut nostra sint tua castra domo
  . . . .
ferrea non Venerem sed Praedam saecula laudant;
  Praeda tamen multis est operata malis.   40
Praeda feras acies cinxit discordibus armis:
  hinc cruor, hinc caedes mors propiorque uenit.
Praeda uago iussit geminare pericula ponto,
  bellica cum dubiis rostra dedit ratibus.
praedator cupit inmensos obsidere campos   45
  ut multa innumera iugera pascat oue;
cui lapis externus curae est urbisque tumultu
  portatur ualidis mille columna iugis,
claudit et indomitum moles mare, lentus ut intra
  neglegat hibernas piscis adesse minas.   50

At tibi laeta trahant Samiae conuiuia testae
  fictaque Cumana lubrica terra rota.
eheu diuitibus uideo gaudere puellas:
  iam ueniant praedae si Venus optat opes,
ut mea luxuria Nemesis fluat utque per urbem   55
  incedat donis conspicienda meis.
illa gerat uestes tenues quas femina Coa
  texuit, auratas disposuitque uias.
illi sint comites fusci quos India torret,
  Solis et admotis inficit ignis equis.   60
illi selectos certent praebere colores
  Africa puniceum purpureumque Tyros.

Vota loquor: regnum ipse tenet quem saepe coegit
  barbara gypsatos ferre catasta pedes.

At tibi, dura Ceres, Nemesim quae abducis ab urbe,   65
  persoluat nulla semina terra fide.

O Phoebus, where is Delos now, and where your Delphic Pytho?
Love commands your presence in a little hut.
Happy those prehistoric days when the immortal Gods
were not ashamed to be the public slaves of Venus!
Apollo is a byword now, but any man in love
would sooner be a byword than a loveless God.

But you, whoever you are, whom Cupid's frown commands
to make my quarters scene of your campaigning

     . . . .

Not Love but Loot our iron age applauds:
but Loot works many evils.
Loot equips fierce battle-lines with jarring arms;
hence bloodshed, slaughter, sudden death.
Loot has doubled danger on the fickle deep
by giving unsafe galleys beaks of war.
The Looter longs to own measureless plains and pasture
wide acres with innumerable sheep.
He fancies foreign marble and yokes a thousand oxen
to cart his columns, setting Rome in turmoil.
He pens the open sea with moles to make a pond
where cold-eyed fish can disregard the storm.

For you let Samian ware extend a merry party
and cups of clay turned on the wheels of Cumae.
Alas, there's no denying that girls adore the rich.
Then welcome Loot if Love loves affluence.
My Nemesis shall float in luxury and strut
the Roman streets parading gifts of mine.
She shall wear fine silks woven by women of Cos
and patterned with paths of gold.
She shall have swart attendants, scorched in India,
stained by the Sun-God steering near.
Let Africa with scarlet and with purple Tyre
compete to offer her their choicest dyes.

My words are day-dreams. King is the very man whom often
a foreign scaffold forced to mark time with chalked feet.

Ah Ceres, cruel temptress of my Nemesis from Rome,
may earth break faith and pay you back short seed.

et tu, Bacche tener, iucundae consitor uuae,
  tu quoque deuotos, Bacche, relinque lacus.
haud impune licet formosas tristibus agris
  abdere: non tanti sunt tua musta, Pater.   70
o ualeant fruges, ne sint modo rure puellae.
  glans alat et prisco more bibantur aquae.
glans aluit ueteres, et passim semper amarunt.
  quid nocuit sulcos non habuisse satos?
tum, quibus aspirabat Amor, praebebat aperte   75
  mitis in umbrosa gaudia ualle Venus.
nullus erat custos, nulla exclusura dolentes
  ianua. si fas est, mos, precor, ille redi.

. . . .

  horrida uillosa corpora ueste tegant.   80
nunc, si clausa mea est, si copia rara uidendi,
  heu miserum laxam quid iuuat esse togam?
ducite. ad imperium dominae sulcabimus agros:
  non ego me uinclis uerberibusque nego.

IV

Sic mihi seruitium uideo dominamque paratam:
  iam mihi, libertas illa paterna, uale.
seruitium sed triste datur, teneorque catenis,
  et numquam misero uincla remittit Amor,
et seu quid merui seu nil peccauimus, urit.   5
  uror: io, remoue, saeua puella, faces.

O ego ne possim tales sentire dolores,
  quam mallem in gelidis montibus esse lapis!
stare uel insanis cautes obnoxia uentis,
  naufraga quam uasti tunderet unda maris!   10
nunc et amara dies et noctis amarior umbra est;
  omnia nunc tristi tempora felle madent.
nec prosunt elegi nec carminis auctor Apollo:
  illa caua pretium flagitat usque manu.

Ite procul, Musae, si non prodestis amanti: 15
  non ego uos ut sint bella canenda colo,
nec refero Solisque uias et qualis, ubi orbem
  compleuit, uersis Luna recurrit equis.

And you too, tender Bacchus, planter of the pleasant vine,
leave your wine-vats with a curse upon them.
It's a punishable trespass to hide Beauty in dull fields:
your vintage, Father Bacchus, costs too much.
Fruits of the field, farewell, if you keep girls on the land.
Let us live on acorns and drink old-fashioned water.
The men of old made love on acorns any time or place,
lost nothing by not having furrows for the seed.
In their day gentle Venus in every shady valley
provided Love's enthusiasts with public joy.
No guard was there or door to bar the broken-hearted.
May God reintroduce that ancient custom.

. . . .

Let them cover their shivering limbs with clothes of fur.
But if my girl's a prisoner now and I can rarely see her,
what good to me, alas, is a toga flowing free?
Lead on. I'll plough the furrows at the bidding of a mistress
and cheerfully accept the leg-irons and the lash.

4

Slave to a mistress! Yes, in recognition of my fate
bidding now farewell to the freedom of my birthright
I accept the harshest slavery — for I am held in chains
and never, to my sorrow, does Love relax the bonds.
He burns me too, regardless of my guilt or innocence.
I'm burning now. Ai-ee, cruel girl, remove the torch!

O that I need never experience this torment
I'd sooner be a stone on some cold mountainside
or standing rock exposed to mad gales, buffeted
by the lonely sea's ship-splintering waves!
Bitter now the daylight, still more bitter the dark night;
every moment now is soaked in sour gall.
Elegies and Phoebus, poet's patron, are no help:
my lady cups her hand and keeps demanding cash.

Leave me alone, O Muses, if you cannot help a lover.
I do not ask your aid to sing of epic wars
nor do I track the Sun-God's path or tell of how the Moon,
her round completed, turns her steeds and gallops back.

ad dominam faciles aditus per carmina quaero:
  ite procul, Musae, si nihil ista ualent.   20

At mihi per caedem et facinus sunt dona paranda,
  ne iaceam clausam flebilis ante domum.
aut rapiam suspensa sacris insignia fanis:
  sed Venus ante alios est uiolanda mihi.
illa malum facinus suadet dominamque rapacem   25
  dat mihi: sacrilegas sentiat illa manus.

O pereat quicumque legit uiridesque smaragdos
  et niueam Tyrio murice tingit ouem!
hic dat auaritiae causas et Coa puellis
  uestis et e Rubro lucida concha Mari.   30
haec fecere malas, hinc clauim ianua sensit
  et coepit custos liminis esse canis.
sed pretium si grande feras, custodia uicta est
  nec prohibent claues et canis ipse tacet.
heu quicumque dedit formam caelestis auarae,   35
  quale bonum multis attulit ille malis!
hinc fletus rixaeque sonant, haec denique causa
  fecit ut infamis nunc deus esset Amor.

At tibi quae pretio uictos excludis amantes
  eripiant partas uentus et ignis opes.   40
quin, tua tunc iuuenes spectent incendia laeti
  nec quisquam flammae sedulus addat aquam.
heu, ueniet tibi mors, nec erit qui lugeat ullus
  nec qui det maestas munus in exsequias.

At bona quae nec auara fuit, centum licet annos   45
  uixerit, ardentem flebitur ante rogum;
atque aliquis senior, ueteres ueneratus amores,
  annua constructo serta dabit tumulo,
et 'bene' discedens dicet 'placideque quiescas,
  terraque securae sit super ossa leuis.'   50

Vera quidem moneo, sed prosunt quid mihi uera?
  illius est nobis lege colendus Amor.
quin etiam sedes iubeat si uendere auitas,
  ite sub imperium sub titulumque, Lares.

By poetry I look for easy access to a mistress.
Leave me alone, O Muses, if your magic does not work.

I must take to crime and bloodshed to provide her with the gifts
that save me from those weeping vigils at her door;
or steal the sacred offerings hung up on temple walls:
and Venus shall be first to be profaned.
She tempts me to do evil and devotes me to a grasping
mistress; she deserves to suffer sacrilege.

Death to all the dealers in green emerald, to all
who dip the snow-white sheep in Tyrian murex.
They and Coan silks and lucent pearls from the Red Sea —
these are the incentives of avarice in girls.
This is why they're faithless, why doors experience keys
and why a dog keeps guard upon the entrance.
But if you bring big money, the guard makes no resistance
nor do keys exclude and even the dog is dumb.
Alas, whichever God it was gave grasping woman beauty,
what a good he added to a load of ill!
Hence the noisy tears and quarrels; here the reason why
Love is now a God of evil reputation.

But you who lock out lovers outbidden in your auction,
may wind and fire rob you of the money you've amassed.
Yes, and may the young men laugh to see your goods ablaze
and no one busily throw water on the flames.
Death, alas, will come for you, but there'll be none to mourn
or share the cost of your sad funeral.

But any kind and generous girl can live a hundred years
and tears will still be shed beside her pyre.
Some elder man in fond remembrance of his former love
each year will bring her flowers to the grave
and as he leaves will say 'Sleep soundly and in peace,
and earth be light on your untroubled bones.'

True prophecy. And yet what help to the true prophet?
Love's worship means obedience to her laws.
Why, even if she bade me sell my ancestral home
I'd pack the Lares off under a bill of sale.

quicquid habet Circe, quicquid Medea ueneni,   55
  quicquid et herbarum Thessala terra gerit,
et quod, ubi indomitis gregibus Venus afflat amores,
  hippomanes cupidae stillat ab inguine equae,
si modo me placido uideat Nemesis mea uultu,
  mille alias herbas misceat illa, bibam.   60

V

Phoebe, faue: nouus ingreditur tua templa sacerdos:
  huc, age, cum cithara carminibusque ueni.
nunc te uocales impellere pollice chordas,
  nunc precor ad laudes flectere uerba mea.
ipse triumphali deuinctus tempora lauro   5
  dum cumulant aras ad tua sacra ueni.
sed nitidus pulcherque ueni: nunc indue uestem
  sepositam, longas nunc bene pecte comas,
qualem te memorant Saturno rege fugato
  uictori laudes concinuisse Ioui.   10

Tu procul euentura uides, tibi deditus augur
  scit bene quid fati prouida cantet auis;
tuque regis sortes, per te praesentit haruspex
  lubrica signauit cum deus exta notis;
te duce Romanos numquam frustrata Sibylla,   15
  abdita quae senis fata canit pedibus.
Phoebe, sacras Messallinum sine tangere chartas
  uatis, et ipse, precor, quid canat illa doce.

Haec dedit Aeneae sortes postquam ille parentem
  dicitur et raptos sustinuisse Lares.   20
nec fore credebat Romam cum maestus ab alto
  Ilion ardentes respiceretque deos.
Romulus aeternae nondum formauerat Vrbis
  moenia, consorti non habitanda Remo,
sed tunc pascebant herbosa Palatia uaccae   25
  et stabant humiles in Iouis arce casae.
lacte madens illic suberat Pan ilicis umbrae
  et facta agresti lignea falce Pales,
pendebatque uagi pastoris in arbore uotum
  garrula siluestri fistula sacra deo,   30

All Circe's magic potions, all Medea's drugs
and all the herbs that sprout in Thessaly,
horse-madness too, that exudation from the mare in season
when Venus breathes her longing into the wild herds,
and a thousand other simples, brewed by Nemesis, I'd drink
if only to find favour in her eyes.

5

Bless, O Phoebus, the new priest entering your temple;
make haste and hither come with psalm and cithara.
Pluck now, I pray you, with your thumb the singing strings
and tune my utterance to hymns of praise.
Bind your brow with bays triumphant: come among us,
while they heap the altar, for your sacrifice.
In brightness and in beauty come, putting on today
the robe of state and combing your luxuriant hair,
as on that legendary day when Saturn fled his kingdom
and you sang the glory of victorious Jove.

You see the future from afar. Your votary the augur
understands the song of the prophetic bird.
You rule the lots. Through you the soothsayer interprets
the signature of God on slippery entrails.
Inspired by you the Sibyl singing destiny obscure
in Greek hexameters has never failed the Romans.
O Phoebus, grant that Messallinus touch her sacred scrolls
and teach him, I beseech you, the meaning of her song.

She gave Aeneas oracles, after (as legend tells)
he carried father and homeless Gods to safety,
incredulous of future Rome when from the deep in grief
he gazed at Troy and Trojan temples burning.
Not yet had Romulus drawn up the Eternal City's walls,
where Remus as co-ruler was fated not to live;
but cows were grazing then a grassy Palatine
and hovels raised low roofs on the hill of Jove.
There drenched with milk was Pan, half seen in ilex shade,
and wooden Pales hewn by rustic hook,
and on the tree in dedication to Silvanus
hung a wandering shepherd's tuneful pipe,

fistula cui semper decrescit harundinis ordo,
    nam calamus cera iungitur usque minor.
at qua Velabri regio patet, ire solebat
    exiguus pulsa per uada linter aqua.
illa saepe gregis diti placitura magistro   35
    ad iuuenem festa est uecta puella die,
cum qua fecundi redierunt munera ruris,
    caseus et niueae candidus agnus ouis.

'Impiger Aenea, uolitantis frater Amoris,
    Troica qui profugis sacra uehis ratibus,   40
iam tibi Laurentes assignat Iuppiter agros,
    iam uocat errantes hospita terra Lares.
illic sanctus eris cum te ueneranda Numici
    unda deum caelo miserit indigetem.

Ecce, super fessas uolitat Victoria puppes: 45
    tandem ad Troianos diua superba uenit.
ecce, mihi lucent Rutulis incendia castris:
    iam tibi praedico, barbare Turne, necem.
ante oculos Laurens castrum murusque Lauini est
    Albaque ab Ascanio condita Longa duce.   50
te quoque iam uideo, Marti placitura sacerdos,
    Ilia, Vestales deseruisse focos,
concubitusque tuos furtim, uittasque iacentes,
    et cupidi ad ripas arma relicta dei.

Carpite nunc, tauri, de septem montibus herbas   55
    dum licet: hic magnae iam locus urbis erit.
Roma, tuum nomen terris fatale regendis
    qua sua de caelo prospicit arua Ceres,
quaque patent ortus et qua fluitantibus undis
    Solis anhelantes abluit amnis equos.   60
Troia quidem tunc se mirabitur et sibi dicet
    uos bene tam longa consuluisse uia.
uera cano: sic usque sacras innoxia laurus
    uescar et aeternum sit mihi uirginitas.'
haec cecinit uates et te sibi, Phoebe, uocauit,   65
    iactauit fusas et caput ante comas.

Quicquid Amalthea, quicquid Marpesia dixit
    Herophile, Phoeto Graia quod admonuit,

the pipe with reeds set in descending order,
each stalk wax-welded to a shorter one.
But where today Velabrum stretches, little dinghies
driven by oars would ply across the shallows.
Often the likely favourite of the flock's rich master
travelled that way at feasts to her young man,
returning with the gifts of country plenty,
cheeses and a snowy ewe's white lamb.

'Unwearying Aeneas, brother of winged Love,
sailing with Ilium's sacred gear in exile,
now Jupiter apportions you Laurentine fields
and welcome land invites your wandering Lares.
There you shall be hallowed when Numicus' holy stream
to heaven sends you as a hero-god.

See where Victory hovers over your worn fleet — at last
the overbearing goddess stoops to Trojans.
See where fire blazes in the encampment of the Rutuli,
foreboding sudden death for savage Turnus.
Laurentum's fort, Lavinium's wall are there before my eyes,
and Alba Longa, founded by Ascanius.
Ilia also I behold, the priestess loved by Mars,
her dereliction of the vestal hearth,
her secret intercourse, the sacred fillet thrown aside
with the lustful God's armour on the bank.

Crop while ye may, O bulls, the grass on the Seven Hills:
here shall be the site of a mighty city —
Rome, the name predestined for empire of the world
where Ceres looks from heaven upon her fields,
where rising up the Sun-God spreads his beams and where in Ocean's
tidal stream he bathes his panting steeds.
Then truly Troy in self-amaze will tell herself
you served her well by so long wandering.
It is the truth I sing — so may I feed unscathed
on sacred bay and be forever virgin.'
Thus sang the Sibyl, Phoebus, and called you to her aid
tossing the long loose hair over her eyes.

The rede of Amalthea and Marpessian Herophile,
the admonitions of Hellenic Phoeto,

quasque Aniena sacras Tiburs per flumina sortes
    portarat sicco pertuleratque sinu —   70
haec fore dixerunt belli mala signa cometen,
    multus ut in terras deplueretque lapis.
atque tubas atque arma ferunt strepitantia caelo
    audita, et lucos praecinuisse fugam.
ipsum etiam Solem, defectum lumine, uidit   75
    iungere pallentes nubilus annus equos,
et simulacra deum lacrimas fudisse tepentes,
    fataque uocales praemonuisse boues.
haec fuerunt olim, sed tu iam mitis, Apollo,
    prodigia indomitis merge sub aequoribus.   80

Vt succensa sacris crepitat bene laurea flammis!
    omine quo felix et satur annus erit.
laurus ubi bona signa dedit, gaudete, coloni:
    distendet spicis horrea plena Ceres,
oblitus et musto feriet pede rusticus uuas   85
    dolia dum magni deficiantque lacus,
ac madidus Baccho sua festa, Palilia, pastor
    concinet (a stabulis tunc procul este, lupi).
ille leuis stipulae sollemnes potus aceruos
    accendet, flammas transilietque sacras,   90
et fetus matrona dabit, natusque parenti
    oscula comprensis auribus eripiet,
nec taedebit auum paruo aduigilare nepoti
    balbaque cum puero dicere uerba senem.
tunc operata deo pubes discumbet in herba,   95
    arboris antiquae qua leuis umbra cadit,
aut e ueste sua tendent umbracula sertis
    uincta, coronatus stabit et ipse calix.
at sibi quisque dapes et festas exstruet alte
    caespitibus mensas caespitibusque torum.   100
ingeret hic potus iuuenis maledicta puellae
    postmodo quae uotis irrita facta uelit;
nam ferus ille suae plorabit sobrius idem
    et se iurabit mente fuisse mala.

Pace tua pereant arcus pereantque sagittae,   105
    Phoebe, modo in terris erret inermis Amor.
ars bona, sed postquam sumpsit sibi tela Cupido,
    eheu quam multis ars dedit ista malum!

the sacred lots which Tibur's Sibyl carried as she swam
down the Anio and brought them dry to land —
all these foretold a comet, the wicked sign of war,
and a rain of stones falling on the earth.
Men say the clang of arms was heard and trumpets in the sky
and voices from the sacred groves forechanting rout.
That year of cloud beheld even the Sun himself
harnessing pale horses in eclipse,
and images of Gods that shed warm tears,
and cattle speaking, prophesying doom.
These omens came to pass of old, but now in mercy, Phoebus,
drown prodigies beneath the untamed sea.

How the kindled bayleaves crackle in the sacred flames,
promising a year fortunate and fruitful!
Rejoice, you tenant-farmers, when the bay gives lucky signs,
for Ceres will cram full your granaries with grain,
and peasants daubed with wine-lees will trample out the grapes
till vat and ample cistern overflow.
Shepherds also drinking deep will sing at the Palilia
their special feast (that day let wolves avoid the fold!)
and when they're drunk will set alight the customary heaps
of straw and overleap them through the sacred flames.
Then Roman wives will all be mothers and the growing boy
will grip his father's ears and steal a kiss.
Grandfathers will be glad to take full charge of little grandsons
and old men talk with children in child language.
Then serving God the folk will lie in groups upon the grass
where lightly falls the shadow of an ancient tree,
or spread their cloaks as canopies and garland them with flowers
and decorate the wine-bowls too with chaplets.
Everyone will pile his plate with food and build up high
a table and a dining-couch of turf;
and here the youth will fling drunken curses at his girl
which later he will wish made void by lover's vows,
weeping when he's sober at his former beastliness
and swearing he was out of his right mind.

O Phoebus, by your leave, perish bow and perish arrows
if only Love can wend his devious way unarmed.
Art is good, but after Cupid took to archery,
alas, how much misfortune your archer's art has brought!

et mihi praecipue, iaceo cum saucius annum
    et faueo morbo, cum iuuat ipse dolor.   110
usque cano Nemesim, sine qua uersus mihi nullus
    uerba potest iustos aut reperire pedes.

At tu, nam diuum seruat tutela poetas,
    praemoneo, uati parce puella sacro,
ut Messallinum celebrem cum praemia belli   115
    ante suos currus oppida uicta feret,
ipse gerens laurus, lauro deuinctus agresti
    miles 'io' magna uoce 'Triumphe' canet.
tunc Messalla meus pia det spectacula turbae
    et plaudat curru praetereunte pater.   120
annue: sic tibi sint intonsi, Phoebe, capilli,
    sic tua perpetuo sit tibi casta soror.

VI

Castra Macer sequitur: tenero quid fiet Amori?
    sit comes et collo fortiter arma gerat?
et seu longa uirum terrae uia seu uaga ducent
    aequora, cum telis ad latus ire uolet?
ure, puer, quaeso, tua qui ferus otia liquit,   5
    atque iterum erronem sub tua signa uoca.
quod si militibus parces, erit hic quoque miles,
    ipse leuem galea qui sibi portet aquam.
castra peto, ualeatque Venus ualeantque puellae:
    et mihi sunt uires, et mihi facta tuba est.   10

Magna loquor, sed magnifice mihi magna locuto
    excutiunt clausae fortia uerba fores.
iuraui quotiens rediturum ad limina numquam!
    cum bene iuraui, pes tamen ipse redit.
acer Amor, fractas utinam tua tela sagittas,   15
    si licet, extinctas aspiciamque faces!
tu miserum torques, tu me mihi dira precari
    cogis et insana mente nefanda loqui.

Iam mala finissem leto, sed credula uitam
    Spes fouet et fore cras semper ait melius.   20

On me especially, for I have lain a year now stricken,
clinging to my sickness, finding pleasure in the pain,
singing of my Nemesis, without whom not one line
of mine can rediscover true rhythm or right phrase.

But since divine protection watches over poets,
I warn you, girl, take pity on a sacred bard,
so that I may honour Messallinus when he drives
the spoils of conquered towns before his chariot,
crowned with bay himself, his troops with wild bay garlanded,
chanting in loud voices the ritual Triumph cry.
Then let my Messalla give the crowd a fond display
by cheering as his son's chariot passes by.
O Phoebus, grant me this, and may your locks remain unshorn
and your sister virgin to the end of time.

6

Macer joins the army. What will tender Love do now?
Go with him as comrade, shouldering a pack,
bearing arms beside a mortal on the endless road
leading over land and never-resting sea?
No, Cupid: brand the ruffian who has left your life of leisure,
recalling the deserter to the flag of love.
But if you're lenient to soldiers, I will soldier too,
carrying the ration of water in my casque.
I'm off to camp and bid goodbye to Venus and the girls.
I too can take the trumpet; I too can be tough.

Brave words, but when I've said them with magnificent bravado
the slamming of a door sends every brave word flying.
I've sworn so often nevermore to set foot on her doorstep,
but after all the swearing my feet still take me there.
O cruel Love, if it be lawful, let me see your weapons,
the arrows and the torches, broken and burnt out.
You torture my unhappiness. You make me curse myself
and with a mind unbalanced utter blasphemy.

Death would have ended my distress but Hope's credulity
nurses life and says 'Tomorrow will be better.'

Spes alit agricolas, Spes sulcis credit aratis
  semina quae magno faenore reddat ager.
haec laqueo uolucres, haec captat harundine pisces
  cum tenues hamos abdidit ante cibus.
Spes etiam ualida solatur compede uinctum: 25
  crura sonant ferro, sed canit inter opus.
Spes facilem Nemesim spondet mihi, sed negat illa:
  ei mihi, ne uincas, dura puella, deam.

Parce, per immatura tuae precor ossa sororis:
  sic bene sub tenera parua quiescat humo.   30
illa mihi sancta est, illius dona sepulcro
  et madefacta meis serta feram lacrimis,
illius ad tumulum fugiam supplexque sedebo
  et mea cum muto fata querar cinere.
non feret usque suum te propter flere clientem: 35
  illius ut uerbis, sis mihi lenta ueto,
ne tibi neglecti mittant mala somnia Manes
  maestaque sopitae stet soror ante torum,
qualis ab excelsa praeceps delapsa fenestra
  uenit ad infernos sanguinolenta lacus.   40

Desino, ne dominae luctus renouentur acerbi:
  non ego sum tanti, ploret ut illa semel,
nec lacrimis oculos digna est foedare loquaces.
  lena nocet nobis; ipsa puella bona est.
lena uetat miserum Phryne, furtimque tabellas   45
  occulto portans itque reditque sinu.
saepe ego cum dominae dulces a limine duro
  agnosco uoces, haec negat esse domi.
saepe ubi nox mihi promissa est, languere puellam
  nuntiat aut aliquas extimuisse minas.   50
tunc morior curis, tunc mens mihi perdita fingit
  quisue meam teneat quot teneatue modis;
tunc tibi, lena, precor diras: satis anxia uiuas,
  mouerit e uotis pars quotacumque deos.

Hope feeds the farmer. Hope entrusts the furrow with a loan
of seed to be repaid at compound interest.
Hope entices birds with snares and fish with rods of reed
hiding a thin hook underneath the bait.
Hope comforts even those whose legs are bound in heavy fetters;
the iron clanks on their ankles but while they work they sing.
Hope guarantees me Nemesis, but Nemesis says No.
Ah, cruel girl, you ought to let a goddess win.

Take pity, I implore you, by your little sister's bones:
so may the child sleep softly under gentle earth.
I hold her sacred and will lay upon her burial-mound
offerings and a garland sprinkled with my tears.
I'll fly for refuge to the grave, sit there a suppliant
and to her dumb ashes utter my complaint.
She will not suffer me to weep on your account for ever.
In her name I forbid you to use me heartlessly,
for fear the blessed dead neglected send you evil dreams
and you behold her standing by your bed in grief,
just as when she fell head foremost from the upper window
and went with blood upon her to the lakes below.

Enough, lest I renew the bitter sorrow of my mistress;
that she should weep once only is more than I am worth.
Nor ought she to disfigure her clear-speaking eyes with tears:
the bawd is our undoing; my girl herself is good.
Phryne the bawd debars me as she slily comes and goes
bearing in her bosom secret messages.
On the cruel threshold often I can recognise
the sweet voice of my mistress when Phryne says she's out.
Often, when a night was promised, Phryne brings me word
my girl's unwell or victim of intimidation.
I die then of frustration and despairingly imagine
who's embracing her and in how many ways.
Bawd, I curse you then, and pain enough would be your life
were the Gods to grant the least of all my prayers.

LIBER TERTIVS

LYGDAMI ELEGIAE

I

Martis Romani festae uenere kalendae:
    exoriens nostris hic fuit annus auis,
et uaga nunc certa discurrunt undique pompa
    perque uias urbis munera perque domos.
dicite, Pierides, quonam donetur honore   5
    seu mea, seu fallor, cara Neaera tamen.

'Carmine formosae, pretio capiuntur auarae:
    gaudeat, ut digna est, uersibus illa tuis.
lutea sed niueum inuoluat membrana libellum,
    pumex et canas tondeat ante comas,   10
summaque praetexat tenuis fastigia chartae
    indicet ut nomen littera facta tuum,
atque inter geminas pingantur cornua frontes:
    sic etenim comptum mittere oportet opus.'

Per uos auctores huius mihi carminis oro   15
    Castaliamque umbram Pieriosque lacus,
ite domum cultumque illi donate libellum
    sicut erit: nullus defluat inde color.
illa mihi referet si nostri mutua cura est
    an minor an toto pectore deciderim.   20
sed primum meritam larga donate salute
    atque haec submisso dicite uerba sono:
'haec tibi uir quondam, nunc frater, casta Neaera,
    mittit et accipias munera parua rogat,
teque suis iurat caram magis esse medullis,   25
    siue sibi coniunx siue futura soror.
sed potius coniunx: huius spem nominis illi
    auferet exstincto pallida Ditis aqua.'

II

Qui primus caram iuueni carumque puellae
    eripuit iuuenem, ferreus ille fuit.
durus et ille fuit qui tantum ferre dolorem,
    uiuere et erepta coniuge qui potuit.
non ego firmus in hoc, non haec patientia nostro   5
    ingenio: frangit fortia corda dolor.
nec mihi uera loqui pudor est uitaeque fateri
    tot mala perpessae taedia nata meae.

BOOK THREE

THE ELEGIES OF LYGDAMUS

1

The holiday Kalends of Roman Mars have come:
this used to be our ancestors' New Year,
and travelling gifts now, carefully despatched, are rushing
from all sides through the City's streets and houses.
Pierians, say what special honour shall be given
to my (or, if I'm wrong, at least to dear) Neaera.

'Lovely women are taken with song, the greedy with cash;
let your verses give her the pleasure she deserves.
But let saffron parchment wrap a snowy papyrus roll,
and first let pumice shave off the white hairs,
and at the very top of the fine papyrus fix
a lettered label to make known your name,
and see that the horns between the twin edges are coloured;
that's how one should send out stylish work.'

I beg you as the sponsors of this song of mine
by Castalian shade and Pierian pools,
go to her home, present her with the polished volume
just like that: let none of its colour fade.
She'll tell me in answer if her love for me is mutual
or less or if I've quite slipped from her heart.
But first wish her unstinted health as she deserves,
then very humbly speak these words:
'Your sometime man and present brother, chaste Neaera,
sends this small gift and begs you to accept it,
and swears that you are more dear to him than his own soul
whether as his future wife or sister,
but sooner as his wife — hope of that name the wan water
of Dis will take away from him in death.'

2

He had a heart of iron who first robbed a young man
of his dear girl and a girl of her dear young man.
Unfeeling too was he who could endure such grief
and go on living when robbed of his wife.
I'm not strong-minded enough for that; such unconcern
is against my nature. Grief can break brave hearts,
I'm not ashamed to speak truth and confess I'm tired
of a life that has suffered so much trouble.

Ergo cum tenuem fuero mutatus in umbram
  candidaque ossa supra nigra fauilla teget,   10
ante meum ueniat longos incompta capillos
  et fleat ante meum maesta Neaera rogum.
sed ueniat carae matris comitata dolore:
  maereat haec genero, maereat illa uiro.

Praefatae ante meos manes animamque recentem   15
  perfusaeque pias ante liquore manus,
pars quae sola mihi superabit corporis, ossa
  incinctae nigra candida ueste legent.
et primum annoso spargent collecta Lyaeo,
  mox etiam niueo fundere lacte parent,   20
post haec carbaseis umorem tollere uelis
  atque in marmorea ponere sicca domo.
illic quas mittit diues Panchaia merces
  Eoique Arabes diues et Assyria,
et nostri memores lacrimae fundantur eodem.   25
  sic ego componi uersus in ossa uelim.

Sed tristem mortis demonstret littera causam
  atque haec in celebri carmina fronte notet:
LYGDAMVS HIC SITVS EST. DOLOR HVIC ET CVRA NEAERAE
CONIVGIS EREPTAE CAVSA PERIRE FVIT.   30

III

Quid prodest caelum uotis implesse, Neaera,
  blandaque cum multa tura dedisse prece,
non ut marmorei prodirem e limine tecti
  insignis clara conspicuusque domo,
aut ut multa mei renouarent iugera tauri   5
  et magnas messes terra benigna daret,
sed tecum ut longae sociarem gaudia uitae,
  inque tuo caderet nostra senecta sinu,
tunc cum permenso defunctus tempore lucis
  nudus Lethaea cogerer ire rate?   10

Nam graue quid prodest pondus mihi diuitis auri,
  aruaque si findant pinguia mille boues?
quidue domus prodest Phrygiis innixa columnis,
  Taenare, siue tuis, siue, Caryste, tuis,
et nemora in domibus sacros imitantia lucos   15
  aurataeque trabes marmoreumque solum?
quidue in Erythraeo legitur quae litore concha
  tinctaque Sidonio murice lana iuuat,
et quae praeterea populus miratur? in illis
  inuidia est. falso plurima uulgus amat.   20

Therefore, when I am changed into a feeble ghost
and black ash covers the white bones over,
before my pyre in mourning may Neaera come,
long hair uncombed, and weep before my pyre.
But may she come companioned with her dear mother's grief,
one mourning a son-in-law, the other a husband.

After addressing my mortal remains and the new-born soul
and pouring pure water on devout hands,
wrapped in black robes they will gather up the only part
to survive of my body — the white bones,
and first, when gathered, sprinkle them with old Lyaean,
then prepare to pour on snow-white milk also,
thereafter with fine linen cloths remove the moisture
and lay them dry in their house of marble.
There let the merchandise that rich Panchaia sends
and Eoan Arabs and rich Assyria,
and tears in memory of me be poured on the same.
Thus would I wish to be laid to rest when turned to bones.

But let an inscription show the sad cause of death
and mark these verses on the frequented side:
HERE LYGDAMUS IS LAID. GRIEF AND LOVE FOR NEAERA,
THE WIFE WHO WAS STOLEN FROM HIM, CAUSED HIS DEATH.

3

What is the good, Neaera, of filling heaven with vows
and giving fulsome incense with much prayer
not that I might emerge from the door of a marble mansion,
impressive and renowned for a fine house,
or that my bulls might recondition many an acre
and bounteous earth bestow great harvests,
but that I share with you the joys of a long life
and my old age end in your embrace at last
when having fully spent my allotted span of light
I'm forced to go naked on Lethe's raft?

What good is a heavy load of precious gold to me
or a thousand oxen cleaving the fat soil?
What good a house supported on Phrygian pillars,
whether yours, Taenarus, or, Carystus, yours,
indoor plantations imitating sacred groves
and gilded beams and marble floors?
What help the shells men gather on the Erythraean shore
and wool dyed in Sidonian murex
and whatever else the public admires? For there
lies Envy. Most things the crowd loves are sham.

non opibus mentes hominum curaeque leuantur,
    nam Fortuna sua tempora lege regit.

Sit mihi paupertas tecum iucunda, Neaera,
    et sine te regum munera nulla uolo.
o niueam quae te poterit mihi reddere lucem!   25
    o mihi felicem terque quaterque diem!

At si pro dulci reditu quaecumque uouentur
    audiat auersa non meus aure deus,
nec me regna iuuant nec Lydius aurifer amnis
    nec quas terrarum sustinet orbis opes.   30
haec alii cupiant, liceat mihi paupere cultu
    securo cara coniuge posse frui.

Adsis et timidis faueas, Saturnia, uotis,
    et faueas concha, Cypria, uecta tua.
aut si fata negant reditum tristesque sorores   35
    stamina quae ducunt quaeque futura neunt,
me uocet in uastos amnes nigramque paludem
    diues in ignaua luridus Orcus aqua.

IV

Di meliora ferant, nec sint mihi somnia uera
    quae tulit hesterna pessima nocte quies.
ite, procul, uani, falsumque auertite, uisus!
    desinite in nobis quaerere uelle fidem!

Diui uera monent, uenturae nuntia sortis;   5
    uera monent Tuscis exta probata uiris:
somnia fallaci ludunt temeraria nocte
    et pauidas mentes falsa timere iubent;
et natum in curas hominum genus omina noctis
    farre pio placant et saliente sale.   10

Et tamen, utcumque est, siue illi uera moneri
    mendaci somno credere siue uolent,
efficiat uanos noctis Lucina timores
    et frustra immeritum pertimuisse uelit,
si mea nec turpi mens est obnoxia facto   15
    nec laesit magnos impia lingua deos.

Iam nox, aetherium nigris emensa quadrigis
    mundum, caeruleo lauerat amne rotas,
nec me sopierat menti deus utilis aegrae
    Somnus (sollicitas deficit ante domos).   20
tandem, cum summo Phoebus prospexit ab ortu,
    pressit languentis lumina sera quies.

Money cannot lighten the minds and cares of men,
for the times are ruled by Fortune's law.

Poverty with you, Neaera, would be bliss for me
and I want no royal gifts without you.
O bright would be the light that brought you back to me!
O three and four times lucky for me that day!

But if whatever vows are made for your sweet return
a God not mine should hear with ear averted,
then kingdoms cannot help me or Lydia's golden stream
nor all the wealth the round world holds.
Others can covet these, if only I, content
with simple living, can enjoy a dear wife.

Be with me, Saturn's daughter, and grant my anxious prayers;
grant them, Lady of Cyprus, voyaging in your shell.
Or if the Fates forbid her return — and the stern sisters
who draw the thread and spin the future,
then let sallow Orcus, rich in stagnant water,
call me to desolate streams and his black swamp.

4

May the Gods bring better things and those dreams not be true
which a sleep of the worst brought me last night.
Away, unreal visions, and turn aside your falsehood!
Cease wanting to find faith in us!

The Gods give true warnings, news of our coming lot;
Tuscan men give true warnings, testing entrails.
But dreams delude at random in the deceitful night
and scare excitable minds with lies;
and the human race, being born to trouble, propitiates
night's omens devoutly with spelt and leaping salt.

And yet however it is, whether they wish to believe
true warnings or deceptive sleep,
may Lucina make night's fears vain and grant
that the innocent were frightened needlessly,
provided my mind is guilty of no shameful deed
nor has my tongue blasphemed the mighty Gods.

Night, in black four-horse chariot measuring Aether's world,
had already washed its wheels in the blue stream,
but Sleep who restores afflicted minds had not put me
to rest — he fails before homes in trouble.
At last, when from his rising's top Phoebus looked forth,
late slumber pressed my tired eyes shut.

hic iuuenis casta redimitus tempora lauro
    est uisus nostra ponere sede pedem.
non illo quicquam formosius ulla priorum   25
    aetas aut hominum nunc uidet ulla domus.
intonsi crines longa ceruice fluebant;
    stillabat Syrio myrrea rore coma.
candor erat qualem praefert Latonia Luna,
    et color in niueo corpore purpureus,   30
ut iuueni primum uirgo deducta marito
    inficitur teneras ore rubente genas,
et cum contexunt amarantis alba puellae
    lilia et autumno candida mala rubent.
ima uidebatur talis illudere palla   35
    (namque haec in nitido corpore uestis erat).
artis opus rarae, fulgens testudine et auro,
    pendebat laeua garrula parte lyra.
hanc primum ueniens plectro modulatus eburno,
    felices cantus ore sonante dedit;   40
sed postquam fuerant digiti cum uoce locuti,
    edidit haec tristi dulcia uerba modo:

'Salue, cura deum: casto nam rite poetae
    Phoebusque et Bacchus Pieridesque fauent.
sed proles Semeles Bacchus doctaeque sorores   45
    dicere non norunt quid ferat hora sequens:
at mihi fatorum leges aeuique futuri
    euentura pater posse uidere dedit.
quare ego quae dico, non fallax, accipe, uates,
    quodque deus uero Cynthius ore feram.   50

Tantum cara tibi quantum non filia matri,
    quantum nec cupido bella puella uiro,
pro qua sollicitas caelestia numina uotis,
    quae tibi securos non sinit ire dies,
et cum te fusco Somnus uelauit amictu,   55
    uanum nocturnis fallit imaginibus,
carminibus celebrata tuis formosa Neaera
    alterius mauult esse puella uiri,
diuersasque tuis agitat mens impia curas,
    nec gaudet casta nupta Neaera domo.   60

A crudele genus nec fidum femina nomen!
    a pereat, didicit fallere si qua uirum!
sed flecti poterit; mens est mutabilis illis:
    tu modo cum multa bracchia tende fide.
saeuus Amor docuit ualidos temptare labores,   65
    saeuus Amor docuit uerbera posse pati.
me quondam Admeti niueas pauisse iuuencas
    non est in uanum fabula ficta iocum.

Then a young man, his brow with chaste bay garlanded,
seemed in my dream to set foot in our dwelling.
No former generation, no human household now
sees anything more beautiful than him.
Down the long neck unshorn the hair was flowing;
myrrh-scented tresses dripped Syrian dew.
Such was his whiteness as Leto's daughter the Moon displays,
and rose-red the colour on his snowy body,
as a virgin, first escorted to her youthful husband,
blushing dyes her tender cheeks,
and as when girls twine amaranthus with white lilies,
and pale apples redden in autumn.
The hem of a long mantle seemed to tease his ankles
(for this was the garment on his glowing body).
A work of rare art, gleaming with tortoiseshell and gold,
hung on his left side — a tuneful lyre.
When he first appeared, playing this with ivory plectrum,
he opened his mouth in a cheerful song.
But after his fingers and voice had finished speaking together,
sadly he uttered these sweet words:

'Greetings, belov'd of the Gods! For the chaste poet rightly
finds favour with Phoebus, Bacchus and Pierians.
But Semele's offspring Bacchus and the learned Sisters
do not know how to tell what the next hour brings.
Yet I have received from my Father the power to see
Fate's laws and what will happen in the future.
Wherefore accept what I say as no deceitful seer
and what I bring on true lips as God of Cynthus.

She who is dear to you as neither daughter to mother
nor pretty girl to a man's desire,
she for whom you importune the heavenly powers with vows,
who does not allow your days to pass serenely,
and who, when Sleep has wrapped you in his dark mantle,
deceives your vanity with nightly imaginings,
the lovely Neaera celebrated in your songs,
prefers to be the girl of another man.
Her wicked mind is busy with worries other than yours,
and a chaste home brings Neaera the bride no joy.

Ah, cruel the sex nor faithful the name of woman!
Ah, death to her who has learnt to deceive her man!
But she can be won over. Their minds are changeable:
only stretch out your arms with much faith.
Savage Love has taught the braving of tough labours,
savage Love has taught endurance of the lash.
That long ago I pastured Admetus' snow-white heifers
is no story invented as an idle joke.

tunc ego nec cithara poteram gaudere sonora
    nec similes chordis reddere uoce sonos,   70
sed perlucenti cantum meditabar auena,
    ille ego Latonae filius atque Iouis.
nescis quid sit amor, iuuenis si ferre recusas
    immitem dominam coniugiumque ferum.

Ergo ne dubita blandas adhibere querelas;   75
    uincuntur molli pectora dura prece.
quod si uera canunt sacris oracula templis,
    haec illi nostro nomine dicta refer:
"Hoc tibi coniugium promittit Delius ipse;
    felix hoc, alium desine uelle uirum." '   80

Dixit, et ignauus defluxit corpore somnus.
    a ego ne possim tanta uidere mala!
nec tibi crediderim uotis contraria uota
    nec tantum crimen pectore inesse tuo.
nam te nec uasti genuerunt aequora ponti   85
    nec flammam uoluens ore Chimaera suo
nec Canis anguina redimitus terga caterua,
    cui tres sunt linguae tergeminumque caput,
Scyllaque uirgineam canibus succincta figuram;
    nec te conceptam saeua leaena tulit   90
barbara nec Scythiae tellus horrendaue Syrtis,
    sed culta et duris non habitanda domus
et longe ante alias omnes mitissima mater
    isque pater quo non alter amabilior.

Haec deus in melius crudelia somnia uertat   95
    et iubeat tepidos irrita ferre Notos.

V

Vos tenet Etruscis manat quae fontibus unda,
    unda sub aestiuum non adeunda Canem,
nunc autem sacris Baiarum proxima lymphis
    cum se purpureo uere remittit humus.
at mihi Persephone nigram denuntiat horam: 5
    immerito iuueni parce nocere, dea.

Non ego temptaui nulli temeranda reorum
    audax laudandae sacra docere deae.
nec mea mortiferis infecit pocula sucis
    dextera nec cuiquam trita uenena dedit.   10
nec nos sacrilegos templis admouimus ignes,
    nec cor sollicitant facta nefanda meum,
nec nos insanae meditantes iurgia mentis
    impia in aduersos soluimus ora deos.

Then neither could I take delight in the plangent lyre
nor could I sing in harmony with its strings,
but I used to practise tunes on a perforated oat-stalk —
I the son of Jupiter and Leto.
You know not what love is if you refuse in youth
to bear a cruel mistress and wild marriage.

Then do not hesitate to use coaxing complaints;
hard hearts are won by gentle pleas.
And if the oracles sing true in holy temples
repeat these words to her in our name:
"This is the marriage promised you by the Delian Himself;
happy in this, cease wanting another man." '

He spoke and inactive sleep flowed away from my body.
Ah, grant me power not to see such evil!
I would not credit *you* with vows that cancelled vows
or think that guilt so great was in your heart.
For you were not brought forth by the barren sea's expanse
nor by Chimaera, rolling flame from her fierce mouth,
nor by the Dog whose back is wreathed with clustering snakes,
who has three tongues and a triple head,
nor by Scylla whose virgin shape is girdled with dogs;
no savage lioness, conceiving, bore you,
nor the barbarous land of Scythia or dreaded Syrtis,
but a cultured home where cruelty should not dwell
and a mother far beyond all others in gentleness
and a father than whom none is more lovable.

God change these cruel dreams for better and command
the warm South winds to bear them empty away.

5

You are detained by waves that flow from Etruscan springs,
waves one should waive beneath the summer Dog-star,
next best, however, to Baiae's holy waters now
when the soil loosens in purple springtime.
But on me Persephone serves notice of the black hour.
Goddess, do not harm an innocent youth.

I have not rashly dared make known the rites no guilty man
may sully — those of the Goddess who must be praised,
nor has my hand infected cups with deadly juices
nor given anyone powdered poison
nor have I sacrilegiously set fire to temples,
nor do unspeakable deeds trouble my heart,
nor, harbouring an unsound mind's rebellious thoughts,
have I opened my mouth to curse unfriendly gods.

Et nondum cani nigros laesere capillos,　　　　　　　　　　15
　　nec uenit tardo curua senecta pede.
natalem primo nostrum uidere parentes
　　cum cecidit fato consul uterque pari.
quid fraudare iuuat uitem crescentibus uuis
　　et modo nata mala uellere poma manu?　　　　　　　　20

Parcite, pallentes undas quicumque tenetis
　　duraque sortiti tertia regna dei.
Elysios olim liceat cognoscere campos
　　Lethaeamque ratem Cimmeriosque lacus,
cum mea rugosa pallebunt ora senecta　　　　　　　　　25
　　et referam pueris tempora prisca senex.

Atque utinam uano nequiquam terrear aestu!
　　languent ter quinos sed mea membra dies.
at uobis Tuscae celebrantur numina lymphae,
　　et facilis lenta pellitur unda manu.　　　　　　　　　30
uiuite felices, memores et uiuite nostri,
　　siue erimus seu nos fata fuisse uelint.
interea nigras pecudes promittite Diti
　　et niuei lactis pocula mixta mero.

VI

Candide Liber, ades (sic sit tibi mystica uitis
　　semper, sic hedera tempora uincta feras)
aufer et ipse meum pariter medicando dolorem:
　　saepe tuo cecidit munere uictus Amor.
care puer, madeant generoso pocula Baccho,　　　　　　5
　　et nobis prona funde Falerna manu.
ite procul, durum curae genus; ite, labores:
　　fulserit hic niueis Euhius alitibus.
uos modo proposito dulces faueatis amici,
　　neue neget quisquam me duce se comitem;　　　　　　10
aut si quis uini certamen mite recusat,
　　fallat eum tecto cara puella dolo.

Ille facit mites animos deus; ille ferocem
　　contudit et dominae misit in arbitrium;
Armenias tigres et fuluas ille leaenas　　　　　　　　　15
　　uicit et indomitis mollia corda dedit.
haec Amor et maiora ualet; sed poscite Bacchi
　　munera. quem uestrum pocula sicca iuuant?
conuenit ex aequo nec toruus Liber in illis
　　qui se quique una uina iocosa colunt.　　　　　　　　20
conuenit iratus nimium nimiumque seueros;
　　qui timet irati numina magna, bibat.

And not as yet has my black hair been spoilt by grey
nor bent old age arrived, slow-footed.
My parents saw my birthday for the first time
when the two consuls fell by the same fate.
What good is it to cheat a vine of growing grapes
and viciously tear off the new-born fruit?

Have mercy, whatever Gods possess the pale waves
and own by lot the harsh Third Kingdom.
Allow me hereafter to get to know the Elysian Fields
and Lethe's raft and the Cimmerian lakes
when my face grows pale with wrinkled age and I tell
the children an old man's tales of the past.

And would I were needlessly scared by imaginary fever,
but my limbs have been weak these thrice five days.
Yet you are honouring the powers of the Tuscan stream
and part the yielding waves with persistent hands.
May you all live happily and live remembering me,
whether I am spared or Fate should will my death.
Meanwhile make promise of black beasts to wealthy Dis
and bowls of snow-white milk mixed with neat wine.

6

Fair Liber, come (so may the mystic vine be yours
always, so may your brow be bound with ivy)
and at the same time cure my pain with present treatment;
often Love falls, defeated, thanks to you.
Dear boy, see that the cups are bathed in noble Bacchus
and pour us Falernian with down-turned hand.
Cares and troubles, dreary brood, away with you!
shine here the Euhian with happiest omens.
Only, sweet friends, you must fall in with my intention
and none of you refuse my lead.
Or if there's anyone says No to wine's soft contest
let his dear girl trick him and not be found out.

The God makes tempers gentle; he can crush the proud,
subjecting them to the will of a mistress.
Armenian tigresses and tawny lionesses
he tames and gives soft hearts to savages.
These things and greater Love can do, but call for Bacchus'
gifts. Can anyone enjoy dry drinks?
As Liber he meets on the level and does not frown at
those who honour him and the merry wine.
But he meets inordinate abstainers angrily;
who fears his angry Godhead's power should drink.

quales his poenas qualis quantusque minetur,
    Cadmeae matris praeda cruenta docet.

Sed procul a nobis hic sit timor, illaque, si qua est,   25
    quid ualeat laesi, sentiat, ira dei.
quid precor, a, demens? uenti temeraria uota
    aeriae et nubes diripienda ferant.
quamuis nulla mei superest tibi cura, Neaera,
    sis felix et sint candida fata tua.   30
at nos securae reddamus tempora mensae:
    uenit post multas una serena dies.

Ei mihi, difficile est imitari gaudia falsa,
    difficile est tristi fingere mente iocum;
nec bene mendaci risus componitur ore,   35
    nec bene sollicitis ebria uerba sonant.

Quid queror infelix? turpes discedite curae:
    odit Lenaeus tristia uerba pater.
Cnosia, Theseae quondam periuria linguae
    fleuisti ignoto sola relicta mari: 40
sic cecinit pro te doctus, Minoi, Catullus
    ingrati referens impia facta uiri.
uos ego nunc moneo: felix quicumque dolore
    alterius disces posse cauere tuo.
nec uos aut capiant pendentia bracchia collo   45
    aut fallat blanda sordida lingua prece.
etsi perque suos fallax iurauit ocellos
    Iunonemque suam perque suam Venerem,
nulla fides inerit: periuria ridet amantum
    Iuppiter et uentos irrita ferre iubet.   50
ergo quid totiens fallacis uerba puellae
    conqueror? ite a me, seria uerba, precor.

Quam uellem tecum longas requiescere noctes
    et tecum longos peruigilare dies,
perfida nec merito nobis inimica merenti,   55
    perfida, sed quamuis perfida, cara tamen!

Naida Bacchus amat. cessas, o lente minister.
    temperet annosum Marcia lympha merum.
non ego, si fugit nostrae conuiuia mensae
    ignotum cupiens uana puella torum,   60
sollicitus repetam tota suspiria nocte.
    tu, puer, i, liquidum fortius adde merum.
iamdudum Syrio madefactus tempora nardo
    debueram sertis implicuisse comas.

What punishments he threatens, in what guise and strength,
we learn from the Cadméan mother's bloody victim.

But let such fear be far from *us*, and if there's anger
on the injured God's part let *her* feel its force.
Ah, madman, what a prayer! Let winds and airy clouds
carry that rash vow off to be torn to shreds.
Although you've no thought left for me, Neaera,
may you be happy and your fate be bright.
As for us, let us pass our time at the carefree table;
after so many days has come one cloudless.

Alas, it's hard to imitate joy one can't feel;
it's hard to joke when thoughts are sad.
Nor can one well contrive a smile on lying lips
nor do drunken words sound well from the distressed.

Wretch, stop complaining! Rid yourself of shameful cares:
father Lenaeus hates sad talk.
The girl from Knossos wept at Theseus' perjuries,
forsaken once beside a foreign sea —
thus for Minos' daughter learned Catullus sang,
recalling an ingrate husband's wickedness.
I give you all this warning: happy the man who learns
from another's pain to beware of his own.
And don't either be caught by arms flung round your neck
or deceived by a mean tongue's coaxing plea.
Even if the deceiver swears by her own eyes,
by her Juno and by her Venus,
there'll be no good faith in her. At lovers' perjuries
Jove laughs and bids winds bear them empty away.
Then why should I complain so much about the word
of a deceitful girl? No more solemnity.

How I could wish to rest long nights with you
and keep vigil with you long days.
You traitor, and enemy (undeserved) of my deserts,
you traitor, but though treacherous still dear!

Bacchus loves Nais. Waiter, you're wasting time.
Blend the old vintage wine with Marcian water.
If a silly girl has fled the party at our table
in her eagerness for an unknown bed,
I shall not heave sighs of distress the whole night long.
Come, boy, mix the clear wine stronger.
Long since I should have bathed my brow in Syrian nard
and twined my hair with garlands.

VII (iv.i)

LAVDES MESSALLAE

Te, Messalla, canam, quamquam me cognita uirtus
terret ut infirmae valeant subsistere uires.
incipiam tamen, ac meritas si carmina laudes
deficiant, humilis tantis sim conditor actis
nec tua praeter te chartis intexere quisquam   5
facta queat dictis ut non maiora supersint.
est nobis uoluisse satis, nec munera parua
respueris. etiam Phoebo gratissima dona
Cres tulit, et cunctis Baccho iucundior hospes
Icarus, ut puro testantur sidera caelo   10
Erigoneque Canisque, neget ne longior aetas.
quin etiam Alcides, deus ascensurus Olympum,
laeta Molorcheis posuit uestigia tectis;
paruaque caelestes placauit mica, nec illis
semper inaurato taurus cadit hostia cornu.   15
hic quoque sit gratus paruus labor, ut tibi possim
inde alios aliosque memor componere uersus.

Alter dicat opus magni mirabile mundi:
qualis in immenso desederit aere tellus,
qualis et in curuum pontus confluxerit orbem,   20
et, uagus e terris qua surgere nititur aer,
huic ut contextus passim fluat igneus aether,
pendentique super claudantur ut omnia caelo.
at quodcumque meae poterunt audere Camenae,
seu tibi par poterunt seu (quod spes abnuit) ultra,   25
siue minus (certeque canent minus), omne uouemus
hoc tibi, nec tanto careat mihi carmine charta.
nam quamquam antiquae gentis superant tibi laudes,
non tua maiorum contenta est gloria fama,
nec quaeris quid quaque index sub imagine dicat,   30
sed generis priscos contendis uincere honores,
quam tibi maiores maius decus ipse futuris.
at tua non titulus capiet sub nomine facta,
aeterno sed erunt tibi magna uolumina uersu,
conuenientque tuas cupidi componere laudes   35
undique, quique canent uincto pede quique soluto.
quis potior, certamen erit. sim uictus in illis,
ut nostrum tantis inscribam nomen in actis.

Nam quis te maiora gerit castrisue foroue?
nec tamen hic aut hic tibi laus maiorue minorue,   40
iusta pari premitur ueluti cum pondere libra,
instabilis natat alterno depressior orbe,   44
prona nec hac plus parte sedet nec surgit ab illa,   42

7 (4.1)

THE PRAISES OF MESSALLA

Of you, Messalla, I'll sing, although your proven virtue
frightens me, lest my feeble powers may not suffice.
Still I'll begin, and if my song should fail your well-earned
praises I'll be the humble scribe of such great actions
and none but you be competent to inweave your deeds
upon papyrus so that greater than those told
are not left out. For me the will's enough. Don't spurn
small presents. Even Phoebus found the gifts a Cretan
brought most welcome, and Icarus was host more cordial
than all to Bacchus, as stars in the cloudless sky bear witness,
Erigone and the Dog, lest lapse of time deny it.
Yes, and Alcides too, about to ascend Olympus
as God, placed happy footprints in Molorchus' house.
A crumb has appeased Celestials, nor is the victim
that falls to them always a bull with gilded horns.
May this small work be welcome too, so that rememb'ring
later I may compose more and more verses for you.

Others can tell of the great world's wondrous workmanship:
how Earth sank downwards in the immensity of Air
and how the Ocean flowed together on the curved globe
and where the wandering air strives to rise from the earth
how interwoven with this on all sides fiery Ether
flows and how Heaven hanging above encloses all.
But whatever my Camenae will have the power to dare —
whether power matching you, or beyond (which hope refuses),
or less (and certainly they will sing less) — we vow it
all to you, lest my paper lack so great a name.
For though the praises of your ancient clan still flourish,
your glory is not content with fame of ancestors;
you don't ask what the label under each portrait says
but strive to outdo your family's old honours, bringing
more kudos to successors than your forbears to you.
Yet no inscription under your name will take your deeds
but you will have great volumes in everliving verse,
and they'll assemble eager to compose your praises
from every quarter — singers in metre and in prose,
competing to be best. Among them let me lose
provided I may write my name on such great actions.

For who does greater things than you in Camp or Forum?
Yet neither there nor here is your praise less or greater,
as, when one loads a true balance with equal weights,
it floats unsteady, weighing down each scale in turn,
nor sits on that side lower down nor higher on that,

qualis inaequatum si quando onus urget utrimque.   43

Nam seu diuersi fremat inconstantia uulgi,   45
non alius sedare queat; seu iudicis ira
sit placanda, tuis poterit mitescere uerbis.
non Pylos aut Ithace tantos genuisse feruntur
Nestora uel paruae magnum decus urbis Ulixem,
uixerit ille senex quamuis dum terna per orbem   50
saecula fertilibus Titan decurreret horis,
ille per ignotas audax errauerit urbes
qua maris extremis tellus includitur undis.

Nam Ciconumque manus aduersis reppulit armis,
nec ualuit lotos temptatos uertere cursus,   55
cessit et Aetnaeae Neptunius incola rupis
uicta Maroneo foedatus lumina Baccho;
uexit et Aeolios placidum per Nerea uentos,
incultos adiit Laestrygonas Antiphatemque,
nobilis Artacie gelida quos irrigat unda;   60
solum nec doctae uerterunt pocula Circes,
quamuis illa foret Solis genus, apta uel herbis
aptaque uel cantu ueteres mutare figuras;
Cimmerion etiam obscuras accessit ad arces,
quis numquam candente dies apparuit ortu,   65
seu supra terras Phoebus seu curreret infra.
uidit ut inferno Plutonis subdita regno
magna deum proles leuibus ius diceret umbris,
praeteriitque cita Sirenum litora puppi;
illum inter geminae nantem confinia mortis   70
nec Scyllae saeuo conterruit impetus ore,
cum canibus rabidas inter freta serperet undas,
nec uiolenta suo consumpsit more Charybdis,
uel si sublimis fluctu consurgeret imo
uel si interrupto nudaret gurgite fundum.   75
non uiolata uagi sileantur pascua Solis,
non amor et fecunda Atlantidos arua Calypsus,
finis et errorum miseri Phaeacia tellus.
atque haec seu nostras inter sunt cognita terras,
fabula siue nouum dedit his erroribus orbem,   80
sit labor illius, tua dum facundia, maior.

Iam te non alius belli tenet aptius artes:
qua deceat tutam castris praeducere fossam;
qualiter aduersos hosti defigere ceruos,
quemue locum ducto melius sit claudere uallo,   85
fontis ubi dulces erumpat terra liquores
et facilisque tuis aditus sit et arduus hosti;
laudis ut assiduo uigeat certamine miles,
quis tardamue sudem melius celeremue sagittam

as happens if unequal burdens press the scales.

For if the motley crowd's caprice should raise a clamour
no other man could calm it, or if juror's wrath
must be appeased it will grow gentle at your words.
Not Pylos or Ithaca are said to have borne such men
in Nestor or (small city's great pride) Ulysses,
though the old man lived while Titan with his fruitful hours
travelled around his orbit for three generations,
and the other wandered fearlessly through unknown cities
wherever Earth's enclosed by the sea's farthest waves.

For though out-armed he drove off the Ciconian bands
nor could the Lotus turn him from his attempted course,
and the Neptunian dweller on Etna's crag gave way,
maimed in the eyes Maronian Bacchus overcame.
He bore the winds of Aeolus over tranquil Nereus,
he approached wild Laestrygonians and Antiphates,
whom famed Artacie waters with her icy wave,
and him alone wise Circe's potions could not turn
although she was the Sun-God's daughter, skilled in herbs
and skilled too in enchantments to change former shapes.
He also reached the Cimmerians' twilit citadels
on whom day never dawned with radiant rising,
whether above the lands or under them ran Phoebus.
He saw how, subject to the infernal rule of Pluto,
the Gods' great offspring gave their judgement on the ghosts,
and in his swift ship he passed by the Sirens' shore.
While swimming in-between the confines of twin death
he feared not the attack of Scylla's savage mouth
when she would crawl the dog-mad waves between the straits,
nor could wild Charybdis devour him in her fashion
either with lowest billow rising up on high
or when she bared the sea-bed with a yawning gulf.
The journeying Sun's pastures profaned must not be hushed up
nor the love of Atlantid Calypso and her luxuriant fields
and the end of his wretched wanderings — Phaeacian land.
Now whether all this really happened on our earth
or fable set these wanderings in an unknown world,
his be the greater hardship, yours the eloquence.

Next, no one has a surer grasp of the arts of war
than you: how one can draw a safe trench to protect
the camp, how fix up 'stags' to obstruct the enemy,
or which position is best surrounded by a rampart,
where the ground gives outlet to a spring's sweet water
with easy access your side but steep for the enemy;
how daily competition for praise keeps soldiers fit —
who's best at shooting speedy arrow or slow stake

iecerit aut lento perfregerit obuia pilo; 90
aut quis equum celeremque arto compescere freno
possit et effusas tardo permittere habenas,
inque uicem modo derecto contendere passu
seu libeat curuo breuius conuertere gyro;
quis parma seu dextra uelit seu laeua tueri, 95
siue hac siue illac ueniat grauis impetus hastae,
aptior, aut signata cita loca tangere funda.

Iam simul audacis uenient certamina Martis
aduersisque parent acies concurrere signis,
tunc tibi non desit faciem componere pugnae, 100
seu sit opus quadratum acies consistat in agmen,
rectus ut aequatis decurrat frontibus ordo,
seu libeat duplicem seiunctim cernere Martem,
dexter uti laeuum teneat dextrumque sinister
miles, sitque duplex gemini uictoria casus. 105

At non per dubias errant mea carmina laudes,
nam bellis experta cano. testis mihi uictae
fortis Iapydiae miles; testis quoque fallax
Pannonius, gelidas passim disiectus in Alpes;
testis Arupinis et pauper natus in armis, 110
quem si quis uideat uetus ut non fregerit aetas,
terna minus Pyliae miretur saecula famae.
namque senex longae peragit dum tempora uitae,
centum fecundos Titan renouauerit annos,
ipse tamen uelox celerem super edere corpus 115
audet equum ualidisque sedet moderator habenis.
te duce, non alias conuersus terga, Domator
libera Romanae subiecit colla catenae.

Nec tamen his contentus eris: maiora peractis
instant, compertum est ueracibus ut mihi signis, 120
quis Amythaonius nequeat certare Melampus.
nam modo fulgentem Tyrio subtegmine uestem
indueras oriente die duce fertilis anni,
splendidior liquidis cum Sol caput extulit undis
et fera discordes tenuerunt flamina uenti, 125
curua nec assuetos egerunt flumina cursus;
quin rapidum placidis etiam mare constitit undis,
ulla nec aerias uolucris perlabitur auras
nec quadrupes densas depascitur aspera siluas;
quin largita tuis sunt muta silentia uotis. 130
Iuppiter ipse, leui uectus per inania curru,
adfuit et caelo uicinum liquit Olympum
intentaque tuis precibus se praebuit aure
cunctaque ueraci capite adnuit. additus aris
laetior eluxit structos super ignis aceruos. 135

or breaking through resistance with the tough *pilum*,
and who can master a speedy mount with a tight bridle
and let a slow one have his head on a loose rein,
and as required can ride at a canter straight ahead
or if need be can turn around in a narrow circle;
who can protect his right or left side with the *parma*
if the weight of the spear's attack should come from here or there,
more skilfully, or hit the target with whirling sling.

Again, soon as the contest comes of daring Mars
and lines prepare to engage under opposing standards,
then you are quick to decide upon battle-formation,
whether the line should be drawn up in square column
so that dressed ranks can launch the attack with fronts aligned,
or whether you prefer to fight two separate battles
so that your right engages their left, and your left
their right, giving twin chance of double victory.

No unattested praises lead my song astray;
I sing from war-experience. Witness for me
defeated Iapydia's brave troops. Witness too
the sly Pannonian routed in the frozen Alps.
Witness the needy Arupine, born under arms —
if you could see how old age fails to enfeeble him
you'd marvel less at the three generations of Pylian fame.
For while the old man's completing his long span of life
the Titan has renewed a hundred fruitful years,
yet without help he dares to leap with nimble body
on a fast horse and, seated, guides him with firm rein.
Under your leadership Domator, who before
never retreated, bowed free neck to Roman chain.

Nor will you be content with all this. Greater feats
draw closer, as is known to me from truthful signs
which Amythaon's son Melampus could not fault.
For you had just donned robes that shone with Tyrian weave
at dawning of the day that leads the fruitful year,
when from clear waves a brighter Sun lifted his head
and the contending winds withheld their savage blasts
nor winding rivers moved on their accustomed courses;
no, even the raging sea stood still with waves becalmed
and no winged creatures glided on the airy breeze
nor rough four-footed beast pastured the dense forests.
No, rather was dumb silence lavished on your vows.
Jupiter's self, borne in light chariot through the void,
was present and deserted sky-neighbouring Olympus,
and lending to your prayers an attentive ear
granted them all with truthful nod, while altar-kindled
a happier fire flared up above the ordered heaps.

Quin hortante deo magnis insistere rebus
incipe: non idem tibi sint aliisque triumphi.
non te uicino remorabitur obuia Marte
Gallia nec latis audax Hispania terris
nec fera Theraeo tellus obsessa colono;   140
nec qua uel Nilus uel regia lympha Choaspes
profluit, aut rapidus, Cyri dementia, Gyndes
aret Araccaeis aut unda Oroatia campis;
nec qua regna uago Tomyris finiuit Araxe,
impia nec saeuis celebrans conuiuia mensis   145
ultima uicinus Phoebo tenet arua Padaeus,
quaque Hebrus Tanaisque Getas rigat atque Magynos.
quid moror? Oceanus ponto qua continet orbem,
nulla tibi aduersis regio sese offeret armis.
te manet inuictus Romano Marte Britannus,   150
teque interiecto mundi pars altera sole.

Nam circumfuso consistit in aere tellus
et quinque in partes toto disponitur orbe.
atque duae gelido uastantur frigore semper:
illic et densa tellus absconditur umbra,   155
et nulla incerto perlabitur unda liquore,
sed durata riget densam in glaciemque niuemque,
quippe ubi non umquam Titan super egerit ortus.
at media est Phoebi semper subiecta calori,
seu propior terris aestiuum fertur in orbem   160
seu celer hibernas properat decurrere luces:
non igitur presso tellus exsurgit aratro,
nec frugem segetes praebent neque pabula terrae;
non illic colit arua deus, Bacchusue Ceresue,
nulla nec exustas habitant animalia partes.   165
fertilis hanc inter posita est interque rigentes
nostraque et huic aduersa solo pars altera nostro,
quas similis utrimque tenens uicinia caeli
temperat, alter et alterius uires negat aer.
hinc placidus nobis per tempora uertitur annus,   170
hinc et colla iugo didicit submittere taurus
et lenta excelsos uitis conscendere ramos,
tondeturque seges maturos annua partus,
et ferro tellus, pontus confinditur aere;
quin etiam structis exsurgunt oppida muris.   175

Ergo ubi praeclaros poscent tua facta triumphos,
solus utroque idem diceris magnus in orbe.
non ego sum satis ad tantae praeconia laudis,
ipse mihi non si praescribat carmina Phoebus.
est tibi qui possit magnis se accingere rebus   180
Valgius: aeterno propior non alter Homero.
languida non noster peragit labor otia, quamuis

Yes, at God's prompting start to press on with great deeds.
Triumphs are not the same for you as for the others.
Gaul will not hold you up, confronting you with nearby
Mars, nor the spacious territory of valiant Spain,
nor the wild land Theraean settlers occupied
nor where the Nile debouches or Choaspes' royal
stream, or Cyrus' folly, impetuous Gyndes,
or the Oroatian wave parches Araccan plains,
nor where Araxes' windings bound Tomyris' realm,
or, celebrating impious feasts at savage tables,
Padaeans, Phoebus' neighbours, own their distant fields,
and Getae and Magyni drink Tanais and Hebrus.
Why stop? Wherever Ocean girds the globe with sea
no region with opposing arms will bar your way.
Unbeaten by Roman Mars the Briton waits for you
and our world's other part with the Sun interposed.

For Earth remains at rest upon circumfluent Air
and as a whole its globe divides into five parts.
Now two through icy cold are always desolate
and there the land is hidden away in thick shadow
and not a wave of shifting liquid glides along
but stiffens solid into thick-packed ice and snow,
since there the Titan never makes his uprising.
But the mid-part lies always under Phoebus' heat
whether he travels nearer the earth in summer orbit
or hastens to run quickly through the winter daylight.
Therefore the land rises not up at the plough's pressure
neither do sown fields offer crops nor earth pasture.
No God can there till ploughland — Bacchus or Ceres —
nor any animal inhabit this burnt part.
Between it and the frozen parts is placed a fertile,
ours and another, opposite this soil of ours,
which similars the neighbouring sky on either side
containing tempers, one air denying the other's force.
Hence for us the year turns mildly through its seasons;
hence the bull has learned to lower neck to yoke
and the flexible vine to climb up lofty branches
and the sown field each year is shorn of ripened produce
and earth by iron, sea by bronze is cloven through;
yes, and towns too rise up inside their high-built walls.

Therefore when your achievements earn their splendid Triumphs
you only shall be hailed as great in either world.
I am not adequate to celebrate such praise,
not even if Phoebus' self wrote out the poem for me.
In Valgius you have someone who can gird himself
to great things; no one else is nearer deathless Homer.
Our labour spends no idle leisure, though Fortune

Fortuna, ut mos est illi, me aduersa fatiget.
nam mihi, cum magnis opibus domus alta niteret,
cui fuerant flaui ditantes ordine sulci   185
horrea fecundas ad deficientia messis,
cuique pecus denso pascebant agmine colles
(et domino satis et nimium furique lupoque),
nunc desiderium superest; nam cura nouatur
cum memor anteactos semper dolor admonet annos.   190

Sed licet asperiora cadant spolierque relictis,
non te deficient nostrae memorare Camenae.
nec solum tibi Pierii tribuentur honores:
pro te uel rapidas ausim maris ire per undas,
aduersis hiberna licet tumeant freta uentis;   195
pro te uel densis solus subsistere turmis
uel paruum Aetnaeae corpus committere flammae.
sum quodcumque, tuum est. nostri si paruula cura
sit tibi — quantalibet, si sit modo — non mihi regna
Lydia, non gnati potior sit fama Philippi,   200
posse Meleteas nec mallem uincere chartas.

Quod tibi si uersus noster, totusue minusue,
uel bene sit notus, summo uel inerret in ore,
nulla mihi statuent finem te fata canendi.
quin etiam mea cum tumulus contexerit ossa,   205
seu matura dies celerem properat mihi mortem,
longa manet seu uita, tamen, mutata figura
seu me finget equum rigidos percurrere campos
doctum, seu tardi pecoris sim gloria taurus,
siue ego per liquidum uolucris uehar aera pennis,   210
quandocumque hominem me longa receperit aetas,
inceptis de te subtexam carmina chartis.

VIII (iv.ii)

Sulpicia est tibi culta tuis, Mars magne, Kalendis:
    spectatum e caelo, si sapis, ipse ueni.
hoc Venus ignoscet. at tu, uiolente, caueto
    ne tibi miranti turpiter arma cadant.

Illius ex oculis, cum uult exurere diuos,   5
    accendit geminas lampadas acer Amor.
illam, quidquid agit, quoquo uestigia mouit,
    componit furtim subsequiturque decor.
seu soluit crines, fusis decet esse capillis;
    seu compsit, comptis est ueneranda comis.   10
urit, seu Tyria uoluit procedere palla:
    urit, seu niuea candida ueste uenit.

as is her custom wearies me with adversity.
For I who, when my high house shone in affluence,
had once had golden furrows in long rows enriching
barns not big enough to take the abundant harvests,
and whose livestock would graze the hills in close-packed column
(enough for owner and too much for thief and wolf),
I now am left with a sense of loss, for care revives
when grief, remembering, brings to mind years past and gone.

But even if worse befall and I'm stripped of the leavings
still my Camenae will not fail to tell of you
nor will Pierian homage only be offered you.
For you I'd even defy the sea's devouring waves
though wintry straits were swollen by opposing winds.
For you I'd even stand alone against a troop
of cavalry or consign my small self to Etna's flames.
Whatever I am is yours. If you've some small regard
for me — small as you please if real — not Croesus' kingdom,
not Alexander's fame would gratify me more
nor would I wish to be able to beat the Homeric scrolls.

But if my verse, in whole or part, should either be
well-known to you or only sometimes pass your lips,
no fate will fix a limit to my singing of you.
No, even when the burial mound entombs my bones,
whether an early date hastens my speedy death
or a long life awaits, still, whether a change of shape
fashions me as a stallion trained to gallop over
hard plains or were I pride of the slow herd — a bull,
or borne through liquid air on feathers as a bird,
whenever the long ages take me back as man
I'll weave more songs about you on to these first pages.

8 (4.2)

Great Mars, on your Kalends Sulpicia's dressed for you;
if you're wise, you'll come from heaven to see her.
Venus will pardon it. But, forceful though you are,
don't drop your guard in ignominious wonder.

At her eyes, when he wants to scorch the Gods,
passionate Love kindles twin torches.
Whatever she does, wherever she turns her steps,
unconscious grace serenely attends her.
If she unbinds her hair, flowing tresses suit her;
if she sets it, the setting is adorable.
She burns one if she opts to appear in Tyrian robes;
she burns one if she arrives dressed in snowy white.

talis in aeterno felix Vertumnus Olympo
    mille habet ornatus, mille decenter habet.

Sola puellarum digna est cui mollia caris   15
    uellera det sucis bis madefacta Tyros,
possideatque metit quicquid bene olentibus aruis
    cultor odoratae diues Arabs segetis,
et quascumque niger rubro de litore gemmas
    proximus Eois colligit Indus aquis.   20

Hanc uos, Pierides, festis cantate Kalendis,
    et testudinea Phoebe superbe lyra.
hoc sollemne sacrum, multos consummet in annos;
    dignior est uestro nulla puella choro.

IX (iv.iii)

Parce meo iuueni, seu quis bona pascua campi
    seu colis umbrosi deuia montis aper,
nec tibi sit duros acuisse in proelia dentes:
    incolumem custos hunc mihi seruet Amor.

Sed procul abducit uenandi Delia cura.   5
    o pereant siluae deficiantque canes!
quis furor est, quae mens, densos indagine colles
    claudentem teneras laedere uelle manus?
quidue iuuat furtim latebras intrare ferarum
    candidaque hamatis crura notare rubis?   10

Sed tamen, ut tecum liceat, Cerinthe, uagari,
    ipsa ego per montes retia torta feram;
ipsa ego uelocis quaeram uestigia cerui
    et demam celeri ferrea uincla cani.
tunc mihi, tunc placeant siluae, si, lux mea, tecum   15
    arguar ante ipsas concubuisse plagas.
tunc ueniat licet ad casses, inlaesus abibit,
    ne Veneris cupidae gaudia turbet, aper.

Nunc sine me sit nulla Venus, sed lege Dianae,
    caste puer, casta retia tange manu;   20
et quaecumque meo furtim subrepit amori
    incidat in saeuas diripienda feras.

At tu uenandi studium concede parenti
    et celer in nostros ipse recurre sinus.

Just so lucky Vertumnus on everlasting Olympus
wears a thousand outfits and all thousand suit him.

She is the only girl who ought to be given by Tyre
soft wools twice dipped in precious dyes,
and to own whatever fragrant crop rich Arab planters
reap in their sweet-smelling fields,
and all the pearls dark Indians, neighbouring Eoan
waters, pick up on the red seashore.

Of her on the holiday Kalends sing, Pierides
and Phoebus, proud of your tortoiseshell lyre.
May she celebrate this solemn rite for many years;
no girl is worthier of your choir.

9 (4.3)

Spare my young man, wild boars that haunt the plain's good pastures
or solitudes of the shadowy mountain,
nor be it yours to sharpen cruel tusks for battle;
may Love as minder keep him safe for me.

But the Delian leads him far astray for joy of hunting.
O perish the woods and let hounds drop dead!
What madness it is! What sense in ringing tree-clad hills
with nets that damage tender hands?
Or what's the good of entering wild beasts' lairs by stealth
and scratching white legs on prickly brambles?

And yet, Cerinthus, could I roam the hills with you,
I'd carry the twisted nets myself;
I'd look myself for the slot of the running deer
and let the swift hound off his chain.
Then, O then I'd love the woods, could I be proved
to have lain with you, my light, beside the snares.
Then wild boars could approach the trap and go away unharmed
so as not to spoil eager Venus' joys.

But now, no Venus without me! Obey Diana
chastely, boy, and touch the nets with chaste hands.
And any girl that creeps up on my love by stealth,
may she meet wild beasts and be torn to bits.

But you should leave the craft of hunting to your father
and run back fast yourself to my embrace.

X (iv.iv)

Huc ades et tenerae morbos expelle puellae;
    huc ades, intonsa Phoebe superbe coma.
crede mihi, propera, nec te iam, Phoebe, pigebit
    formosae medicas applicuisse manus.
effice ne macies pallentes occupet artus,   5
    neu notet informis candida membra color;
et quodcumque mali est et quicquid triste timemus
    in pelagus rapidis euehat amnis aquis.

Sancte, ueni tecumque feras quicumque sapores,
    quicumque et cantus corpora fessa leuant.   10
neu iuuenem torque metuit qui fata puellae
    uotaque pro domina uix numeranda facit.
interdum uouet, interdum, quod langueat illa,
    dicit in aeternos aspera uerba deos.

Pone metum, Cerinthe; deus non laedit amantes.   15
    tu modo semper ama: salua puella tibi est.
nil opus est fletu: lacrimis erit aptius uti   21
    si quando fuerit tristior illa tibi.   22
at nunc tota tua est; te solum candida secum   17
    cogitat, et frustra credula turba sedet.

Phoebe, faue: laus magna tibi tribuetur in uno
    corpore seruato restituisse duos.   20
iam celeber, iam laetus eris, cum debita reddet   23
    certatim sanctis laetus uterque focis.
tunc te felicem dicet pia turba deorum,   25
    optabunt artes et sibi quisque tuas.

XI (iv.v)

Qui mihi te, Cerinthe, dies dedit, hic mihi sanctus
    atque inter festos semper habendus erit.
te nascente nouum Parcae cecinere puellis
    seruitium et dederunt regna superba tibi.
uror ego ante alias; iuuat hoc, Cerinthe, quod uror,   5
    si tibi de nobis mutuus ignis adest.
mutuus adsit amor, per te dulcissima furta
    perque tuos oculos per Geniumque rogo.

Mane Geni, cape tura libens uotisque faueto,
    si modo cum de me cogitat ille calet.   10
quod si forte alios iam nunc suspiret amores,
    tunc precor infidos, sancte, relinque focos.

10 (4.4)

Come here and cure the sickness of a tender girl,
come here, Phoebus, proud of your unshorn hair.
Believe me, hurry, Phoebus, and you will not regret
laying healing hands on beauty.
Make sure those pale limbs do not waste away
and no bad colour marks her fair body.
And whatever's wrong, whatever trouble frightens us,
let the river's rushing stream carry it out to sea.

Come, Holy One, and bring with you whatever tastes
and incantations relieve a weary frame.
Don't torture a young man who fears his girl will die
and makes vows without number for his mistress.
Sometimes he vows, sometimes as she grows weaker
he says hard things of the deathless Gods.

Put away fear, Cerinthus. God will not hurt lovers.
Only keep loving: your girl is safe.
No call for weeping. You had better save your tears
for times, if any, when she's angry with you.
Now she's all yours — in kindness only thinks of you;
the mistaken crowd sit by her in vain.

Be gracious, Phoebus. Great praise will be given you
if you restore two lives by saving one.
Famous and glad you'll be when the two pay their debts
at your holy altar in glad rivalry.
Then the faithful crowd of Gods will call you fortunate
and every one of them covet your skill.

11 (4.5)

The day that gave me you, Cerinthus, shall be sacred
for me always and kept as a festival.
When you were born the Parcae sang new slavery
for girls and gave you a proud sovereignty.
I burn more than the rest, but am glad to burn, Cerinthus,
provided you catch mutual fire from me.
Catch mutual fire, I beg you, by those sweetest thefts
and by your eyes and by your Genius.

Good Genius, take this incense gladly and hear my vows
if only he grows hot at the thought of me.
But if he sighs already for another love,
then, Holy One, please leave his faithless hearth.

Nec tu sis iniusta, Venus: uel seruiat aeque
   uinctus uterque tibi, uel mea uincla leua.
sed potius ualida teneamur uterque catena,   15
   nulla queat posthac quam soluisse dies.
optat idem iuuenis quod nos, sed tectius optat;
   nam pudet hic illum dicere uerba palam.

At tu, Natalis, quoniam deus omnia sentis,
   adnue. quid refert clamne palamne roget?   20

XII (iv.vi)

Natalis Iuno, sanctos cape turis aceruos
   quos tibi dat tenera docta puella manu.
lota tibi est hodie, tibi se laetissima compsit,
   staret ut ante tuos conspicienda focos.
illa quidem ornandi causas tibi, diua, relegat;   5
   est tamen occulte cui placuisse uelit.

At tu, sancta, faue, neu quis diuellat amantes,
   sed iuueni, quaeso, mutua uincla para.
sic bene compones. ullae non ille puellae
   seruire aut cuiquam dignior illa uiro.   10
nec possit cupidos uigilans deprendere custos,
   fallendique uias mille ministret amor.
adnue purpureaque ueni perlucida palla:
   ter tibi fit libo, ter, dea casta, mero.

Praecipit et natae mater studiosa quod optet;   15
   illa aliud tacita, iam sua, mente rogat.
uritur ut celeres urunt altaria flammae,
   nec, liceat quamuis sana fuisse, uelit.
sit iuueni grata ac, ueniet cum proximus annus,
   hic idem uotis iam uetus extet amor.   20

XIII (iv.vii)

Tandem uenit amor qualem texisse pudore
   quam nudasse alicui sit mihi fama magis.
exorata meis illum Cytherea Camenis
   attulit in nostrum deposuitque sinum.
exsoluit promissa Venus. mea gaudia narret   5
   dicetur si quis non habuisse sua.
non ego signatis quicquam mandare tabellis
   ne legat id nemo quam meus ante, uelim.
sed peccasse iuuat, uultus componere famae
   taedet. cum digno digna fuisse ferar.   10

And, Venus, don't be unfair: either let both serve you,
bound equally, or else lighten my bonds.
But sooner let us both be held by a strong chain
that no day yet to come can break.
The young man prays the same as I, but secretly;
he is ashamed to speak openly here.

Grant it, Natalis: as God you know everything.
What matter if his prayer be spoken or silent?

12 (4.6)

Birthday Juno, accept these holy heaps of incense
from the soft hand of an educated girl.
For you today she bathed and gladly adorned herself
to stand in the public eye before your altar.
Or at least she claims her finery's for you, Goddess;
but secretly there's someone else she wants to please.

Be gracious, Holy One. Let no one split up lovers,
but please make mutual bonds for the young man.
That way you'll match them well. He ought not to be slave
to another girl nor she to another man.
Nor let the watchful chaperone surprise their passion,
but love invent a thousand subterfuges.
Nod your assent and come, brilliant in purple robe:
thrice we give you cake, thrice, chaste Goddess, wine.

And the anxious mother tells her daughter what to pray for,
but she, now grown-up, silently asks for something else.
She's burning, as the swift flames burn upon the altar,
and though she could be cured she would not wish it.
Let her please her young man and, when next year comes, thanks to
her vows then make this same love permanent.

13 (4.7)

At last has come a love which it would disgrace me more
to hide out of shame than expose to someone.
Prevailed upon by my Camenae Cytherea
delivered him into my arms on trust.
Venus has kept her promise. My joys can be the talk
of all who are said to have none of their own.
I would not wish to send a message under seal
so no one could read it before my man.
But I'm glad to sin and tired of wearing reputation's
mask. The world shall know I've met my match.

XIV (iv.viii)

Inuisus natalis adest qui rure molesto
  et sine Cerintho tristis agendus erit.
dulcius urbe quid est? an uilla sit apta puellae
  atque Arretino frigidus amnis agro?
iam, nimium Messalla mei studiose, quiescas. 5
  non tempestiuae saepe, propinque, uiae.
hic animum sensusque meos abducta relinquo,
  arbitrio quamuis non sinis esse meo.

XV (iv.ix)

Scis iter ex animo sublatum triste puellae?
  natali Romae iam licet esse suo.
omnibus ille dies nobis natalis agatur,
  qui necopinanti nunc tibi forte uenit.

XVI (iv.x)

Gratum est securus multum quod iam tibi de me
  permittis, subito ne male inepta cadam.
sit tibi cura togae potior pressumque quasillo
  scortum quam Serui filia Sulpicia.
solliciti sunt pro nobis quibus illa dolori est 5
  ne cedam ignoto maxima causa toro.

XVII (iv.xi)

Estne tibi, Cerinthe, tuae pia cura puellae,
  quod mea nunc uexat corpora fessa calor?
a, ego non aliter tristes euincere morbos
  optarim quam te si quoque uelle putem.
at mihi quid prosit morbos euincere, si tu 5
  nostra potes lento pectore ferre mala?

XVIII (iv.xii)

Ne tibi sim, mea lux, aeque iam feruida cura
  ac uideor paucos ante fuisse dies,
si quicquam tota commisi stulta iuuenta
  cuius me fatear paenituisse magis
hesterna quam te solum quod nocte reliqui, 5
  ardorem cupiens dissimulare meum.

14 (4.8)

That hateful birthday's near, which must be sadly spent
in tedious countryside and without Cerinthus.
What's sweeter than the city? Can country house and cold
river by Arretium suit a girl?
Messalla, you worry too much about me. Stay put now.
Journeys, kinsman, are often ill-timed.
If dragged away, I leave my heart and senses here,
even though you don't allow me charge of them.

15 (4.9)

That dreary journey's lifted, you know, from your girl's heart.
Now she can be in Rome for her birthday.
Let the day that chance now brings you unexpectedly
be spent as a birthday by us all.

16 (4.10)

I'm glad you're so permissive to yourself *re* me,
unfussed that I may fall into some folly.
You're welcome to toga-love and a basket-laden strumpet
instead of Servius' daughter Sulpicia.
Concern for me is felt by those whose greatest worry
is that I may submit to a low-born bedmate.

17 (4.11)

Do you feel real concern, Cerinthus, for your girl
now that a fever afflicts my tired body?
Ah, I would not choose to conquer wretched illness
unless I thought that you too wished it.
What should I gain by conquering illness if you
can bear my suffering with a cold heart?

18 (4.12)

Let me no more, my light, be loved as fervently
by you as I seem to have been a few days past,
if in all my youth I committed any folly
which I should own I more regretted
than leaving you alone yesterday night
from a wish to keep my passion secret.

XIX (iv.xiii)

Nulla tuum nobis subducet femina lectum:
    hoc primum iuncta est foedere nostra Venus.
tu mihi sola places, nec iam te praeter in urbe
    formosa est oculis ulla puella meis.

Atque utinam posses uni mihi bella uideri!   5
    displiceas aliis; sic ego tutus ero.
nil opus inuidia est. procul absit gloria uulgi.
    qui sapit, in tacito gaudeat ille sinu.
sic ego secretis possim bene uiuere siluis,
    qua nulla humano sit uia trita pede.   10
tu mihi curarum requies, tu nocte uel atra
    lumen, et in solis tu mihi turba locis.

Nunc licet e caelo mittatur amica Tibullo,
    mittetur frustra deficietque Venus.
hoc tibi sancta tuae Iunonis numina iuro,   15
    quae sola ante alios est mihi magna deos.

Quid facio demens? eheu mea pignora cedo.
    iuraui stulte. proderat iste timor.
nunc tu fortis eris, nunc tu me audacius ures.
    hoc peperit misero garrula lingua malum.   20

Iam facias quodcumque uoles: tuus usque manebo,
    nec fugiam notae seruitium dominae,
sed Veneris sanctae considam uinctus ad aras:
    haec notat iniustos supplicibusque fauet.

XX (iv.xiv)

Rumor ait crebro nostram peccare puellam:
    nunc ego me surdis auribus esse uelim.
crimina non haec sunt nostro sine facta dolore:
    quid miserum torques, rumor acerbe? tace.

19 (4.13)

No woman shall rob me of your bed: on this condition
our Venus was first joined.
You alone please me, nor is any girl in Rome
beautiful in my eyes save you.

And would I were the only one to find you pretty!
Displease the others — that way I'll be safe.
But envy must be avoided. Away with vulgar boasting!
The wise man keeps his joy to himself.
I'd live the good life thus in secret woods
where human foot has worn no path —
with you as my rest from worry, you in darkest night
my light and you my crowd in lonely places.

Were Venus now sent down from heaven as Tibullus' girl-friend,
she'll be sent in vain and love be lacking.
This I swear to you by your Juno's holy power,
who is great beyond the other Gods for me.

What am I doing? I'm mad, alas, to give such pledges,
foolish to swear. Your fear was an advantage.
Now you'll be strong, you'll burn me now more boldly.
Loose talk has brought this trouble on a wretch.

Then do as you please. Yours forever, I shan't run away
from the service of the mistress I know,
but sit in chains at holy Venus' altar —
she marks the unjust and favours suppliants.

20 (4.14)

Gossip says frequently my girl's unfaithful.
Just now I wish I had deaf ears.
The accusation can't be made without my hurt.
Why rack the lovesick, cruel Gossip? Hush!

EPITAPHIVM TIBVLLI

Te quoque Vergilio comitem non aequa, Tibulle,
  Mors iuuenem campos misit ad Elysios,
ne foret aut elegis molles qui fleret amores
  aut caneret forti regia bella pede.

VITA TIBULLI

Albius Tibullus, eques Romanus, insignis forma cultuque corporis ob-
seruabilis, ante alios Coruinum Messallam oratorem dilexit, cuius etiam
contubernalis Aquitanico bello militaribus donis donatus est. hic multorum
iudicio principem inter elegiographos optinet locum. epistolae quoque eius
amatoriae, quamquam breues, omnino utiles sunt. obiit adulescens, ut
indicat epigramma supra scriptum.

TIBULLUS'S EPITAPH

Inequitable Death sent you, Tibullus, also
as Virgil's comrade young to Elysian Fields,
lest any live to weep soft loves in elegiacs
or sing of royal wars in brave rhythm.

THE LIFE

Albius Tibullus, Roman knight, noted for good looks and remarkable for
personal adornment, beyond others loved Corvinus Messalla the orator, as
whose aide also in the Aquitanian War he was awarded military decorations.
In the judgement of many he occupies first place among the elegiographers.
His amatory epistles too, though short, are thoroughly useful. He died
young, as the epigram quoted above testifies.

TEXTUAL NOTE

The editor of a literary text is also a scribe who must copy, or otherwise reproduce, his text for the printer from some reliable source, printed or in manuscript. I accordingly chose to type out the text of Tibullus from a photograph of the earliest MS, the Ambrosian of 1374 (*R* 26 *sup.* in the Biblioteca Ambrosiana, Milan, discovered by Baehrens in 1876), simply recording departures from it — some 364 in all — in the list that follows. To settle questions about first and second hands I examined the actual MS.

For the readings of other MSS, readings which, though appearing in my text, for the sake of brevity are not attributed to their source, I have used photographs of the Vaticanus, the next earliest MS (3270 in the Vatican Library), of the Guelferbytanus, an important fifteenth-century MS (*Aug.* 82.6 *fol.* in the Herzog August Library at Wolfenbüttel), and of the tenth-century Freising Excerpts (6292 in the Bavarian State Library, Munich). For the rest, including the conjectures of scholars, I have relied on the critical apparatuses of Calonghi (1928) and Lenz-Galinsky (1971), the Additional Variants recorded by O'Neil, and Valpy's reprint of Huschke.

The punctuation is modern. The spelling has been brought into line with what may be called the vulgate orthography. Spelling departures from the Ambrosian are not listed (this includes *tum* for *tunc* and *eheu* for *heu heu*), nor do I record the unimportant spelling mistakes of my source (e.g. 1.2.54 *perdonuisse*, 1.5.65 *ocultos*).

With these omissions the readings quoted below are those of the Ambrosian. When the reading printed in my text is not found in a MS, the name of the scholar whom I believe to have first conjectured it is given; a colon separates this name from the Ambrosian reading. Where there might be a doubt which word in the Latin text replaces the Ambrosian reading, that word is quoted and followed either by a square bracket or by a scholar's name. My own emendations are attributed to *Translator*.

BOOK ONE

1   14 agricolae   19 felices   24 clamat   25 non possum   29 ludentes   37 et   44 scilicet   49 si   54 exiles   59 te] et   60 te] et   63 dura   64 iuncta   73 posses

2   23 decet   42 rapido   60 ipse   67 possit   71 contextus   80 posset   81 magni   84 diripuisse   89 *Broukhusius:* laetus   90 unus

3   9 quam *Dousa pater:* cum   13 numquam   14 *Aldine edition 1502:* cum   17 aues dant   18 *Some 16th century scholar:* Saturni   21 neu   22 *Doering:* sciat   25 deum   38 ueteris   50 reperte   59 passuque   86 colo   91 nunc

4 8 sit   28 remeatque   29 te perdit   36 illam   40 credas   44 *Crux as yet unsolved*   53 mihi ... cum   54 *Santen:* tamen apta   59 at] iam   62 ne   63 est *omitted*   71 *Heyne:* Venus ipsa   72 flentibus   80 diducat   81 heheu

5 1 dissidium   2 sortis   3 turbo   6 post haec   7 per te] parce   16 uoca nouem creme   28 segete et spicas   30 adiuuet   42 *Lucian Mueller:* et pudet   *Nodell:* mea   45 Nereis quae   55 *Castiglioni:* urbes   60 *Huschke:* nam   61 *Muretus:* praesto tibi praesto   67 iuncta   69 furta   74 usque] ipse   76 nat] nam

6 11 nunc   18 lasso   40 effluit   42 stet procul ante   45 mota   46 non et amans   47 uiolata   52 *Achilles Statius:* didicisse   67 uicta   70 possum   71 putat ducor   72 proprias proripiorque   84 quam] quod

7 4 *Scaliger:* Atax   6 uinctos   9 *Scaliger:* tua bella   12 Carnoti   13 at   16 arat   40 *Muretus:* tristitiae   42 cuspide   49 *Markland:* centum ludos   54 Mosopio ... mella   57 ne ... quae   61 canit   a *omitted*

8 1 celare   2 ferat ... leuia   11 comas   29 ne   49 seu   51 sentita   52 luteo   57 leuis   59 *Kraffert:* quamuis   61 possunt   64 *Francken:* est ... euigilanda   77 *P. Burman II:* at

9 9 petituros   19 O uiciis   23 celanti fas   24 sit ... uetet   25 saepe *Muretus:* leue   31 nullo tibi   35 eriperet   36 *Heyne:* puras   40 sit ... sed   44 sed .. clausos   68 pectore   69 *Postgate:* ista   73 nec] haec   75 huic] hunc   81 dum

10 8 ciphus   11 *Heyne:* uulgi   18 ueteres   21 uua   23 ipsa   30 aduerso   36 puppis   49 uidens *(corrected to* nitens) uomer uiderit. *Guyet proposed* nitent   51 elutoque ... ipso   60 diripit   61 perscindere   68 praefluat

BOOK TWO

1 1 *Scaliger:* ualeat   9 sunt   23 satiri   34 *Scaliger:* ades   38 grande famen   42 suppotuisse   45 antea tunc   49 ingerat   50 et   54 duceret   58 *Postgate and others:* yrcus hauxerat hyrcus oues   65 Mineruam   66 *Muretus:* appulso   73 opus   74 limem   88 thoro   89 fuluis

2 7 distillent   15 undis   19 uinculaque

3 11 armenti   18 *Muretus:* mixtus   45 obsistere   46 et   47 tumulti   57 gerit   63 uota *Kraus:* nota liquor   quem] que   64 bipsatos   65 *Heinsius:* seges Nemesis qui abducit   72 et *omitted*   82 iuuet

4 2 pater ue   4 remittet   5 nil *Heinsius:* quid   10 uasti *omitted*   12 nam   17 equalis ... urbem   33 uicta] incerta   36 ipse   38 nunc

Broukhusius: hic   40 portas   43 *Camps:* seu   44 obsequias
55 quidquam habet   59 modo] non

5   4 *Lachmann:* meas   11 debitus   18 quos canat   20 captos   34 pulla
35 illaque   *Muretus:* ditis   47 rutilis   49 castris   62 longam ... uiam
64 noscar   68 *Lachmann:* Phoebo grata   69 quodque Albana sacras
Tiberis   70 *Postgate:* portarit ... perluerit   72 et ... deplueritque
76 amnis   79 fuerant   81 crepitet   82 *Cornelissen:* sacer
92 compressis   94 puro   95 operta   99 extruat   109 taceo
116 ferent   122 perpetua

6   16 scilicet   32 ferant   45 Phirne   46 itque] tuncque   47 diro

BOOK THREE

1   8 *Muretus:* meis   10 pumicet et   11 protexit   15 paruos
16 umbrosam   21 meritum   26 tibi

2   7 est *omitted*   15 recentem *Bach:* rogatae   21 uentis

3   7 sociarent   14 thariste   17 legiturque in   20 inuida quae
21 homini   22 gerit   28 aduersa

4   3 *Translator:* uisum   4 uotis   9 maturas   14 pertinuisse   17 emersa
26 *Cartault:* humanum nec uidet illud opus   28 tyrio myrtea
50 quidque ... ferat (feram *Broukhusius*)   59 tuis *Lipsius:* suas
60 nerea   65 *omitted*   80 hoc] ac   87 consanguinea   89 submixta
96 impia

5   1 nos   3 *Scioppius:* maxima   7 *Sandbach:* deorum   10 certa
11 sacrilegis ... amouimus egros   13 meditantis   27 necquicquam
29 atque nobis

6   1 uictis   8 pulserit   Euhius *Baehrens:* Delius   13 dites   15 Armenas
17 uolet   21 *Lachmann:* non uenit ... seuerus   23 qualis quantusque]
deus hic quantumque   33 Ei] Si   44 carere   46 fide   51 qui
58 martia   62 i] et

7   1 mea   3 a meritis   10 pura   11 ne *omitted*   13 terris   14 pacauit
18 dictat opus   22 hinc et   24 et   27 nec   30 qua iudex   37 potius
Jortin: uictor   39 nam quique tibi ... cartis ne   55 non ... tempus
uertere   60 artacre gelidos   68 discurreret undis (ius diceret *Postgate*)
70 illum terminae nautem   71 orbe   73 in ore   75 *Cartault:* puntum
77 calipsos   82 nam ... artos   84 ceruos] uernos   86 fontibus ut
88 et   91 *Ayrmann:* celeremue   93 directo   94 *Huschke:* contendere
96 grandis uenit   97 *Francken:* amplior   102 ut] in   103 *Scaliger:* seu
iunctum   104 dexteraque ut   108 iapigiae   110 et arpinis et
113 *Voss:* saecula famae   114 renouerat   128 ulla   130 multa
132 linquit   137 non] nunc   140 Theraeo] te tereo   141 dyaspes

142 cydnus   143 *Postgate:* creteis ardet ... caristia   149 offerret
156 *Guyet:* incepto   162 igitur] ergo   168 utrique   171 huic
174 confunditur   175 exurgitat opida   186 fecundis indeficientia
mensis   190 anteactos] accitos   191 relictus   200 magni ... Gylippi
(gnati *Morgan*)   201 nec *omitted* ... mittere   204 statuunt   205 tunc
... cum texerit   206 celerem] fato   211 inquencunque

8   14 mille habet] mille hunc   23 *Scaliger:* hoc sumet   24 thoro

9   3 proelia] pectore   18 ne] da   19 tunc

10   6 pallida   8 rabidis eueat   17 ac

11   1 Est qui te   4 dederant   6 tibi ne de   10 ualet   16 quam *omitted*
17 tutius   20 referet -ue ... -ue

12   1 Hatalis   3 *Canter:* tota   5 orandi   7 ne nos   10 cuidam   13 -que
omitted   14 fit] sic   15 optat   19 si   ac *omitted*   20 *Baehrens:* esset

13   6 suam   8 me legat id uenio quoniam

14   6 neu

15   2 iam licet] non sinet   suo *Aldine 1502:* tuo

16   1 mihi   6 nec credam (cedam *Statius*)

17   1 placitura   5 at] ha   si] quid   6 laeto

19   3 mihi] modo   8 ipse   9 possum   16 tibi   17 credo   18 prodeat
21 *L.Mueller:* faciam   22 noto   23 confidam   24 nec

VITA TIBVLLI

Romanus] regalis. *Baehrens's conjecture* R. e Gabis (= Romanus e
Gabiis) *may be right.* oratorem] originem   equitanico
superscriptum

EXPLANATORY NOTES

BOOK ONE

1

Inspired by the *Eclogues* and *Georgics* of Virgil, Tibullus dreams of living the simple life on his inherited land, now much reduced (his version of the Stoic and Epicurean ideal of contentment with little). It turns out that he is in the army, perhaps serving abroad, that he is an *amicus* of Messalla (see Introduction xiv), and that he has an *amica* named Delia, whom he imagines holding his hand as he dies and weeping at his funeral pyre (adapting an idea from Propertius 1.17). Meanwhile he urges her to join him on Love's campaign; with his modest independence he can afford to look down on the rich (his version of the philosophical *despicientia rerum humanarum*). The themes of love and death, war and military glory, wealth and a simple country life, basic to his collection of elegies, are here introduced. For a full discussion see Lee 'Otium cum indignitate' (1974).

1-4 Service in the army was one way in which Roman *equites* might with luck become rich; see, for example, Horace *Odes* 1.29.

labor combines the ideas of duty, hard work and hardship, cf. Cicero *Fam.* 7.17.1 *timidus in labore militari*.

terreat: probably generic subjunctive; see Woodcock §155.

As *urbs capta* = 'the capture of the city', so *classica pulsa* = 'the pulse of trumpet-calls' (or 'of trumpets', see Servius on Virgil *Aen.* 7.367).

Perhaps line 4 was suggested by Bacchylides *Fragment* 4.35-7 (in praise of Peace): 'There is no din of brazen trumpets, nor is honeyed sleep stripped from the eyelids'; there too sleep is combined with a military metaphor.

5 traducat: for this military term cf. Caesar *De Bello Gallico* 6.40.7. The metaphor has the effect of personifying *paupertas* (which, of course, is a relative term; an *eques Romanus* who calls himself poor is not exactly on the bread-line).

inerti: as at Virgil *Eclogue* 1.27, almost 'unenterprising'.

6 assiduo igne: contrasts with *labor assiduus*. In the context of *divitiae* here, a Roman reader might remember that in the archaic Latin of the Twelve Tables *assiduus* was equivalent to *locuples* 'rich' (Cairns 17).

7 Cf. Hor. *Epist.* 1.14.39, *rident vicini glaebas et saxa mouentem* (sc. *me*); such work was infra dig. for *equites*.

8 **rusticus** usually has disparaging overtones, e.g. Virgil *Eclogue* 2.50. It is one stage worse than *indoctus,* see Quintilian *Inst.* 12.10.53.

poma: the young trees, not as at line 13 the fruit; cf. Virgil *Georgics* 2.426. 'Maiden' is a nurseryman's term for a one-year-old fruit-tree.

9 Contrast Livy 40.47.9 *destituti ab unica spe auxilii in deditionem uenerunt. Spes* may be the goddess, hence capital *S.*

11-12 Probably refer to the Roman God of boundaries, Terminus; see Ovid *Fasti* 2.641-2.

veneror: the present tense here really does duty for the future, so too *ponitur* (14) and *fertis* (20); for this use cf. 2.6.9 *castra peto.* For the thought, see Introduction xv-xvi.

14 Probably Silvanus, *aruorum pecorisque deus* according to Virgil *Aen.* 8.601. He receives offerings of fruit in Horace *Epode* 2.21-2, a poem which influenced this elegy. Cf. 1.5.27 *deo agricolae.*

17 **ruber:** cf. *Eclogue* 10.27 (of Pan) *minioque rubentem.*

18 A fertility God with a huge phallus. Not a native Italian divinity, he came from Asia Minor via Greece.

19-22 Perhaps the estate had suffered in the confiscations after Philippi, which also deprived Horace and Propertius of their property.

20 For the Lares see Introduction xvi-xvii.

24 **clamet** is probably jussive subjunctive; see Woodcock §109.

26 **deditus:** another military word.

27 Sirius rose some days after the summer solstice (Cicero *De Diuinatione* 2.93).

28 **riuos:** the rhyme with *aestiuos* is attractive.

praetereuntis: i.e. neither stagnant nor dry in summer.

29-30 **tenuisse ... increpuisse:** this use of the perfect infinitive where one expects the present is often found in the Augustan poets; it is not only metrically convenient but has its origin in old Latin where the perfect infinitive occurs in prohibitions, e.g. *ne quis fecisse uelit.*

nec tamen interdum: cf. *Eclogue* 1.57 *nec tamen interea.*

31-32 For the kid abandoned cf. *Eclogue* 1.14-15.

35 **hic** could imply that the poet is on his estate, but 49-50 is against that; therefore like *hic* at 1.3.59.

36 Patron Goddess of flocks and herds, whose festival was celebrated on 21 April, the day of Rome's foundation (Cicero *De Diuinatione* 2.98).

38 **puris fictilibus:** there is perhaps an implicit contrast with *purum argentum* 'plain silver'.

39-40 For the etymological play here see Cairns 94. For the postponement of -*que* cf. 1.3.38 *praebueratque* and Platnauer 91, who remarks that Propertius offers only one example, Tibullus fourteen.

41 **fructus** is also 'produce' here.

43 Cf. Catullus 31.10 *desideratoque acquiescimus lecto*; again a soldier is writing.

46 **continuisse:** witty use of a military word; the ordinary one would be *tenuisse*. For the tense see note on 29-30 above.

47 Cf. Isidore *Etymologiae* 18.10.1 *funda* (a sling) *dicta eo quod ex ea fundantur lapides, id est emittantur.*

51 The logical order would be *smaragdique potius*.

For *que* kept short before *sm-* see Platnauer 62.

53 **decet:** because *noblesse oblige.*

54 The rhyme with 52 and 50 is remarkable, cf. 28 note.

55 **retinent:** cf. Caesar *De Bello Gallico* 3.9.3 *legatos ... retentos ab se et in uincla coniectos.*

56 The real-life doorkeeper is chained too, but sits *pone fores* 'behind the door'; Tibullus sits *ante* because he is an *exclusus amator*, as *duras* implies.

58 **segnis inersque** are words of military disapproval.

59-60 The poet does not want to die 'on the field of honour', but ingloriously; cf. Propertius 1.6.25-6.

61-62 For the postponement of *et* cf. 1.2.6 *clauditur et.*

67-68 The Manes, from old Latin *manus* 'good', were the deified spirits of the dead. Delia may weep (despite line 52) and unbind her hair, but the more extreme tokens of grief would maltreat her beauty and thus give pain to the poet's sensitive ghost.

69 Cf. Catullus 64.372 *coniungite amores* (picked up in the next line by *coniunx*).

70 **tenebris:** can go with *ueniet* (cf. 1.2.25) and/or with *adoperta*. This striking image is a fine example of Tibullus's originality.

71-72 Ovid neatly sums this up later at *Amores* 1.9.4 *turpe senilis amor.* Lysidamus in Plautus *Casina* is an amusing example.

73-74 Cf. Terence *Adelphi* 101-3 *non est flagitium, mihi crede, adulescentulum/ scortari neque potare, non est, neque fores/ ecfringere.* The couplet alludes to the *komos*, Latin *comissatio*; in the evening, after wine, young men would go round to their mistress's house and try to persuade her to let them in, serenading her and sometimes forcing an entry. See Headlam on Herodas 2.34-7 for fullest details.

74 **rixas inseruisse:** cf. Livy 35.17.2 *suas quisque nunc querellas, nunc postulationes inserit.*

75   The conceit of the lover-soldier has been prepared for by military metaphors earlier, in 45-8 and 55. Ovid devotes a whole poem to the idea (*Amores* 1.9).

76   Contains a double pun, for *uiris* 'men' can refer to soldiers or husbands, and they can be *cupidi* 'greedy' for money or sex.

78   It is more usual to despise the poor, cf., in the New Testament, James 2.1-6.

2

This long elegy appears to have a dramatic setting, but readers differ over what that setting is. Some think the whole thing takes place at Delia's closed door (the wine referred to in line 1 could be served there, cf. Plautus *Curculio* 82-5). Others think that it takes place at a drinking-party, at which the poet from line 7 on falls into a reverie, possibly (as Leo suggested) coming out of it at line 89 when someone present laughs. Still others think that the poet is at home, soliloquizing after initially addressing a servant; a variant of this would be that he falls asleep after line 6 and what follows represents his thoughts in a vivid dream. For the fullest discussion see Vretska.

In any case the elegy (which follows on from 1.1.56) is a Tibullan variation of the type of poem technically known as *paraklausithyron* (sc. *melos*) or Song at the Closed Door. We find another variation at Propertius 1.16 where the door speaks throughout and quotes the lover's song, and at Ovid *Amores* 1.6 where the serenade has a refrain and is addressed not to the girl but to the doorkeeper. For an interesting study of these three elegies see Yardley.

5   **custodia:** abstract for concrete; again the language is military, cf. Caesar *De Bello Gallico* 1.20.6 *Dumnorigi custodes ponit ut quae agat, quibuscum loquatur, scire possit.*

7   **difficilis:** could go with *ianua*, but is best taken with *domini*, which needs an adjective; to take *domini* apo koinou with *Iouis*, as some do, is unnecessarily complicated.

11   **mala:** *male dicere* is the ordinary expression.

13   **peregi:** see *OLD* s.v. 11 (a).

14   Cf. Catullus 63.66 *mihi floridis corollis redimita domus erat.*

16   Presupposes the Latin proverb *fortes Fortuna adiuuat* (Cicero *Tusculans* 2.11).

18   **fixo dente:** 'with an inserted spike'; *OLD dens* 3.

In this and the following couplets the anaphora of *illa* (characteristic of hymns) imparts a religious tone, which is continued in 29ff. and carries on from the address to the Door as a god. In fact the elegy's atmosphere is religious, mysterious and romantic throughout, though there is wit too, e.g. 23-4.

19 **molli lecto:** i.e. the bed of love, cf. 58. For the idea of love's teaching cf. Callimachus *Aetia* 67.1 'Eros himself taught Akontios craft'.

21-22 Ovid expands this couplet into a complete elegy, dramatising it in *Amores* 1.4.

26 Missing in the archetype from which all our MSS derive.

28 Probable allusion to the old Latin word *praemiator* 'robber'.

29-34 See Introduction xi.

29-30 The first appearance of the idea that the lover is a sacred person, divinely protected from harm. Tibullus may well have developed it from the Greek epigrammatist Posidippus (*AP* 5.213): 'Drunk and through thieves have I come, using bold Love as a guide'.

eat is potential subjunctive, see Woodcock §118.

32 There is hyperbaton of *imber*; = *non mihi <nocet> imber cum decidit multa aqua*.

34 **ad:** see *OLD ad* 39.

35 For the meaning of the high-style expression *parcite luminibus* see Ovid *Metamorphoses* 5.248.

Being engaged on *furtum*, he naturally does not want to be reecognised hanging around Delia's door.

36 Contradicts Catullus 55.20 *uerbosa gaudet Venus loquela*.

38 I.e. *neu ferte prope lumina <de> fulgenti face*, again avoiding more ordinary idiom.

39 **et:** 'even', with *imprudens*.

41-42 For the birth of Venus-Aphrodite see Hesiod *Theogony* 176-206. Kronos castrated his father Ouranos and threw his genitals into the sea; Aphrodite grew from the foam (*aphros*) that they produced, and when full-grown stepped ashore on the island of Kythera.

43 **coniunx** need not be 'husband', cf. *vir*; he could be the lover (usually rich) under whose protection the courtesan has placed herself.

44 Magic first appears in love elegy at Propertius 1.1.19-22, on which see Cairns (1974). Some ten years earlier Virgil had latinized Theocritus *Idyll* 2, The Sorceress, in *Eclogue* 8.64-109.

45 The third-century AD Greek Christian Father, Hippolytus, reveals how this and other such tricks were done in his *Refutation of all Heresies* 4.28-42 (Cairns (1974) 100-1).

46 The sound of *iter* partially reverses that of *uertit* (Putnam).

48 **deuocat:** the witch not only 'lures' (*elicit*) ghosts (*manes*) up from the underworld, but also 'calls down' corpses from the still warm pyre. For the theme of bringing burnt corpses back to life, cf. Horace *Epode* 17.79 *possim cremos excitare mortuos*.

52   **orbe:** of the sky's vault; *OLD s.v.* 7 (c).

53   Medea, the Colchian princess who by her magic enabled Jason to win the Golden Fleece, was for antiquity the prime human example of a sorceress.

54   A formidable Greek Goddess of the Underworld, worshipped by witches; she was Medea's patroness (Euripides *Medea* 395); her hell-hounds first appear in Apollonius *Argonautica* 3.1217.

55   *quis* for *quibus* again at 1.6.13.

61-62   'Why should I believe her? (or 'What am I to believe?'). Why, she even (*eadem*) said she could get rid of (*OLD soluo* 15) my love ...', a thing which the poet thinks impossible, nor in any case would he wish it (66). Clearly 'my love' here can't mean Delia, because of 65 *totus abesset amor*. I agree with Dissen that the rhetorical point of 61-6 is to demonstrate the poet's strong and faithful love for Delia and with K.F. Smith that *quid credam?* suddenly doubts the efficacy of the aforesaid spell and is tantamount to saying 'Better not risk using it'.

67   It is simplest to take *ille* here as = *ille* (57). We now gather that the *coniunx* is fighting in Cilicia and infer that that is why he has put a guard on Delia. This avoids either multiplying characters or splitting Tibullus in two.

69   Messalla made an expedition to Cilicia some time after the battle of Actium (see 1.7.13-16). The Cilicians were noted for their toughness, piracy and saffron.

71   *contextus* is usually read, but 'a man all interwoven with silver and gold' strains belief. The most famous set of gold armour is that of Glaucus at *Iliad* 6.236.

75   **retinere:** the military overtones (cf. 1.1.55 note) are not heard in this context, I should now guess; see *OLD s.v.* 4.

79   **stragula:** strictly not coverlets but under-blankets; 'painted' in Latin is used of embroidery.

80   Refers to a fountain playing in the peristyle, or inner court, of some wealthy Roman's house.

81   **uiolaui:** cf. 1.3.8; 6.51; 9.2 and 19; and Introduction xix-xx.

83   **incestus:** cf. 2.1.13-14 *casta placent superis ...*

84   I.e. to hang on his mistress's door, as at line 14.

90   I.e. *mox tibi deus <saeuiet>, non usque saeuiet uni <mihi>.*

91ff   *senilis amor* again; cf. 1.1.70-71.

98   Both among Greeks (Theophrastus *Characters* 16.15) and Romans (Pliny *Natural History* 28.35) this was a way of averting bad luck. For *molles sinus* see *OLD mollis* 3 (b), and for the postponement of *et* cf. 1.3.82.

100   Probably adapts a proverb, as does 16; cf. Horace *Epistles* 2.1.220 *ut uineta egomet caedam mea.*

3

Some time after Actium (September, 31 BC) and perhaps before the Aquitanian campaign mentioned in 1.7, Messalla was sent on a mission to the East (but see *KP* 3.1244-45). The general and his staff were in Corcyra when Tibullus fell ill and was unable to accompany them further. The elegy recording this occasion is a meditation on love and death, the war-torn present and the Golden Age. Remembering how unwilling Delia was for him to leave her, the poet imagines that his illness is a punishment for that offence against the god Amor. Afraid to die in a strange land where his family are not present to give him the customary burial rites, he prays that Delia's vows to Isis for his safe return may be fulfilled, and looks back nostalgically to the days when war was unknown, the fabled reign of Saturn (thrust from power by his son Jupiter). He is now prepared to accept death, if such is his destiny, for he looks forward, having done his duty in Jupiter's violent world, to a Lovers' Paradise and contrasts it with a Hell reserved for sinners against Amor. He therefore begs Delia to be faithful to him and ends with a picture of their joyful reunion.

This elegy is one of his very best, and reading it is a spiritual experience akin to hearing a Chopin Nocturne. For a perceptive discussion see Campbell.

1-6   See Introduction x-xi.

1-3   For Messalla's expedition to the East see 1.7.13-22.

cohors = *cohors praetoria*, the bodyguard and staff of a Roman general.

Phaeacia was the land of Homer's Phaeacians where Odysseus was shipwrecked on his journey home to Ithaca. In the *Odyssey* the island is called Scherie; Callimachus *Fragment* 13 identifies it with Corcyra, the modern Corfu.

5-8   Again he pictures his own funeral, as at 1.1.61-8, this time imagining his family mourning.

9   **mitteret:** cf. Catullus 66.29 *sed tum maesta uirum mittens quae uerba locuta es!*

10   **ante** goes with *quam*; for the order cf. Lucretius 3.973 *quam nascimur ante.*

11-12   Sortilege was a common way among the superstitious of coming to a decision. Cicero *De Diuinatione* 2.86 reports that in the temple of Fortune at Praeneste the lots were shuffled and drawn *pueri manu*. The repetition of the pronoun *illa ... illi* here suggests two different types of divination are being referred to. In 11 Delia consults the boy's lots. In 12 the boy reports back (*rettulit*) clear omens from the crossroads (*e triuiis*). Omens in the strict sense were signs taken not from lots but from utterances (cf. Varro *De Lingua Latina* 6.76 *ab ore ... omen ... quod ex ore primum elatum est*). Crossroads were sacred places (cf. 1.1.12) and also full of people talking — a good place to pick up omens.

14   respiceret: 'thinking of', cf. Lucretius 4.1159 *nec sua respiciunt miseri mala maxima saepe.*

15   solator: 'as comforter', perhaps standing for a final clause *ut solarer.* It may be a Tibullan coinage, cf. 2.3.67 *consitor.*

16   tardas ... moras: cf. Virgil *Georgics* 1.32 *tardis mensibus.*

18   A reference to the Jewish Sabbath and also evidence that the seven-day week was known in the Augustan age (cf. *CIL* 4.6779). See K.F. Smith's note.

19-20   Or possibly 'O how often I started the journey and said <to Delia> that a stumble in the gateway had given me an unlucky sign!'

22   This line makes it clear that *inuito amore* is now taken as ablative absolute, 'against the will of Amor'. It is hard to represent that ambiguity in English.

23   The cult of the Egyptian Mother-Goddess Isis, often represented in art as a seated Madonna suckling the child Horus, spread through the Mediterranean world in the Hellenistic age, reaching Rome in the time of Sulla. Tibullus first introduces her into extant love elegy.

24   aera: the famous *sistrum* (Gk. *seistron*, from *seio* 'shake').

26   Usually ten nights of ritual chastity were offered to the goddess (Propertius 2.33.2).

28   The pictures, on tablets fixed to the wall, were thank-offerings made to the Goddess by those who had recovered from illness and other dangers. 'Who does not know that painters are fed by Isis?' asks Juvenal at *Satires* 12.28.

29   uotiuas ... uoces: this periphrasis for *uota* makes the reader think of Delia's voice, the plural suggesting its varied inflexions.

31   resoluta comas: see Woodcock §19, and cf. 'tongue-tied', 'muscle-bound', 'foot-loose' in English.

32   Pharos, a small island at the entrance to the harbour of Alexandria with a famous light-house, was one of the cult centres of Isis. Pharian here is used by metonymy (see Quintilian 8.6.32) for Egyptian.

33   Penates: the Roman gods of the household, cf. Cicero *De Natura Deorum* 2.68 *siue a penu* ('store') *ducto nomine ... siue ab eo quod penitus insident.* For the Lares see Introduction xvi.

35ff   This new section has been prepared for by 18 *Saturni* and 33 *antiquo.* Saturn was the Roman equivalent of the Greek Kronos and his reign was the Golden Age (Hesiod *Erga* 109-20), the *Saturnia regna* of Virgil *Eclogue* 4.6. After his ejection from Olympus by Jupiter he is reported to have 'lain hid' (*latuisse*) in Latium (Virgil *Aeneid* 7.319-27), where Tibullus had an inherited estate. See Cairns 106 on this whole passage for a salutary warning against reading by conditioned reflex.

38   praebueratque: cf. 1.1.40 note.

39-40 Cf. Aratus *Phaenomena* 110-11 (from a description of the Golden Age): 'Beyond them lay the cruel sea/ and ships were not yet bringing livelihood from afar'.

compendia: a mercantile word not found in the other elegists; its opposite is *dispendia*.

repetens by association with *repetundae* might suggest extortion.

43-44 **fixus ... finibus:** cf. 1.1.39-40 **fictilia ... fecit ... facili** and Cairns 100.

regeret: *regula* = 'ruler', *rectus* = 'straight'.

45 **ipsae:** 'of themselves', i.e. without bees. Cf. Virgil *Eclogue* 4.21-2 *ipsae lacte domum referent distenta capellae/ ubera.*

47 Cf. Aratus *Phaenomena* 108-10: 'Not yet at that time did they know of wretched strife/ or blameful dissension or the din of battle/ but simply they lived'.

48 A 'golden' pentameter. This arrangement (adjective, adjective, verb, noun, noun) is very rare before Catullus 64. See Wilkinson 215-18.

49 **Nunc:** 'now' is the Age of Iron (Hesiod *Erga* 176-201).

Tibullus leaves the reader to draw the inference expressed in Lactantius *Epitome* 10: *rex et pater Iuppiter quem tenere in caelo summam credunt potestatem, quid habuit pietatis qui Saturnum patrem regno expulit et armis fugientem persecutus est?* He commits no blasphemy (52).

50 **repente:** with *leti* 'death suddenly', cf 2.5.53 *concubitusque tuos furtim.*

54 **fac:** this use, though with infinitive for dependent subjunctive, comes through to the Christian Collect, e.g. for the XIVth Sunday after Trinity (= XIIIth after Pentecost) *fac nos amare quod praecipis.*

55-56 It is Tibullus who first introduces the Epitaph into extant love elegy. It is remarkable that Delia gets no mention in this epitaph, though Messalla does. Contrast Propertius 2.13.35-6

immiti: 'unripe' (cf. *mitia poma* at *Eclogue* 1.80) and 'ungentle'. As usual it is hard to keep the double meaning in translation.

dum sequiturque: cf. 1.1.40 note.

58 The Elysian 'plain' (*pedion*) first occurs in *Odyssey* 4.563-9. The idea of an Elysium reserved for lovers is perhaps Tibullus's own; so also the substitution of Venus for Mercury as guide of the souls of the departed. More probably Propertius 4.7.59-69 indicates a common source in Greek poetry. The nearest one gets to the description here in surviving Greek poetry is Pindar *Fragments* 129-30, which also has the contrast with Tartarus. For a full discussion see Cairns 44-54.

59-60 The assonances *-que uigent ... -que uagantes ... -ce sonant* etc. are attractive; in fact this whole section, despite the sigmatism, is one of the most musical in Tibullus.

64 **proelia miscet Amor:** cf. Livy 41.19.4 *miscente Perseo inter Dardanos*

Bastarnasque certamina.

65   rapax: in this context it would seem natural to derive the adjective from *OLD rapio* 4 'To carry off (and violate), ravish'.

66 Because myrtle is sacred to Venus. I take *insigni* as equivalent to *insignita* here.

67 The Greek Tartaros, equivalent of the Christian Hell. Cf. 2 Peter 2.4 (of the rebel angels) *Deus ... in Tartarum tradidit cruciandos.*

69 Tisiphone means 'Avenger of Bloodshed' (cf. 49 *caedes*). She is one of the three Erinyes or Furies.

71 The monstrous dog of Hades (Hesiod *Theogony* 311).

73-74 See Pindar *Pythians* 2.21-48.

75 Tityos tried to rape Leto (Homer *Odyssey* 11.576-81) and was slain by Artemis (Pindar *Pythians* 4.90-92).

77 Tantalus raped Ganymede, Jupiter's favourite (Orosius 1.12.4: citing Phanocles' version of the story, a Hellenistic poet). For full discussion see Cairns 54-7, who refers to this as a typical example of Tibullus's unobtrusive *doctrina*; contrast Propertius and Ovid, who usually parade theirs.

78   iam iam poturi: 'on the point of drinking', cf. Ovid *Tristia* 1.2.20 *iam iam tacturos* (sc. *fluctus*) *sidera summa putes.*

79 The Danaids murdered their husbands on the wedding night (Aeschylus *Prometheus Vinctus* 853-64).

81-82   uiolauit ... optauit: for the perfect in a generalizing *qui* clause see Woodcock §230.2 and 2.5.83 note.

82   et: for this postponement cf. 1.2.98; 1.9.16; 2.5.66 and 98.

84-92 For this domestic picture cf. Terence *Heautontimorumenos* 275-307.

87   puella: here collective singular, as *pensis* shows; cf. 1.4.58 *puer.*

89 Not, surely, as a ghost, which would conflict with the final couplet, there being no dawn in the underworld.

91-92 For Tibullus's obsession with hair and feet see Delatte, and O'Neil's concordance under *capillus, coma, crinis* and *pes.*

93   hunc illum: 'Notat *hic* diem paullo ante descriptum, *ille* praestantiam eius' (Dissen). Cf. Virgil *Aeneid* 7.255-6 *hunc illum fatis externa ab sede profectum/ portendi generum.*

94 'The star of Venus which is called *Phosphoros* in Greek, in Latin Lucifer' Cicero *De Natura Deorum* 2.53. The Latin name translates the Greek — 'Light-bringer'.

4

This is the most Callimachean of the elegies of the first book, in both matter and manner. The basic idea may have come from Callimachus *Iambus* 9, where someone (perhaps the poet himself) asks an ithyphallic Hermes why he is in that state: is it because of the boy Philetadas? Anyhow, Tibullus, in reply to a question of his own, puts a miniature Art of homosexual Love (clearly the inspiration of Ovid's later full-scale heterosexual work) into the mouth of Priapus, who in suitably pompous and hieratic tones (after a cursory couplet counselling total avoidance of pederasty) proceeds to reveal his technique. It boils down to this: persevere; have the courage to commit perjury; never hang back; above all, indulge him. The lecturer then turns to the boys, solemnly warning them not to be mercenary but to prize the art of poetry and to love poets, who have power to immortalize them and who are under the protection of Venus. At this point the poem takes an unexpected turn and ends with yet another surprise. It is a brilliant performance, and at the same time poetry of subtle elegance and beauty. For its relationship to Callimachus see Luck 92-9 and Bulloch 75-6, 78-80.

1 For Priapus see 1.1.18 note.

2 For the position of *-que* in this line cf. 1.3.56.

5 **nudus:** not only 'naked' but also 'destitute' (*OLD s.v.* 10, and Cairns 37-8).

producis: cf. Terence *Adelphi* 591 *hunc producam diem* 'pass', but in this context one can hardly help thinking of the god's *fascinum*.

6 Cf. 1.1.27.

7 Priapus was the son of Bacchus and Aphrodite (Pausanias 9.31.2).

9 **fuge ... credere:** this high-style construction may be taken from Lucretius 1.1052 *fuge credere, Memmi*, where it is first found.

10 **causam ... habent:** cf. Cicero *De Natura Deorum* 1.35 *omnem uim diuinam in natura sitam esse censet, quae causas gignendi, augendi, minuendi habeat.*

iusti ... amoris: to get the full effect of this one must remember that homosexuality was an offence under the Lex Scantinia; see Williams 551.

11 **angustis:** cf. our 'on a tight rein'.

12 **hic placidam** echoes *hic placet*. 'Equo rapido, habenis compescendo, opponitur placida aqua' (Dissen). 'The epithet may have suggested itself because the grace of the swimmer in calm (and so, clear) water is visible to the eye; cf. *niueo pectore*' (Camps).

The alliteration is not mere ornament here.

17-18 **docuit ... peredit:** the so-called 'gnomic' past tense can occur in English too, e.g. 'Faint heart never won fair lady'.

21 The first surviving Latin example of the famous commonplace that lovers' perjuries go unpunished.

23-24   Zeus swore falsely to Hera his wife that he had not had intercourse with Io and 'from then on he made the oath without penalty for men, concerning the covert deeds of Cypris' (Hesiod *Fragment* 187). Catullus's friend Calvus had written an epyllion, or short narrative poem in epic hexameters, about Io and there may be a reference to that here.

25-26   Like 23-4 clearly an allusion to some literary context. Dictynna, 'Lady of the Net', was a cult title of Artemis-Diana as Goddess of the chase. The occurrence of this rare name in a line by Helvius Cinna — *saecula permaneat nostri Dictynna Catonis* (*Fragment* 14) — suggests that the reference may be to Valerius Cato's epyllion of that name.

crines perque: the order is metrically convenient but *per* could be postponed in prose, e.g. Cicero *De Lege Agraria* 2.81 *agrum ... quem per iter qui faciunt.* I suspect that Tibullus wrote *crinis*, to avoid homoeoteleuton of consecutive words; our MSS are not reliable in such matters.

27   **eris:** for the rare lengthening of a short final syllable at the caesura cf. 2.2.5 and Platnauer 59.

transiet: this very rare alternative to *transibit* is found at Seneca *Natural Questions* 3.10.4 and in Apuleius.

29   **purpureos:** cf. Virgil *Eclogue* 9.40 *hic uer purpureum.*

32   The Olympic Games were held at Elis in the Peloponnese; they included horse- as well as chariot-racing.

34   Or possibly 'that the days of folly had passed him by', i.e. that he had not sown his wild oats.

35   **nouus:** cf. Virgil's snake at *Georgics* 3.437 *positis nouus exuuiis nitidusque iuuenta.*

37-38   Phoebus Apollo is called 'unshorn-haired' (*akersikomes*) at *Iliad* 20.39, and Dionysus's 'beautiful dark locks are shaken around' at *Homeric Hymn* 7.4-5.

40   Presupposes Virgil *Eclogue* 10.69 *omnia uincit Amor.*

44   **amiciat** 'dresses', like the early correction *admittat*, gives poor sense and in any case does not scan, the first syllable being short. I translate Calonghi's *admoneat*. Camps suggests *dicat*, comparing Ovid *Tristia* 1.9.50, and that is closer to the *ductus litterarum*. We must suppose that the last syllable of the verb is lengthened (cf. 27 note) or we must read Heinsius's *nimbifer*.

46   The job of a slave, as is also carrying hunting-nets (50).

47-48   For the perfect infinitives here and at 56 below see 1.1.29-30 note.

atteruisse, first found here, is probably an archaic form for *attriuisse.*

56   Cf. Virgil *Aeneid* 2.723-4 *dextrae se paruus Iulus/ implicuit sequiturque patrem non passibus aequis.*

57   **male ... tractant:** cf. Cicero *Att.* 13.29.2 *male ... audio ipsum esse tractatum* (admittedly of a person and not *artes*, though that could stand for 'artists'). Possibly, 'Alas, this generation wrongfully exercises wretched arts', comparing Cicero *Academica* 2.22 *qui artem tractabit* (but there is no adverb).

59-60   Euripides *Hippolytus* 407-9 provides the earliest surviving example of the curse on the inventor. A famous example occurs in Callimachus *Coma Berenices* 48-50; see Catullus's translation.

61-62   *Pierides* was a title of the Muses from Hesiod *Scutum* 206 onwards; they were born in Pieria, a district of S.W. Macedonia (Hesiod *Theogony* 54). Tibullus here aligns himself, by implication, with the *docti poetae*, a title applied to Catullus and his poet friends. His *doctrina* is evident from the various allusions in this poem and from the technical point of this particular couplet. Clearly Callimachus was an important influence; for his poetic aims see Pfeiffer 137-8.

See Introduction ix.

63   Nisus, king of Megara, had a purple lock of hair on which the safety of the city depended. His daughter Scylla, in love with the enemy commander Minos of Crete, cut off her father's lock and betrayed the city to him.

carmine: the meaning 'spell' or 'incantation' is secondary here but perceptible. In Latin, poetry (*carmen*) is both magic and song; cf. Virgil *Eclogue* 8.69-70.

Nisi ... ni sint: Camps compares 2.5.27 *illic ... ilicis*; one might add *Venerem ... uendere* at 59 above.

64   Tantalus dismembered his son Pelops and served him up at a banquet to the Gods. They were not deceived and reassembled Pelops, apart from one shoulder which Ceres had inadvertently eaten and for which they provided an ivory replacement.

65   **referent:** presumably the literal meaning 'bring back' is also working here.

66   It was thought that the sky revolved with the stars 'fixed' in it; see Cicero *Somnium Scipionis* 17 (= *De Republica* 6.17).

68-70   Ops, wife of Saturn, is the Roman equivalent of Rhea, wife of Kronos. The Greeks identified Rhea with Cybele, the Phrygian Mother-Goddess of Mount Ida. Cybele's priests the Galli were eunuchs and made a living as wandering beggars. This passage has connexions with Callimachus *Fragment* 193.34-6: 'It would be more profitable for me (sc. than being a poet) to toss my hair for Cybele to the sound of the Phrygian flute'.

69   **expleat:** 'complete', cf. Virgil *Aeneid* 12.763 *quinque orbes explent cursu* (I am not suggesting that we should read *orbes* here, though *urbes* perhaps brings in the ghost of that word). Perhaps *OLD expleo* 3 'satisfy the demands or appetites of' is also present.

71   **blanditiis:** cf. 1.1.72 and 9.77. Dissen rightly takes it as referring here to love elegy, comparing Ovid *Amores* 2.1.21 *blanditias elegosque leuis, mea tela, resumpsi*. The translation, of course, goes too far; the Vulgate Latin for the Authorized Version's 'loving-kindness' is *misericordia*.

73   Titio: Cairns 174 makes the attractive suggestion that this was the Marcus Titius (like Messalla an ex-Antonian) who succeeded Messalla in the consulship in 31 BC and who may have been recently married at the time this elegy was written. Perhaps he *asked* Tibullus for a poem.

edidit ore: cf. Virgil *Aeneid* 7.194 *atque haec ingressis placido prior edidit ore*. Perhaps this epic phrase goes back to Ennius.

75-76   celebrate: also 'frequent my company', cf. 1.6.17 note.

magistrum in the same context as *puer* would normally mean *ludi magister* 'schoolmaster'. The idea that you become a *maestro* by listening to a lecture is a good one.

male habet: cf. Lucretius 3.825-6 *aduenit id quod eam* (sc. the soul) *de rebus saepe futuris/ macerat inque metu male habet ...*

77   gloria: perhaps 'boast' is better, considering 81-2.

78   consultent: the word would remind the Roman reader of a jurisconsult.

79-80   Cf. Callimachus *Fragment* 41: 'That old man ages more lightly whom boys love and lead him by the hand to the door of his house like their own parent'.

ferentem: cf. Virgil *Eclogue* 8.9-10 *en erit ut liceat totum mihi ferre per orbem/ sola Sophocleo tua carmina digna coturno?* (= *OLD fero* 26, and possibly, in our context, 20 'endure' as well).

deducat: for the mood see Woodcock §234. Popular teachers of rhetoric or philosophy would be similarly escorted.

81-82   The translation is no doubt too free here!

Marathus: the name is found in the neighbourhood of Capua (*CIL* 10.4044).

artes: those of line 57.

5

Does this poem represent the poet's thoughts unfolding in solitude (see 39-48) or is he all the time at Delia's closed door (see 67-8)? In either case we have a second Tibullan variant on the paraklausithyron (see the introductory note to 1.2). He appeals to Delia's need to dominate (1-8), to her sense of justice (9-18), to her wish to *be* someone (19-34), to her vanity (35-46), to her religious fears and better nature (47-60), to her need to be looked after and protected (61-6). At this point it appears that all these appeals fail. To my mind this is pure guile. The rich lover is to be made uneasy and suspicious, but not of Tibullus; hence 67-8 and the mysterious *quidam* (71). In fact the description of the behaviour of this anonymous is a signal to Delia; this is how the poet will behave on his next visit, so that her servant can recognise him and let him in. This gives double point to *nescioquidfurtiuus Amor parat*; it applies to *quidam* and it applies to the poet's implied arrangement. Cairns is illuminating on the distortions of the temporal sequence in the poem (176-81), Bright on its imagery (160-66) and Lyne on its 'psychological' unity (176-9).

3 turben: the fourth-century grammarian Charisius cites this line for the rare form, which all our MSS of Tibullus have replaced with the familiar *turbo*.

4 ab arte: cf. 1.9.66 and *OLD ab* 15.

puer: one can hardly help thinking of Cupid here. Then, until lines 7-8, it is not clear whether the imperatives in 5-6 may not be addressed to him. This memorable simile appears to be original with Tibullus.

5 ure ... et torque: 'petitum a seruorum tormentis; cf. 1.9.21' (Heyne); and see Lyne's interesting remarks on *seruitium amoris*, 80-1. At the same time the two verbs suit the simile; e.g. Horace *Epistles* 1.16.47 *loris non ureris* and Persius 3.51 *buxum torquere flagello*.

7 *per* governs *foedera*, not *te*; 'the separation is characteristic of this kind of excited appeal and evidently reflects the usage of everyday speech, cf. Terence *Andria* 289 *per ego te hanc nunc dextram oro*' (Camps).

8 compositum caput means (i) 'head placed beside mine', cf. Propertius 2.14.22; (ii) 'well-groomed head', cf. Virgil *Georgics* 4.417; and perhaps (iii) 'heading drawn up', cf. *OLD caput* 17-18.

9 Ille ego: 'this phrase comes in two constructions, either (i) with the verb *sum* present or understood, as in 1.6.31, "I am the one who ..."; or (ii) as here with *ille* reinforcing *ego*, "I, the one you know about ...". Here the effect is: "I, as you well remember ..."' (Camps).

11 The translation paraphrases. 'Pure sulphur' here suggests 'purifying sulphur'; see Cairns 109, who observes that Tibullus likes using 'adjectives more frequently intransitive in an active sense'.

ipseque: see Platnauer 93.

14 deueneranda: for the more usual *deprecanda*. This compound verb is not found elsewhere.

15 filo: cf. Varro *De Lingua Latina* 5.84 *flamines, quod in Latio capite uelato erant semper ac caput cinctum habebant filo, filamines dicti.*

16 Trivia 'Three-ways' (cf. 56) is the title of Hecate as Goddess of the crossroads and translated from the Greek *Trioditis*. For the identification with Artemis-Diana see Catullus 34.15.

20 I.e. *sed <fingebam> renuente deo*. 'A god', 'the god' or 'God'?? Latin is not the language for philosophy, though good for poetry.

23 lintribus: probably portable treading-vats carved out of tree-trunks; see K.D. White 164-5.

25-26   The change of subject with the second *consuescet* is unexpected. For an analogous example see 1.2.63-4.

28   **segete spicas:** for the lengthening of *e* before the double consonant, see Platnauer 63.

30   **at iuuet** comes closest to A's *adiuuet* (*at* was sometimes written as *ad*). For *at* introducing a contrast, cf. 1.3.33. Alternatively read *ac* (*atque*) 'and I should even enjoy' — see *OLD atque* 1 and 2.

31   **meus** denotes close friendship, cf. Horace *Odes* 4.11.19 *Maecenas meus*.

poma: strictly speaking, not 'apples' (*mala*) but 'fruits'.

32   **detrahat:** for this jussive subjunctive see Woodcock § 148.

33   **uirum, hunc:** either Tibullus is treating *h* as a consonant here, or the pause at the caesura permits hiatus; cf. Virgil *Eclogue* 2.53 *addam cerea pruna (honos erit huic quoque pomo)*, and see Platnauer 57.

35   **Eurusque Notusque:** from Homer *Iliad* 2.145, *Euros te Notos te* and later used by Virgil *Aeneid* 1.85.

36   **uota:** predicative 'as vows' after *iactat*. Camps notes that *uotum* 'sometimes has the special sense of a wish not apt to be fulfilled' and compares Quintilian *Institutio Oratoria* 12.5.6 *sed hoc uotum est et rara felicitas* 'an ideal'; R.G. Austin's note there gives other examples.

38   This idea too appears to be original with Tibullus.

39-40   Impotence provides the theme of Ovid *Amores* 3.7.

43   **facit hoc:** unusually placed before the verb it stands for (*deuouet*), which can in fact be understood from *deuotum* in 41. Note the word-play with *facie*.

45-46   Haemonia was the old name for Thessaly, Haemon being the father of Thessalus. Peleus, king of Phthia, in Thessaly, by the will of Zeus married the sea-goddess Thetis, who was fated to produce a son greater than his father: that son was Achilles. Catullus wrote an epyllion about the wedding (Poem 64). This is one of Tibullus's very few mythological comparisons and stands out for that reason.

caerula: Thetis had been so described by Horace at *Epode* 13.16. For the meaning 'blue-eyed' see *Epode* 16.7 *nec fera caerulea domuit Germania pube* (sc. *Romam*).

nocuere: cf. 1.8.23.

47   **quod:** 'as to the fact that' — see *OLD s.v.* 6 — introducing a new idea and looking forward to 48: 'as for her having a rich lover, a crafty procuress has caused my destruction.'

48   Evidently the rich lover employed the *lena*, a new arrival on the scene, as a go-between to negotiate terms on his behalf with Delia. Putnam notes 'the punning connection between *uenit* and *exitium*' in its literal meaning, roughly 'has entered for my exit'; *OLD in* 20 and 21.

49-50   Cf. Callimachus *Fragment* 530 'Flesh like to gall may you eat'. The *deuotiones*, or flyting, in 49-56 can be thought of as arising from *deuotum* in 41; they represent the poet's answer to the bawd, who is also a witch (59). Tibullus here introduces to elegy in miniature what already existed as a full-blown Hellenistic literary form, e.g. the *Arai* (Curses) of Moiro and of Euphorion.

52   Pliny in *Natural History* 11.232 is not sure what bird this is, but Ovid knows it is an owl that screeches horribly and sucks the blood of children (*Fasti* 6.131-42).

56   post = *pone* 'behind', cf. 1.10.24.

57-58   We are left to imagine who the god is and what the sign he gives. — 'Dicit autem hoc manifesto ad terrendam Deliam' (Dissen).

This is one of the rare couplets subdivided into four separate units, and in the hexameter the units lengthen by one syllable.

59   sagae praecepta: 'The typical witch is old, drunken, and a procuress, who in return for pay puts her magic at the disposal of a person wishing to establish or to break an erotic connection' (Liebeschuetz 129) and cf. 1.2.43ff. Ovid (*Amores* 1.8) and Propertius (4.5) later compose dramatic elegies on the theme of *sagae praecepta*; cf. Plautus *Mostellaria* 157ff.

60   donis uincitur omnis amor reverses *omnia uincit amor*, cf. 1.4.40.

61ff   K.F. Smith compares Ovid *Ars* 2.165 *pauperibus uates ego sum quia pauper amaui* etc. See also Cairns 20-21.

62   in is surprising; one would expect *ad* or the dative, cf. Ovid *Amores* 3.11.17 *quando ego non fixus lateri patienter adhaesi*. At Ovid *Ibis* 543 *fixus et in duris ... saxis* the Loeb translator gives 'chained on ...'. Perhaps there is a *double entendre*, see *OLD latus* 2.

For *adibit* Camps compares Catullus 8.16 *quis nunc te adibit?*

64   For the probable secondary meaning cf. Ovid *Amores* 1.4.57-8 *agmine me inuenies aut inuenieris in illo:/ quicquid ibi poteris tangere, tange, mei.*

65   To their dinner parties as 66 shows, but again there could be *double entendre*, see *OLD deduco* 10 (b) and *amicus² 2.

66   Sandals were not worn during a Roman dinner, cf. Horace *Satires* 2.8.77. *Seruitium amoris* again.

67-68   It now turns out that this elegy may be, like the second, a paraklausithyron.

canimus: we should remember that elegies were in fact sometimes sung; see Gellius 19.9.4.

plena ... manu: 1.9.52 is more explicit.

69-70   He now addresses the rich lover of line 47 (= 18 *felix ille*); the *coniunx* of Elegy 2 has faded from the picture, though his continued existence is implied by 7 *furtiui* and 75 *furtiuus*.

71   The mysterious *quidam* is probably the poet himself, as Copley suggests (165 n.33), implying a variant of Occam's razor: 'Personae non sunt multiplicandae praeter necessitatem'.

74   Perhaps it would be better to render *solus* literally. Strictly speaking, the translator's job is to translate and not paraphrase or explain.

75   utere: the colloquialism (cf. Persius 6.22 *utar ego, utar*) echoes 18 *utitur*. Elder 101 is good on such echoes in this poem.

76   For the ending with a disconnected proverb cf. 1.2.98.

6

We are to suppose that the 'husband' is back (cf. 1.2.67 note), that the poet is Delia's lover again and has been for some time (59-62), and that Delia is double-crossing them both. In this rather piquant situation the poet's strategy is fourfold: to appeal man to man to the husband (15-38); to frighten off possible rivals (39-54); to win the total support of Delia's mother (57-72); and to scare Delia herself (55-6, 77-84). This poem is the nearest of the Delia elegies to Comedy, but the ending of Elegy 5 has prepared us for that. Julia Gaisser's study is a great help in getting one's bearings, but her reading of the poem is disturbingly cynical for Tibullus.

3   Cf. Cicero *De Prouinciis Consularibus* 24 *quod mihi odium fuit cum P. Clodio ...?* and Terence *Hecyra* 643 *quid mulieris uxorem habes!* 'What a woman you have to wife!'. It would work equally well as a question 'What sort of ...?'

5   casses carries on the metaphor of *insidias*, cf. 1.4.49.

6   nescioquem is unlikely to refer to the *quidam* of 1.5.71, for that pronoun is not indefinite like *aliquis* but implies 'whom I could name'. Against this it could be argued that *nescioquis* sometimes refers slightingly to a known person.

7   tam multa: feminine, 'so persistently'; see *OLD multus* 6. Or possibly neuter, cf. Propertius 3.12.4 *ne faceres Galla multa rogante tua*, like the Greek *pollá*, *LSJ s.v.* III (a).

10   premor: 'hard pressed'. There may be erotic overtones, see *OLD s.v.* 2.

13   quis for *quibus* as at 1.2.55 at the same point in the line. It looks like an archaism and may lend a touch of pomposity.

16   me quoque seruato: i.e. 'I'd welcome it if by putting a stricter guard on her you put one on me'. For the so-called future imperative, regular in the text of laws and formal instructions, see Woodcock §126 note (i).

nihil: Ovid quoting from memory at *Tristia* 2.458 gives *minus*.

17   celebret: contrast Cicero *Pro Milone* 98 *omni sermone celebramur* 'celebrated in every conversation'. For the meaning 'accompany' cf. Cicero *Ad Atticum* 4.1.5 *frequentia et plausus me usque ad Capitolium celebrauit*.

21   A's *quam* possibly points to original *quom*; cf. 1.3.14 where *cum* may have come via QVM from original QVIN.

seu here is for *uel si*, cf. Propertius 3.21.8 and 33.

22   A Roman fertility Goddess whose cult was confined to women. Her annual celebration was held in December in the house of a magistrate with *imperium* and presided over by his wife assisted by the Vestal Virgins. In 60 BC there had been a famous scandal when Clodius dressed up as a woman and took part in her rites.

23-24   Literally 'I alone would attend her to the altar'. The altar would be outside the temple (see *OCD* 'Temple'), and Tibullus would make sure that no other man followed her there. Thus he would not have to fear for his eyes, because he would neither have committed sacrilege by entering the temple (for which the Goddess might strike him blind), nor have seen Delia in the company of another man.

25   **uelut ... probarem:** literally 'as if I were to examine *or* were examining her jewels and signet'.

29-30   Another 'Ovidian' couplet, both in form and content, cf. 1.5.57-8 and Introduction ix-x.

prudens: 'intentionally', also hints at the belief that *amor* is *insania*, cf Cicero *Tusculans* 4.72 *sin autem est aliquis amor, ut est certe, qui nihil absit aut non multum ab insania*.

contra ... deos: for this separation see Platnauer 99.

32   **instabat:** an unexpected word, considering its literal meaning. Ovid, at *Tristia* 2.459, remembers it as *latrabat*.

33-34   I have gone back to A's punctuation of this couplet, except for his question-mark after *frustra clauis inest foribus*.

For the lengthening of the *e* of *seruare* see Platnauer 63

35   **suspirat:** governing an accusative first here. On the analogy of *flere*?

36   André notes that Phronesium the call-girl in Plautus *Truculentus* uses this excuse verbatim at 632: *nam mihi de uento misere condoluit caput*.

37-38   The girl's *custos* would be a slave and liable to these punishments if he failed in his duty.

39-42   The direct address to potential lovers illustrates the role Tibullus would adopt as Delia's *custos*.

39-40   Dandies, like the young men round Catiline as Cicero describes them: *pexo capillo ... uelis amictos, non togis* (*Catilines* 2.22).

colit: for the third person after *absitis* cf. 1.2.35. It may be colloquial, cf. *CIL* 4 (Pompeii), 5386 *Hospes salue. Sal<u>us sis quisquis est. Val[l]e*.

42   The reading of the majority of MSS is wrongly reported in the Oxford Text; it is *stet procul aut* (*atque* G) *alia stet procul ante uia*. This has been variously emended; *transeat ille* is pure makeshift.

45-46   The Roman Goddess of War, whose temple was in the Campus Martius. Her worshippers were notorious for their religious frenzy, e.g. Juvenal 4.123-4 *fanaticus oestro/ percussus, Bellona, tuo.* In Sulla's time she was identified with the Cappadocian Ma, whose temples 'like those of other Asiatic mother goddesses, were served by sacred prostitutes. It is this fact which may make the priestess of Bellona a suitable erotic teacher and explain her goddess's interest in Tibullus' love-affairs' (Cairns 41).

For *nec ... non* cf. Virgil *Georgics* 3.252-3 *neque uerbera saeua, non scopuli ...*

51-52   Cf. *CIL* 4.1645 *Si quis forte meam cupiet uiolare puellam,/ illum in desertis montibus urat Amor.* Among the Pompeian graffiti there are quotations from Ennius, Lucretius, Virgil, Propertius and Ovid; this might be one from Gallus.

For a discussion of the text of 52 see Lee 54-5.

53   I.e. Delia will fleece any such 'lover'.

attigerit: the sudden change to third person after *parcite* is analogous to that at 39.

55-56   nescioquas ... poenas: menacingly indefinite.

admittas: there must be a *double entendre*: (1) commit (a crime) — *OLD* 13; and (2) receive (a lover) — *OLD* 2b. The reference is to Delia's receiving a rich lover (cf. 51-4).

illa: Bellona.

58   Gaisser wants to take *aurea* ironically, comparing Antipater of Thessalonica's epigram on 'golden Aphrodite' (*AP* 5.30 and cf. 31) and Ovid *Ars* 2.277-8 *aurea sunt uere nunc saecula: plurimus auro/ uenit honos, auro conciliatur amor*, but these places are not parallel to this one, for in both the pun is explained.

59-62   See Introduction xi-xii.

tenebris: plain ablative, perhaps on the analogy of *nocte.*

63-64   contribuisse is treated as though it were *communicauisse.*

66   sanguis: the last syllable *was* originally long, contrast 54.

67-68   sit modo casta doce: i.e. she is not to be promiscuous; only one lover, the poet, is allowed.

quamuis ... pedes: see Introduction xiv-xv. Alternatively, with Gordon Williams 536: 'although her relationship *to me* is not one of marriage'.

69-72   'That there should be terms for T. also is only fair, but anger and jealousy on Delia's part would be welcomed by T. as an indication of her love' (Murgatroyd).

72   pronas proripiarque uias: 'for the postponed *-que* cf. 54 above and 1.3.38, etc. The text is uncertain here; if it is right, the meaning must be "and (I am ready to) be dragged along with my face on the ground". To arrive at this we must suppose (a) that *uias* is an idiomatic plural, as in Prop. 1.2.12 *currere lympha uias*; (b) that it is an internal accusative of the type *ire uiam*, also as in the Propertian passage cited; (c) that *pronas* with *uias* is a "transferred" epithet (instead of *pronus proripiar*)' (Camps).

The original could perhaps have been *pronus proripiarque foras* 'and dragged outside face down'; *pronus* could have become *pronas* by attraction to *foras* and *foras* altered to *uias* to make some sense.

73-74 **iste ... furor:** could that refer to Delia's unfaithfulness?

75 Cairns 94 notes the etymological connexion of *metus* with *mens* according to Varro *De Lingua Latina* 6.45 *metus a mente quodam modo mota*.

77ff Some readers are worried by the slight contradiction of this warning to Delia with 75-6 and suppose a lacuna between 76 and 77.

80 **tracta** is the noun in this line, cf. Varro *Menippeae* 325 *ut suis manibus lanea tracta ministrasset infectori*.

81 **senem:** very rarely of a woman, but cf. the last line of Papinius' epigram, quoted by Varro *De Lingua Latina* 7.28, *nam uere pusus* (a lad) *tu, tua amica senex.*

85 Literally: 'Let these reproaches befall others'; cf. 2.2.17 *uota cadunt.*

86 Lyne 294 n.4 notes a contradiction with 1.1.71-2.

7

A poem written for Messalla's next birthday after his Triumph in 27 BC, celebrating his successful operations in Gaul, his mission to the Near East and his repair of the Via Latina, and including a *kletic* (i.e. invocatory) hymn to Osiris. All are agreed on the influence here of Callimachus and his *Epinikia* (see Bulloch 80) and on the originality of this Tibullan mixture of genres, but there is some disagreement about the precise nature of the mix (see Luck 85, Cairns 171-2, Murgatroyd 209-10) and general uncertainty (*pace* Julia Gaisser) about the relevance of Osiris to Messalla. Few would deny, however, that we have here, for the first time in extant Latin literature, an example of occasional poetry in elegiacs, most elegantly and attractively done.

1 **Hunc ... diem:** Messalla's birthday, cf. 63.

The Parcae were the Roman equivalent of the Greek Moirai, or Fates, who according to Plato *Republic* 617 and Catullus 64.306ff, sang as they spun the thread of destiny.

2 **dissoluenda:** presumably pronounced as usual but *felt*, in this position, to be *dissŏlŭenda*, cf. 40 and Platnauer 70-1.

3 These tribes occupied the area from Pyrenees to Garonne (Caesar *De Bello Gallico* 1.1); for the names of most of them see Caesar *ibid.* 3.27.

'The day does the deeds of him that was born upon it' (K.F. Smith). So we need not suppose that either Messalla's victory or his Triumph fell on his birthday (though it may have done).

4   The MSS give *Atax*, the modern Aude, which was well inside the Roman province of Gallia Narbonensis. Had the Aquitani invaded the province and crossed the Atax it is hard to believe that its recovery by Messalla would have been referred to like this. Therefore read *Atur* with Scaliger; for the form see Vibius Sequester (Riese) p.146. The Atur, modern Adour, was in the territory of the Tarbelli in S.W. Aquitania.

5   **euenere:** cf. 1.5.57 *eueniet*, though one might have expected singular here and plural there.

pubes: an archaic and poetical collective noun for adult males of military age, 'manhood'.

6   **euinctos bracchia:** see 1.3.31 note. For full details of the Triumph see Badian's article in *OCD*.

9-12   Messalla's operations must have taken place in an area bounded by Pyrenees in S., Loire in N., Bay of Biscay in W., Saône and upper Rhone in E. The Santoni (hence modern Saintonge and Saintes) were a Celtic tribe between Charente and Garonne (Caesar *De Bello Gallico* 1.10); the Carnutes (hence Chartres) a Celtic tribe between Seine and Loire. Messalla's Triumph *ex Gallia* is firmly dated by the *Fasti Triumphales* to 25 September, 27 BC (see *CIL* 1², p.180).

13-22   Messalla was in Asia Minor at some time after Actium in 31 and before his Triumph; see introduction to 1.3 and Cairns 44.

13   A Cilician river rising in Mt Taurus and flowing through Tarsus.

16   **alat:** there is an interesting account of the fertility of Mt Taurus at Strabo 12.570.

18   The dove was sacred to the Syrian Goddess Astarte (Lucian *De Syria Dea* 54).

Syro is noun, *Palaestino* adjective — 'for the Syrian of Palestine'. Cf. Mark 7.26 *mulier Gentilis, Syrophoenissa genere* 'a Syrian of Phoenicia'.

19-20   K.F. Smith compares the small island of Tyre with its tall buildings (Strabo 16.757) to Manhattan and its skyscrapers. Pliny *Natural History* 7.208 records the Phoenician invention of *onerariae naues* (they had sails but no oars) and navigation by the stars; he adds the alphabet at 5.67.

21   **Sirius:** see 1.1.27 and note.

23-24   A witty allusion to the then unknown source of the Nile and cause of its floods.

caput: see *OLD s.v.* 1 and 11 (a).

27   Osiris was brother and husband of Isis and identified by the Egyptians with the Nile (Plutarch *Isis* 33).

atque: rarely unelided in elegy. Lee 55 defends *utque*; for the confusion see 2.3.55, where Q (the Quirinianus at Brescia) reads *atque* for *utque* (admittedly after *fluat*).

28   Apis, the sacred bull of Memphis. The line adapts Callimachus *Fragment* 383.16 (also a pentameter) 'knowing to keen the lucent bull'.

29-30   Camps notes an echo of *sollerti* in *sollicitauit*. Isidore *Etymologiae* 10.243 gives an etymological connexion: *sollers quod sit sollicitus in arte et utilis*.

The translation exaggerates a possible pun, which would have to be suggested by *teneram;* see *OLD sollicito* 1 (b) and 5 (c) or 4 (a).

33   **adiungere:** cf. Virgil *Georgics* 1.2 *ulmisque adiungere uitis*.

35-36   Murgatroyd remarks on the heavily spondaic rhythm. Combined with the rarish (see Platnauer 16) trisyllabic ending to the pentameter it must be intended as onomatopoeia.

In the context of the invention of cultivation *incultis pedibus* must be pointed.

38   The translation, while bringing out the contrast in *certos nescia*, doesn't make it clear that the line refers to the invention of metre — 'fixed measures'.

39   The Greeks identified Osiris with Dionysus-Bacchus (Herodotus 2.42).

40   To take A's *tristitiae* as genitive of separation in a context where it is most naturally taken as dative after *dedit* is a clumsy solution. The real question is whether *dare* has to have an indirect object in this construction with the gerundive. If it has, then we must read *laetitiae*. If it has not, then Pucci's *tristitia* (ablative of separation as with *soluere*) is best.

41-54   These lines are notably musical, despite sigmatism.

44-45   *Cantus* is plural (as metre and euphony demand), *aptus* predicate, going with *non tibi* but agreeing with *leuis amor*.

46   **fusa sed:** for postponement of *sed* see Platnauer 95.

48   For the Dionysiac mysteries in Italy see Nilsson's article 'Bacchanalia' in *OCD*.

Despite the translation *sacris* is the noun, and dative after *conscia*: cf. Lucretius 3.1018 *mens sibi conscia factis/ praemetuens* (*sibi* goes with *praemetuens*).

49   The Genius was each man's guardian spirit: 'The companion who tempers the star of our birth, the God of human nature, subject to death in each individual life' (Horace *Epistles* 2.2.187-9). According to Censorinus *De Die Natali* 3, he was identified with the Lar by many.

50   **tempora funde mero:** a recherché construction, as though *funde* were *perfunde*.

51-52 A couplet specially interesting for its sound-patterns.

51 Cf. Callimachus *Fragment* 7.12 'And unguent from your ringlets ever flows'.

53 **sic uenias, hodierne:** 'Genium siue Natalem alloquitur, eo modo quo solebant eos uocare quorum dies natalis erat. Plautus *Pseudolus* 243-244 *hodie nate, heus, hodie nate, tibi ego dico, heus, hodie nate,/ redi et respice ad nos*' (Passeratius in 1608). *Sic* refers to the conditions for his coming (i.e. 50-52).

54 Callimachus referred to Attica as Mopsopia (*Fragment* 709).

55-56 The poet now turns from Messalla's Genius to address Messalla. His elder son Messallinus (see introduction to 2.5) was certainly alive at this time.

facta parentis: Putnam compares Virgil *Eclogue* 4.26.

veneranda: Heyne compares Virgil *Aeneid* 9.276 (Ascanius to Euryalus) *uenerande puer*.

57-58 Between Tusculum and the Alban Mount ran the Via Latina. The *Feriae Latinae* were held annually on the Alban Mount and would draw crowds.

Combination of lines 57-60 with Suetonius *Augustus* 30 allows us to infer that Messalla paid for the repair of this stretch of the Via Latina with money brought in by the sale of booty from his Gallic campaign.

60 **apta ... arte:** Cairns 109 notes the word-play in this context; *OLD aptus* 6 and 1.

61 *canit* is impossible with *cum uenerit* and has clearly come in from 27; *canet* is an obvious correction of *canit*, and a bit odd when the road is already finished; *canat* is parallel to 57 *nec taceat* and unexceptionable.

Baehrens's *a* mends the metre.

62 **rettuleritque:** cf. 1.1.40 note.

63 Natalis, the Birthday Spirit, was probably identical with the Genius; cf. 3.12.1 *Natalis Iuno* — a woman's Genius was called her Juno.

celebrande: probably predicative with *ueni*, cf. Virgil *Aeneid* 2.282-3 *quibus Hector ab oris/ expectate uenis?*

8

Cairns 147-51 is most illuminating on 'the technique of delayed information' in this poem — the way in which the dramatic situation implied by it is gradually revealed. It would be a pity to spoil the effect of this for the reader by summarizing the poem's plot. Suffice it to say (*pace* Cairns 137 who takes the poem as a typical example of a Tibullan 'personal monologue' like Theocritus *Idyll* 11) that it can be taken even more effectively as a dramatic monologue in which the poet and two other characters are imagined to be present together (so K.F. Smith and Murgatroyd). The fact that Tibullus often uses 'personal' monologue does not exclude his occasional use of 'dramatic' monologue. Similarly, of the Catullan elegiac epigrams 101 is clearly dramatic, whereas 83 is not. We unconsciously accept the convention that 83 is a written epigram, not 'dramatically' addressed to Lesbia's husband, although it does address him; in 101, on the other hand, the poet is evidently speaking at his brother's tomb in the Troad — indeed, of all his elegiac epigrams this is the only demonstrably 'dramatic' one.

1   **Non ego celari possum quid ..** looks like a recherché construction but is not; see *OLD celare* 5.

2   **ferant:** the metaphor in English 'convey' is the same.

3-4   The reference is to three kinds of divination: sortilege, haruspicy (examination of entrails), augury (observation of the flight and call of birds). *fibra* is a division or lobe of the liver.

5-6   'Suspenditur a Venere amator, quo modo serui et noxii solebant; sed fune in nodum magicum constricto, ne posset renodari aut solui. deinde crebris uerberibus caeditur, ut addiscat patientiam: hoc est, ut fastum ferat immitis dominae' (Broukhusius in 1708). Cairns 138 sees another way of taking the metaphor: 'Venus, like the *magistra* of a mystery-cult group, has initiated a bound Tibullus with the usual flogging, and has taught him this arcane knowledge'. For the form of the sentence cf. Callimachus *Fragment* 67.1 'Eros himself taught Akontios ...'.

9-14   Cf. Petronius *Satyricon* 126.2 (Chrysis, Circe's maid, to Polyaenus) *quo enim spectant flexae pectine comae, quo facies medicamine attrita et oculorum quoque mollis petulantia, quo incessus arte compositus et ne uestigia quidem pedum extra mensuram aberrantia, nisi quod formam prostituis ut uendas?*

10   Cf. Callimachus *Hymn* 5.22 'Many-times-twice she altered the same hair'.

11   Orchella *alias* orchil *alias* archil is apparently a lichen producing a red dye.

14   **ansa:** 'The loop or eye on the side leather of the Greek shoe called *crepida*, through which the thong or lace was passed and crossed over the instep to bind it on the foot' (Rich).

   arta: Camps compares 1.4.11 *angustis*.

15   **quamuis:** presumably 'however' with *inculto*, and *uenerit* perfect subjunctive; see Woodcock §249(c).

17   **pallentibus:** because they turn one pale, cf. Horace *Epistles* 1.19.18 *exsangue cuminum* 'bloodless cummin'.

19   Cf. Virgil *Eclogue* 8.99. The Twelve Tables specified a punishment for the person *qui fruges excantassit* (Pliny *Natural History* 28.17).

21-22 Cf. Virgil *Eclogue* 8.70. Bronze instruments were clashed and banged to frighten the demons responsible for the moon's eclipse: see Gow on Theocritus 2.36.

23 The translation adds 'boy' to represent the masculine *misero*, anticipating *puero* at 27.

24 A memorable *sententia*, cf. 1.5.43-4.

27 **tamen** here can be translated 'though', cf. Virgil *Eclogue* 1.27 *Libertas, quae sera tamen respexit inertem* and Housman on Lucan 1.333.

28 Another *sententia*, cf. 1.5.58.

29 This *nec* answers the one that begins the paragraph; for its position second in the sentence see Platnauer 95.

30 **molli frigida:** Cairns 94 quotes Paulus Festus 347 in Lindsay's Teubner edition '*rigidum* et praeter modum frigidum significat et durum'.

31-32 Cf. Theocritus 15.130 'The kiss does not prickle; golden down is still about his lips' (of Adonis).

34 **Reges** can be used of patrons (e.g. Terence *Phormio* 70 and 338) and rich men (e.g. Horace *Odes* 2.14.11).

36 **et ... sinus:** 'and continuously joins tender embraces'. The phrase is parallel with *timet* and describes the boy's reaction during the encounter. A slight contradiction may be felt with *timet* but both timidity and impetuosity are characteristic of youth — cf. *anhelanti* (37). To read *conserere* would cause an elision unparalleled in Tibullus (Platnauer 89) and would leave *dum timet* isolated. For *consero* = 'joins', cf. 26. For *sinus* = 'embrace', cf. 30. The closeness of the expression to phrases of the type *manus* and *pugnam conserere* = 'join battle' leads smoothly into the military image of *pugnantibus* in 37.

For an alternative explanation of the phrase = 'keeps pulling together the tender folds «of his *toga praetexta* or tunic»' — i.e. as a gesture of timidity, see Cairns 104-5; an idea he later backs up by reference to vase-paintings in *Vichiana* XII (1983) 75-7.

39 **lapis ... gemmaeque:** samples of the *opes* of 34.

44 The green outer skin of the walnut (Pliny *Natural History* 15.87).

45 There may be an implicit contrast with the lover's *cura*, e.g. Virgil *Eclogue* 10.22 *tua cura Lycoris* and *CIL* 4.7679 *Marcellus Praenestinam amat et non curatur*.

46 Pliny mentions mastic gum (*Natural History* 24.43); Juvenal a dough plaster (6.462).

48 **utere:** possibly as at 1.5.75.

49 One is probably meant to remember 1.4.81 *Eheu, quam Marathus lento me torquet amore*. The tables are turned on Marathus but the *magister amoris* is not vindictive.

50   Cf. 29 *det munera canus amator.*

uetus miles is not *senex miles*; one could translate 'aged veterans'.

51   Cf. Festus p.464 in Lindsay's Teubner edition '*<sontica> causa dicitur a morbo <sontico, propter quem quod est> gerendum agere <desistimus>*'. The pun here is obscure to us, but perhaps means roughly 'his is not a grave illness'.

52   **lūto:** 'with yellow'; distinguish *lŭtum* 'mud'.

53   Murgatroyd convinces me that *Vel* is to be read here. It gives an example of Marathus' *nimius amor*; see *OLD s.v.* 4(b) quoting Terence *Hecyra* 60 *uel hic Pamphylus iurabat quotiens Bacchidi.*

58   It gives best point to take *nec* here as 'not even' with *oscula rapta*; see *OLD s.v.* 2 (b).

59   The trouble with *quamuis* is that it goes awkwardly with *media*, 'however much in the middle of the night'. Therefore read *quauis* or *quouis* with Kraffert.

64   Francken's correction makes the couplet dependent on *quid prosunt artes...?* The MS reading makes it an oddly detached statement. One could get round that difficulty by taking it as part of the *si* clause which begins at 61. But if Tibullus had meant that, surely he would have written *seu* for *uel?*

67-70   Surely this passage compels us to take the poem as a dramatic monologue?

67   **non frangitur illa:** cf. Publilius Syrus *Sententiae* 128 (Loeb) *crudelis lacrimis pascitur, non frangitur.*

68   I.e. you are spoiling your good looks, cf. Catullus 3.17-18 *tua nunc opera meae puellae/ flendo turgiduli rubent ocelli.*

69   The girl's name is at last revealed. It is also found at Horace *Odes* 1.33.9 (see Nisbet and Hubbard).

70   Understand *fastidienti* from *fastidia* in 69.

73   **dolentis:** genitive, of the lover, cf. 2.3.77-8 *nulla exclusura dolentes/ ianua.*

76   **opposita:** understand *illi* from 75.

77   Logically *et* is better here than *at*; see Lee 55.

9

This poem too can most effectively be taken as a dramatic monologue, in which the poet again, as in Poem 8, addresses two characters — this time a boy and an elderly married man — present with him in person, though nameless. The poet is in love with the boy and accuses him of faithlessness: the married man has bought the boy's love with gifts. Three female characters are mentioned, all nameless: a young girl, whose love affair with the boy the poet has furthered; the elderly husband's young wife, who herself has a young lover; and the same husband's drunken and promiscuous sister. What is the relation of this elegy to the eighth? So as not to spoil things for the reader, further comment is delayed.

2   foedera: poetical plural, for the Catullan *foedus amicitiae*. The expression *dare foedus* 'grant a treaty' is used of the superior party; cf. Sallust *Jugurtha* 104.5 *foedus et amicitia dabuntur* (sc. *Boccho*) *cum meruerit*, and Livy 9.20.8 *impetrauere ut foedus daretur*.

4   Literally: 'yet in the end on silent feet comes Punishment'. Cf. Euripides *Fragment* 979 (Nauck²) 'Justice ... in silence and slow-footed/ marching will some day catch the wicked'; see also Cairns 62.

13   iam: as at 1.1.70-71.

16   For *et* third word in the sentence and first in the second half of the pentameter see 1.3.82 note.

uia longa: cf. 1.1.26. 'The rival intends taking Marathus on military campaign or provincial service (*militia*)' (Lyne 173).

19-20   See Introduction xix.

21   If *ure meum ... flamma caput* refers to branding on the forehead (as it possibly may), there is rhetorical exaggeration.

24-28   It is not clear who this mysterious god is; perhaps Amor. Cf. 1.5.20 note.

25   Muretus' *saepe* (scribes would write it *sepe*) at least gives unobjectionable sense; Camps points to 2.5.34 *pulla* for confusion of *l* and *s*, and to 2.1.58 *oues* for confusion of *u* and *p*. Rigler's *lingua* is also good, the hyperbaton bringing out a contrast with *inuitos* in 28. Many editors print *lene*, but it is hard to believe that *lene* could be used adverbially with a verb such as *permisit*. For contexts in which the neuter adjective is so used see K-S 1.281. *laeue* (= *leue*) seems unlikely (see *OLD laeuus* 4 (b)) and to call *deus 'lena'* is surely intolerable here.

32   pondere: for the ablative of price see Woodcock §§86-87.

33   Noted for its fertility; cf. Pliny *Natural History* 3.60 *felix illa Campania*.

34   Cf. Isidore *Etymologiae* 20.3.6 *Falernum uinum uocatum a Falerna regione Campaniae, ubi optima uina nascuntur*.

36   G's reading, *puras fulminis esse uias* 'that the thunderbolt's path is clear', may be right.

37   at ... doctus: hyperbaton for *at ego non doctus fallere*. Cf. Callimachus 193.30 (same situation) 'I was honourably educated'.

41   uerbis ... conscius: cf. 1.7.48 *conscia cista sacris*.

42   The job of a slave.

47   For the full meaning of *attonita* see *OLD attonitus* 2 (c) 'spell-bound', 3 'inspired' and 4 'crazy'.

48   For a defence of *ei mihi* see Lee 55.

49-50   **uelim ... torreat:** for this idiom see Woodcock §130.

   deleat: quite literally — 'delete'.

53-54   **te ... rideat:** contrast *ridere* with dative, e.g. Virgil *Eclogue* 4.62 *qui non risere parenti*.

   inulta: for *impune*.

59   The poet has been addressing the husband, so *soror* is probably *his* sister, cf. 2.6.37-8; Catullus 12.6-7 *non credis mihi? crede Pollioni/ fratri*, and 66.21-2 *et tu non orbum luxti deserta cubile,/ sed fratris cari flebile discidium*; also Virgil *Eclogue* 8.37-8 *saepibus in nostris paruam te roscida mala/ (dux ego uester eram) uidi cum matre legentem.*

60   **emeruisse:** 'It may well ... hint at *meretrix*' (Murgatroyd).

61   **ducere:** 'prolong', cf. Lucretius 3.1087-8 *nec prorsum uitam ducendo demimus hilum/ tempore de mortis.*

62   Literally: 'till Lucifer's rising wheel call forth the day'. *rota* suggests both the Morning Star's chariot and his disc (as Dr Robert Buttimore pointed out to me). For the high-flown description of dawn in a satiric passage cf. Horace *Satires* 1.5.9-10.

63   **consumere** 'spend' hints also at her extravagant 'consumption' of alcohol; one could take *noctem* in the sense of a lover's 'night', cf. Propertius 2.20.25 *nec mihi muneribus nox ulla est empta beatis.*

64   An arch reference to the positions of sexual intercourse.

66   **ab arte:** cf 1.5.4.

68   **denso ... dente:** Cairns 93 points out an etymological connexion according to Varro *De Lingua Latina* 5.113.

69-70   **persuadet** here takes a directly dependent subjunctive (i.e. without *ut*), cf. 84 below *sis ... rogat. Que ... et* links the two subjunctive clauses like Greek *te ... kai*, cf. 1.1.35-6.

70   **apta** is not elsewhere found with clothing, as Murgatroyd points out. The unusual expression probably invites sarcastic emphasis here.

71   **bella:** the colloquial word, only used here by Tibullus; this puts the word in inverted commas, cf. *apta*.

73   Literally: 'Nor does she do this wrongly', cf. Cicero *De Diuinatione* 1.29 *cum uitio nauigassent, uitio* being a term from augury (see Pease on the Cicero passage).

74   **culta** also refers to her turn-out, cf. Propertius 1.2.26 *uni si qua placet, culta puella sat est.*

75   I go back to the MS reading. If *hic* and *illi* at 1.7.34-5 can refer to the same person, why shouldn't *huic* and *hunc* in this line refer to different people?

77-78 The sigmatism probably expresses anger here, cf. Wilkinson 54.

81-82 Literally (taking the subjunctives as potential rather than optative or jussive): 'But then your punishment would delight me, and a golden palm-branch, deservedly hung up to Venus, would mark my fortune'. In the translation the future makes the statement too definite, perhaps.

83 The possibility of taking *fallaci* with *tibi* is difficult to reproduce in English; I have done my best.

84 I.e. 'asks that in gratitude she give me another love and make him grateful'.

Everyone agrees that the boy in this poem is Marathus and the girl Pholoe, as in Elegy 8, but we have Cairns 152 to thank for the elegant suggestion (so obvious *once it has been made*!) that the husband is the *canus amator* of Elegy 8, that his young wife is Pholoe and that her 'young man' is Marathus. Murgatroyd has shrewd things to say about the poet's mixed feelings and about the humorous contrast of his appearing as *magister amoris* and greenhorn in successive poems. Lyne is interesting on Tibullus's 'sacrifice of dignity and freedom for love of *a boy*'.

10

This attractive, but in some respects untypical, elegy has often been regarded as the earliest in the book, as it contains no reference to either Delia or Messalla. On the other hand, it has been argued that since the poem so clearly pairs with the first elegy it must have been designed as the final poem in the collection (which of course does not necessarily follow, for the first might equally well have been designed to pair with this). It is worth remarking that of its thirty-four hexameters no less than eighteen have a weak caesura in the third foot, viz. 9, 15, 19, 25, 27, 37, 39, 41, 43, 45, 49, 51, 53, 55, 59, 63, 65 and 67. This is a very high proportion, the next highest being in Elegy 6 with fifteen out of forty-three, followed by Elegy 3 with twelve out of forty-seven. This feature, characteristic of the hexameter in Greek verse, may suggest that technically the elegy is experimental. It is also unique (if we discount the prayers to the Lares and to Peace) in lacking the dramatic appeals to other characters that are so typical of Tibullan elegy. It can in fact be thought of as a more general meditation on Tibullan themes, arising from the thought *nunc ad bella trahor* and employing a technique of repetition of key words and phrases (see Introduction xii-xiii) perhaps even more pervasively than in other elegies where the same technique is found.

1-2 A variant of the curse on the inventor: cf. 1.4.59-60 note. The existing phrase *ferus et ferreus*, already found in Cicero *Ad Quintum Fratrem* 1.3.31, is given fresh point in the ferrous context. See also Cairns 99.

1 Despite Quintilian's statement at *Institutio Oratoria* 10.1.11 that there is no difference in meaning between *ensis* and *gladius*, Axelson 51 shows that *ensis* is the more poetical word.

3 The translation takes *hominum* pointedly (see *OLD s.v.* 2), as contrasting too with *feras* in 6.

6 **in:** 'against', *OLD s.v.* 22 (b).

dedit: cf. Horace *Odes* 3.6.47-8 *nos ... mox daturos/ progeniem uitiosiorem.*

7-8 Cf. Plato *Phaedo* 66c 'It is in order to get money that all wars are made'.

uitium: Janice M. Gilmartin 234 observes that this word is also used of 'dross', comparing Ovid *Fasti* 4.785-6 *omnia purgat edax ignis uitiumque metallis/ excoquit.* So there is possibly a pun here.

scyphus: Tibullus's point in using this Greek loan-word is lost on us.

9 The translation assumes (perhaps wrongly) that *somnum petere* in this military context recalls *pacem petere.*

10 Spotted fleeces were bad (Varro *Res Rusticae* 2.2.4). In primitive days we are to suppose the profit motive did not operate and there were neither sheep-breeders nor sheep-thieves; spotted was as good as pure white.

The reading *sparsas*, though poorly supported by our MSS, is favoured by some editors. But suppose it had been the original: how, in a context where it so clearly meant *dispersas*, could it possibly have been glossed by *uarias*? More probably it arose either by a curious misreading of *uarias* or by the need to supply an adjective in a MS where *uarias* had inadvertently been omitted, or by quotation from memory.

11 The emendation *Valgi* is uncertain. Anyhow, C. Valgius Rufus, who later held the consulship in 12 BC, was a writer of elegies whose judgement of poetry Horace respected (*Satires* 1.10.82) and who is praised as an epic poet at [Tibullus] 3.7.181. Two pastoral hexameters of his are quoted by a scholiast on Virgil *Georgics* 3.177; their tone is in harmony with this elegy.

tristia: Cairns 104 sees an implicit allusion to *civil* war; this would mean interpreting *aerata* in 25 as André does (see the note below).

13 **trahor:** for the lengthening of *-or* in arsis at the caesura see Platnauer 59.

15 **et** really goes with *aluistis*, cf. Ovid *Metamorphoses* 1.2 *nam uos mutastis et illas.*

18 Closer: 'so shaped you dwelt of old in my grandfather's place'.

23 **atque:** 'yes, and', cf. 2.4.47 and *OLD s.v.* 2.

25-26 A pentameter and a hexameter must have been missing in the archetype between these two lines, in which the poet promised the Lares a thank-offering if he survived.

25 J.H. Voss saw a reference in *aerata* to the copper mined by the Aquitani (Caesar *De Bello Gallico* 3.21.3) and dated the poem accordingly. Postgate in his *Selections* takes it more simply as implying barbarian enemies. André notes that in epic poetry weapons are generally bronze.

26 Though *rustica* goes with *hostia*, *porcus* despite the masculine ending may be feminine, see *OLD s.v.* 1. If so, 'gilt' is a possible translation.

27 **myrto:** cf. Horace *Odes* 3.23.15-16 *paruos coronantem marino/ rore deos fragilique myrto.*

32 **miles:** 'as a soldier'.

pingere castra: Putnam hears an implicit reference to *ponere castra.*

33 **accersere:** see *OLD arcesso* 1 (b).

35 **infra:** i.e. *apud inferos.*

36 **audax** is rather unexpected and looks like a literary allusion. The sound of the adjective, emphatically placed at the line-ending, suggests barking in this context. The *nauita* is Charon, who on payment of an obolus ferried the dead man's spirit across the river Styx.

37 **percussis genis:** because the dead are behaving like mourners. The reading *pertusis* has probably come from *subtusa* in 55.

39-40 The contrast is with those *qui militari laude antecellunt* (Cicero *Pro Murena* 24). Cf. 1.1.57 *non ego laudari curo. Piger* is a word of military disapproval (see L&S).

39 For *quin potius* introducing a question 'why not rather' cf. Virgil *Aeneid* 4.99. Some editors prefer the less well supported *quam potius* 'how rather' here. But *quam potius* at *Copa* 6 means 'than rather'; moreover at *Panegyricus Messallae* 130 original *quin* has been corrupted to *quam* by several MSS, so too by one at line 136 there.

40 Or: 'old age slowly overtakes'. There is perhaps an implied contrast with the sudden death on the battlefield of a young man with no children.

43 Perhaps as opposed to the warrior *aere caput fulgens* (Virgil *Aeneid* 10.869).

44 Contrasts with 31.

45-46 **colat:** both 'abide in' and 'cultivate' (Camps).

candida: see *OLD s.v.* 4, 5 and 7.

araturos: etymologically connected with *arua* (Cairns 93). *curua* chimes pleasantly with both.

49-50 Cf. Bacchylides *Fragment* 4.31-4 (in praise of Peace): 'On the iron-bound handles of shields are shining spiders' webs. Rust overpowers sharp-pointed spears and two-edged swords'. And cf. 1.1.4 note. See also Cairns 103-4.

51 A couplet has possibly dropped out after 50, as Moritz Haupt suggested (*Opuscula* 3.38ff.), because the switch to the drunken peasant is sudden and could be eased by supposing mention of a festival. This lacuna could have been on the verso of a leaf in the archetype, corresponding with the certain lacuna between 25 and 26. Most editors however take *at ... situs* parenthetically and 51 as a continuation of 49 *pace ... nitent*.

e lucoque counts as one word and *que*, though very rarely postponed in either half of the hexameter, is sometimes found attached to the second word of the clause (see Munro on Lucretius 2.1050). Alternatively, just possibly it might be a hyperbaton for *uxoremque*.

53-64   There is probably a criticism of this passage in Propertius 2.5.21-6, as Solmsen has argued in *Philologus* 105 (1961) 273ff. This enables one to date the publication of Tibullus's first book between 25 September, 27 BC, the date of Messalla's triumph, and 25 BC, the probable date of Propertius Book 2.

53   **Veneris bella:** cf. 1.1.75. For the idea of *militia amoris* see Murgatroyd *Latomus* 34 (1975) 59ff. and Lyne 71-8.

54   **conqueriturque:** for postponed *que* at this point in the pentameter cf. 1.1.40.

55   **subtusa:** 'somewhat bruised', only found here; cf. *subustus* 'singed'

58   'The construction of this verse mirrors its sense, with *lentus* occupying the pivotal position between the combatants. Emphasizing the couple's estrangement is the grammatical separation of *inter* from its object; cf. Lucretius 3.860 *inter enim iecta est uitai pausa*, which dramatically depicts the sudden and complete severing of human consciousness at death' (Gilmartin 241).

59   Rhymes interestingly with *utrumque* and *ferrumque*.

60   For the beloved as Goddess cf. Catullus 68.70 *mea ... candida diua* and Lyne 308 n.20.

62   For *ornatus* of hair-style cf. Ovid *Ars* 3.135 *nec genus ornatus unum est* etc.

64   **quo ... irato:** ablative absolute, analogous to *quo consule, me inuito.* There is no need to emend to the dative *quoi.*

65   **sudis** is another word for *uallus* (cf. 9 above), the stake carried by every Roman legionary, cf. Cicero *Tusculans* 2.37.

66   **sit procul:** religious and poetical, cf. 2.5.88, Virgil *Aeneid* 6.258 *procul, o procul este profani*, and I Maccabees 8.23 *gladiusque et hostis procul sit ab eis* (sc. *Romanis et Judaeis*).

68   **ante:** adverbial, 'in front' or 'forward'.

BOOK TWO

1

The first elegy dramatises, on the analogy of Callimachus *Hymn* 5 (also in elegiac couplets), the events of the day of a festival known to Cato as *lustratio agri* (*De Agri Cultura* 141), or the purification of the land, but to modern scholars as the private Ambarvalia, said to have been celebrated annually in May: a ritual circumambulation of the fields, which has a parallel, perhaps a remote continuation, in the Rogation ceremonies of the Christian Church. The dramatisation is selective but includes the morning proclamation of a holy day, the procession behind a sacred lamb, prayer, sacrifice, inspection of entrails, drinking of wine and of the absent Messalla's health, hymn to the country gods and to Cupid, followed by noisy dancing till nightfall. For more detailed interpretation of this fine poem Musurillo is helpful, but the best discussion of its complications will be found in Cairns 126-34.

1 **faueat:** sc. *lingua*, cf. Seneca *Dialogus* 7.26.7 (on *fauete linguis*) *hoc uerbum non, ut plerique existimant, a fauore trahitur sed imperat silentium ut rite peragi possit sacrum, nulla uoce mala obstrepente.*

3 Bacchus is often represented with horns on coins and in works of art; they symbolize strength and fertility.

9 **operata:** cf. 2.5.95 *operata deo pubes.* For evidence that *deo* is dative in this idiom see *OLD operatus* 2.

non audeat: for *non* instead of *ne* in a prohibition see Woodcock § 109 note (ii).

10 **imposuisse:** for this perfect infinitive where one would expect the present see note on 1.1.29-30.

11 **discedat:** there is a slight anacoluthon after *uos*, but cf. the note on 1.6.39-40 *colit.*

13 **casta:** cf. Cicero *De Legibus* 2.19 *ad diuos adeunto caste.*

15 **fulgentes:** sc. *igne*, see *OLD fulgeo* 1 (b).

19-20 The prayer here is that the crop (*seges*) should not cheat the harvest (*messem*) with young growths (*herbis*) that prove deceptive (*fallacibus*) and do not fulfil their promise. For the contrast between *herba*, the young green corn (*OLD herba* 4), and *seges*, the mature crop, cf. Ovid *Remedia Amoris* 84 *ualidos segetes, quae fuit herba, facit* (sc. *mora*). If in the early stages the young growth becomes too luxuriant then the final crop can be damaged, cf. Virgil *Georgics* 1.111-2.

21 **nitidus:** hard to translate, see *OLD s.v.* 3, 5 and 6.

22 **ligna** is 'firewood'; 'timber' *materies.*

24 **casas:** cf. Horace *Satires* 2.3.247 *aedificare casas*, of a children's game.

25 **Euentura:** cf. 1.5.57 *eueniet: dat signa deus.*

27-28 It was believed that smoke in moderation matured wine more quickly (Columella *De Re Rustica* 1.6.20). The Chian would be mixed with the Falernian (cf. Horace *Satires* 1.10.24).

Falernos: sc. *cados* from *cado* in the next line.

29 **madere:** cf. Plautus *Mostellaria* 331 *madet homo* 'the man's tight'.

30 **rubor:** more lively than *pudor.*

31 **bene Messallam:** sc. *ualere iubeo.* Cf. Plautus *Stichus* 709 *bene uos, bene nos, bene te, bene me, bene nostram etiam Stephanium!*

ad pocula: cf. Cicero *Pro Caelio* 67 *ad uina diserti sint* 'at wine'.

32 **singula uerba:** literally 'every utterance', as Fletcher explains, comparing Livy 8.30.13 *alternis paene uerbis T. Manli factum laudantem.*

33 **triumphis:** rhetorical plural as at 1.7.5; see Quintilian *Institutio Oratoria* 9.3.20.

34 According to Varro the Romans started shaving in 300 BC (Pliny *Natural History* 11.211).

victor: 'as conqueror'.

35 We are used to Virgil and Horace addressing Octavian as a god (e.g. *Georgics* 1.24-42), but it comes as a surprise when Tibullus does the same to Messalla, much as it illuminates the social set-up in the Roman world at the time. One can imagine Cato the Censor's comment.

39 **tigillum** is a diminutive of *tignum*, cf. *sigillum.*

41 **feruntur:** there may well have been some prose source for the history of the development of civilisation sketched in this hymn to the country gods.

47 **sideris:** of the sun, see *OLD s.v.* 2 (c), and 1.5.22 *sole calente.*

49 Strangely enough from Aristotle onwards classical writers assert that bees carry flowers. See Gow on Theocritus 7.81.

leuis could go with *flores* and *uerno* with *alueo.* For the scansion of *alueo* see Platnauer 68.

52 There is a pun on *pede* if he dances while he sings; cf. 1.7.37-8.

53 **satur** after *satiatus* seems to be making a point and looks like an etymological reference to *satura*, cf. Livy 7.2.7.

55-58 There seems to be a fusion here of the Aristotelian theory of tragedy's origin in the dithyramb (*Poetics* 1449a) and the later idea that the name tragedy arose because a goat (*tragos*) was the prize for the best singing (*ode*). See Brink on Horace *Ars Poetica* 220.

56 **ab arte:** cf. 1.5.4.

58 The scribe of the archetype looked ahead and inadvertently replaced an adjective with an anticipation of *hircus*; he has made this sort of mistake more than once, see 1.1.54 *exiles*, 2.1.34 *ades*, 2.2.15 *undis*.

66. The weights which keep the warp tight are made of brick (*later*). For an account of all the technicalities see Postgate's excellent note in *Selections*.

a: causal here, *OLD s.v.* 15. *appulso* was perhaps due to the unconscious influence of *apposito* in the pentameter above.

68   **dicitur:** we don't know by whom. This is the first mention of this tradition, which re-appears in *Peruigilium Veneris* 77 *ipse Amor puer Dionae rure natus creditur*. Tibullus may have got the idea from Virgil *Georgics* 3.209-41 (*armenta*) and 266-83 (*equae*).

74   **limen ad iratae:** for this word-order see Platnauer 97.

76   G's *in tenebris* is unnecessary, cf. 1.2.25 and 1.6.59.

77   'Tiptoe' because of the suggestion in this context of *suspenso pede*, cf. Phaedrus *Fabulae* 2.4.18 (of a cat) *inde euagata noctu suspenso pede*.

80   **afflat:** cf. 2.3.75 *quibus aspirabat Amor*.

81   **Sancte:** see Introduction xviii-xix.

83   I punctuate like A after *uocate*, because the sense is then complete and it would not occur to anyone reading aloud to continue to *uoce*. For *uoce palam* cf. Cicero *Verrines* 5.41 *omnium palam ... uoce damnatus est*.

86   **tibia curua:** for a picture of this see Rich *tibia* 6. The 'Phrygian sound' was orgiastic, cf. 1.4.70.

87-88   Cf. Aeschylus *Choephori* 660 'Hurry, for Night's dark chariot hastens on', Euripides *Ion* 1150-51 'Black-robed Night shook her yoke-drawn/ car and stars accompanied the goddess' and Theocritus 2.166 'The stars that follow still Night's wheel'.

89   For *circumdatus* 'flanked' Camps compares Livy 30.19.8 *hinc patre, hinc Catulo lateri* (sc. *Seruilii*) *circumdatis*.

2

A birthday poem (*genethliakon*) for the poet's friend Cornutus, to whom the third elegy in this book is also addressed. If at the time of its writing he was an Arval Brother (see note on 9 below), then according to Scheid he is not likely to have been younger than forty.

For the structure of the poem as an example of 'ring-composition' see Cairns 204. It is an elegant piece of Tibullan 'occasional' verse.

1   For Natalis see 1.7.63 note.

2   **lingua ... faue:** see note on 2.1.1 *faueat*.

4   **tener:** cf. Catullus 11.5 *Arabasue molles*.

diuite: cf. Pliny *Natural History* 5.65 'Beyond Pelusium is Arabia, extending to the Red Sea and to the Arabia known by the surname of Blest and famous for its perfumes and wealth' — *ad ... odoriferam illam ac diuitem et Beatae cognomine inclutam.*

5   For the Genius see 1.7.49 note. Maybe the image of the Genius would be carried from the Lararium to the scene of the birthday ceremonies. The nodding in line 10 would then not be pure fantasy; cf. Ovid *Amores* 3.2.58 where the statue of Venus is being carried in procession and a tilt of the head is taken as a nod.

For the lengthening of the last syllable of *Genius* in arsis at the caesura see Platnauer 59. Tibullus could have written *adsit Genius*, but that would involve an homoeoteleuton of successive words which (apart from final *a* e.g. *callida turba*, *mala uerba* etc.) he usually avoids.

6   **decorent:** jussive subjunctive.

7-8   This couplet is very like 1.7.51-2. The assonance of *illius* and *destillent* seems to be paralleled in the pentameter by *atque* and *madeatque*. For a discussion of the possibility of reading *ille* for *atque* see Lee 56.

9   **Cornute:** identified by Cichorius (*Roemische Studien*, Leipzig (1922) 264) and Scheid (13ff.) with the M. Cornutus who appears with Messalla Corvinus in an inscription of the Fratres Arvales dated about 21/20 BC (*CIL* 6.32338).

11   'A wife's': alternatively 'the wife's', as many interpret. I am with those who read the line as implying that he is *not* married (though he may have a fiancée).

auguror: paratactic as in English 'I augur you will choose', cf. the frequent use of *credo, opinor, puto* thus. By its etymology (*au* from *aui*) the word looks forward to *auis* in 21.

15   **gemmarum quicquid:** cf. 1.1.51 *quantum ... auri.*

17   **Vota cadunt:** not 'your prayers are granted' as most commentators take it, since this would be illogical before *utinam*, but rather 'your prayers are made'. For *cado* in the sense of 'fall from one's lips', 'be uttered' of words and prayers see *OLD* 14. Cornutus finally makes his request, as Tibullus had asked him to do in 10.

utinam ... aduolet: the poet prays for the epiphany of winged *Amor* to grant his friend's request for marriage.

18   For saffron or yellow as a colour connected with marriage see Catullus 61.8-10 where the Marriage-God wears the *flammeum* or flame-coloured veil of the bride and yellow slippers.

21-22   Text and interpretation uncertain. Keeping A's reading, *hic* would refer to *Amor* and *ueniat* would repeat the wish for his epiphany made in 17-18. *hic* would also be the subject of *ministret. Natalis* would be vocative of the God this wish is addressed to, and *auis* would be dative plural of *auus*. Other interpretations are possible, including changing *hic ueniat* to *eueniat* and taking *auis* as nominative singular 'bird' = 'omen', but on the whole A's text can be made to give tolerable sense and should be retained.

22   Cf. 1.10.15-16.

3

The tone of this second elegy addressed to Cornutus is light-hearted and *galant*, as immediately appears from the second couplet, is underlined by the wit at Apollo's expense and confirmed by the sheer fantasy of line 69 to the end, in particular by the last couplet where the *eques Romanus* is keen to turn ploughman and even prepared to join a chain-gang of convicts. Evidently the revision of Tibullus's familiar attitude to the country is not exactly serious. Evidently too the deification of Nemesis the gold-digger has somewhat cheapened the poet's Muse, though his verse is more elegant than ever. As regards content the poem is unique for Tibullus in containing a full-scale mythological *exemplum* and a miniature diatribe against *Praeda*. He is experimenting, and the experiment is chiefly interesting as an anticipation of the light verse of Ovid, who must have been about twenty at the time. The detailed studies by Gaisser and Whitaker are worth consulting; for the poem's structure in comparison with that of 2.4, its pair, see Cairns 209-12.

3   **ipsa Venus:** 'a compliment to (the still unnamed) Nemesis' (Putnam).

4   **uerbaque aratoris rustica** perhaps implies the contrast *uerba amatoris urbana*.

5   For this use of *cum* where one might expect *si* consult L&S 2 *cum* V.1.

8   **dum subigunt:** it was unusual to retain the present indicative with *dum* in an unfulfilled condition.

11ff   This is by far the longest of the very few mythological illustrations in the work of Tibullus and clearly has a Greek poetical source behind it. One notices the Alexandrian treatment (Apollo's love for Admetus is first mentioned in Callimachus *Hymn* 2.49), exploiting paradox and incongruity and describing the technique of cheese-making in detail (cf. the detailed description of spinning in Catullus 64.311-19). See also Cairns 120f. and 154.

11   Cf. Virgil *Eclogue* 10.18 *et formosus ouis ad fluminua pauit Adonis.*

12   **profuĕrunt:** for the shortening of *e* see Platnauer 53.

15   It is customary to number this line and 17-18 as 14a, 14b, 14c; my numbering also includes a missing pentameter. Therefore add 4 to all references to this poem in other books from their line 15 on.

17   The subject must be *deus* with the verb *dicitur* or *fertur* understood from the missing pentameter. At 18 the subject suddenly changes to *liquor*. With *mixtis* understand *coagulis*.

21   'Any country boy knows that neither gods nor men can carry a calf ... and retain their dignity' K.F. Smith.

22   'His sister' is Diana.

23   **caneret:** another recherché construction with *dum*.

24 **carmina docta:** Apollo, god of poetry, is a *doctus poeta*, cf. 1.4.61 note. It is difficult to make this point in English, so the translation substitutes another — the implied play on 'moos' and 'Muse'.

28 Juno was Apollo's stepmother (*nouerca*).

31 Delos, the island where Apollo was born, and Delphi were the chief centres of his cult; Pytho was the name of the district round Delphi.

35-36 A difficult couplet. I take *fabula* as at 1.4.83. Alternatively: 'Apollo is a fable now, but he who loves his girl/ prefers the god to be a fable rather than <real and> without love'; but people *did* believe in Apollo then, notably Augustus. Moreover it is *not* true, as some have maintained, that verbs of wishing, preferring etc. *must* take the infinitive when the wisher is also subject of the wish clause; e.g. Cicero *Pro Cluentio* 198 *uellem ... possem* (not *posse*) and, even clearer, Cicero *Ad Atticum* 8.9.4 *aiebat nihil malle Caesarem quam ut Pompeium adsequeretur* (sc. *Caesar*), and a line or two later *scribit nihil malle Caesarem quam principe Pompeio sine metu uiuere*.

37-38 I assume the poet slightingly addresses his rival and use Camps's translation of 38. For this metaphorical *castra* see Propertius 4.8.27-8. For *domus* from the point of view of man and mistress cf. Isidore *Etymologiae* 9.4.3 *est autem domus ... coniunctio uiri et uxoris*. Or the house will be that of Nemesis, cf. Ovid *Amores* 3.8.63-4 *me prohibet custos, in me timet illa maritum;/ si dederim, tota cedet uterque domo*.

39-40 This couplet leaves *tu* (37) hanging and for this reason a lacuna seems likely after 38.

ferrea and *Venerem* echo 2 *ferreus* and 3 *Venus*.

40 **operata:** 'is engaged in' personifies *Praeda*.

42 **Mors propiorque:** *que* is not misplaced here but joins *propior* closely to *Mors*, making it clear that the adjective is not predicative with *uenit*.

48 As *iugis* already has an adjective, perhaps *mille* could go (irregularly) with *columna*, collective singular, 'a thousand column'.

51-52 Samian and Cumaean ware was elegant but relatively inexpensive.

I agree with Dissen in taking this couplet as addressed to Nemesis. Then in 53-4 the poet suddenly sees that the opposition he set up in 39 between Venus and *Praeda* is false if, as he implied in line 3, Nemesis is Venus, and having seen this he changes tack accordingly.

57 **tenues:** Tibullus may have written the other form *tenuis*, see note on 1.4.26.

63-64 **Vota:** cf. 1.5.36 note.

Slaves on sale from abroad had their feet coated with chalk as a distinguishing mark (Pliny *Natural History* 35.199). When on the platform in the market they would have to mark time at the double to prove their physical fitness to prospective buyers.

65-66 Alternatively read:

> At tibi dura seges, Nemesim qui abducis ab urbe,
> persoluat nulla semina certa fide
>
> But you, the kidnapper of Nemesis from Rome,
> may hard ground pay you treachery for trusty seed

taking *seges* as the field in which the seeds of corn are sown and reading *certa* for *terra* with the *recentiores*.

71   ne ... modo: usually *modo ne*, see *OLD modo*[1] 4, but cf. Cicero *Academica* 2.87 *denique uideantur sane, ne adfirmentur modo*.

73   amarunt: the so-called 'syncopated' form of *amaverunt*.

75-76   Cf. 33-4; also Apollonius *Argonautica* 3.396-7 'On thee neither Cypris (i.e. Venus) nor the gentle Loves breathe friendly'.

79   A hexameter was omitted in the archetype, something like *quin etiam, modo sint admissi, rursus amantes* 'what's more, provided they're admitted, let lovers again ...'.

80   I.e. like early man dressed in the skins of animals. For *uilli* 'fur' cf. Pliny *Natural History* 7.2.

81   nunc: 'As things are now'.

82   Literally: 'Alas, what help to a wretched lover that his toga is roomy (unrestricted)?' *Miser* is almost the technical term for a lover, e.g. Lucretius 4.1075-6. This line may perhaps have given rise to *cultuque corporis observabilis* in the *Vita Tibulli*, for a *toga laxa* was the sign of a dandy; see 1.6.39-40 note. Ovid's description of Tibullus as *cultus* at *Amores* 1.15.28 and 3.9.66 may also have helped, see *OLD cultus*[1] 3.

4

What does it feel like to be a Roman poet infatuated by a beautiful but grasping courtesan? This elegy attempts an answer. It is interesting that Postgate and K.F. Smith thought very highly of it. 'I should agree with Mr Postgate' writes the latter 'that as an expression of genuine feeling it has no equal in the work of Tibullus.' For my part, I should certainly rate it higher than the third and the sixth elegies in this book. The tone is more harmonious and the various emotional outbursts are for the most part credibly handled, lines 7-12 being particularly impressive and 45-50 memorably appealing. But 21-2 strain belief and so too does the witch's brew of the conclusion — not however so grossly as to make the reader laugh or ruin his pleasure in the poem as a whole.

1   Literally: 'Yes (*OLD sic* 5a), I realize that slavery and a mistress have been planned (*OLD paro* 8) for me.' He could also be saying: 'that slavery and a mistress have been bought (*OLD paro* 3 and 4) by me (dative of the agent)'; in the second case *datur* in line 3 would be as at *OLD do* 6b.

3   sed: qualifies *triste* 'and harsh too'; *OLD sed* 3.

teneorque catenis: plays on an etymology of *catena*, see Cairns 95. These *catenae*, like the *seruitium*, are metaphorical; contrast *uinclis uerberibusque* at 2.3.80.

6   Nemesis is identified with Amor and his burning torch; at the same time there is a reference to the punishment of a slave by branding or burning.

8   For *quam* 'how' cf. 1.4.81.

10   **tunderet unda:** if Cairns 96 is right, in addition to the onomatopoeia there is etymological play.

uasti: missing in the archetype, but a very likely supplement on the part of the Guelferbytanus.

11   **amara** fits well after –*a maris*.

12   A's *nam* is feeble; *iam* is an attempt to improve it. Trouble probably arose from confusion of the abbreviations for *nam* and *nunc* through attraction of the *am* of *amara* just above.

13   **nec prosunt elegi** for *nec elegi prosunt*.

17   I.e., didactic poetry such as the *Phaenomena* of Aratus.

orbem: both 'orb' and 'orbit'; *OLD s.v.* 6 and 15.

20   Plays on the other meaning of *carmina*, 'incantations'.

22   **flebilis:** first here in the active sense; see Cairns 109.

24-26   Cf. *CIL* 4.1824 *quisquis amat ueniat. Veneri uolo frangere costas/ fustibus et lumbos debilitare deae./ si potest illa mihi tenerum pertundere pectus,/ quit ego non possim caput illae frangere fuste?*

25   **rapacem** gives point to *rapiam* in 23 (Gilmartin).

26   **sacrilegas** refers in its literal meaning 'stealing sacred objects' to line 23, and in its usual meaning to 24 (Gilmartin).

27   **legit:** etymological connexion with *sacrilegas* (Gilmartin).

uiridesque: the *que* really goes with *legit* (see Platnauer 92) and is kept short before *sm* as at 1.1.51.

31   **clauim:** this recherché form is vouched for here by the fourth-century grammarian Charisius.

33-34   Cf. Antipater of Thessalonica (*Anthologia Palatina* 5.30.3-4) 'For if you bring the coin, friend, no keeper stands in the way, no dog is chained at the front door'. Gow and Page date this epigram as later than Tibullus, however. Cf. 1.6.58 note.

38   The archetype's *hic* must have arisen from confusion of the abbreviations for *nunc* and *hic*, abetted by *hinc* and *haec* in 37.

For *esset* where one might expect *sit* see Woodcock §140 note.

42   **nec quisquam ... sedulus:** possibly 'and no guileless person'. The adjective was formed from the adverb *sedulo* which in its turn came from *se dolo* 'without deceit' (see Ernout-Meillet *dolus*).

43 For the reading *heu* see Lee 57 and for the confusion with *seu* cf. app. crit. at Horace *Epistles* 1.3.33.

44 The archetype's *obsequias* is medieval Latin; this reading might enable one roughly to date the archetype.

45 I.e. *at quae bona fuit et non auara ...*

47 **ueneratus:** for the use of perfect participles of deponent verbs in a present sense see Woodcock §103.

'The possible pun here, on the etymological connexion of *ueneror* with Venus, appears as early as Plautus *Rudens* 1349' (Putnam).

48 **constructo ... tumulo:** literally 'the heaped-up burial-mound', The implication seems to be that the lover caused the mound to be made — in other words, paid for her decent burial (contrast 44).

50 The common formula was *sit tibi terra leuis*, so *securae* here would probably be felt as dative rather than genitive.

52 Also *colendus amor*, in the other sense; cf. *colere amicitiam*.

54 **titulus** is the placard advertising the sale, cf. Ovid *Remedia* 302 *sub titulum nostros misit auara Lares.*

sub imperium is not so clear. Dissen has an excellent note, finally agreeing with Voss in understanding *illius* from 54 and comparing 2.3.79 *ad imperium dominae.*

55 Circe is the divine witch of the *Odyssey*, who turned Odysseus' comrades into swine. For Medea see 1.2.53 note.

56 Cf. Apuleius *Metamorphoses* 2.1: 'Thessaly, celebrated by the concordant voice of all the globe as birthplace of the magic art's cantillations.'

58 For more about mares and *hippomanes*, the reputed aphrodisiac first mentioned by Aristotle, see Virgil *Georgics* 3.266-83.

59 **placido ... uultu:** cf. Horace *Odes* 4.3.2-3 (of his Muse) *Quem tu, Melpomene, semel/ nascentem placido lumine uideris.*

60 To get the effect of the Latin asyndeton before *mille* (*'dissolutio' uocatur apta cum quid instantius dicimus* Quintilian *Institutio Oratoria* 9.3.50) simply omit 'and' in the English translation.

misceat: jussive subjunctive, representing an 'if' clause.

Dissen sums up the last section of the poem memorably: 'Offert se totum puellae in omne obsequium.'

5

In this his longest and most ambitious elegy Tibullus celebrates the induction of Messalla's son Messallinus into the priestly college of fifteen members known as the *Quindecimuiri*; it was the duty of this college to guard the

Sibylline Books and to consult them when the Senate thought fit. There is inscriptional evidence for Messallinus as the junior member of the college in 17 BC (*CIL* 6.32323.152).

The poet's affection for pre-Aenean pastoral 'Rome' is evident, also his belief that in his own day the Palilia reflected the simple happiness of that early time. Nevertheless, 'barbarous Turnus' in 48 implies that Aeneas brought civilisation to Italy. Moreover, although the recent Civil Wars are hinted at as something monstrous and against Nature, there is no implied condemnation of the murder of Remus or of war *per se*. Indeed, lines 57-62 express unqualified pride in the might of the Roman empire and 115-18 imply the hope that its profitable conquests will be extended.

For an illuminating analysis of the poem's 'ring-composition' see Cairns 204-7, who also draws attention to the repetition of *Phoebe* at 1, 17, 65, 106 and 121, *Amor* at 39 and 106, *laurus* at 5, 63, 83 and 117, and to the mention of long hair at 8, 66 and 121, and the symmetrical placing of *triumphali* at 5 and *Triumphe* at 118. Clearly the elegy is intricately wrought in detail; as a whole it is a fine example of Tibullan poetry. For an interesting study with full bibliography see Merklin.

1-10 Tibullus probably has in mind the statue of Apollo Citharoedus by Scopas (fourth century BC) which Augustus had placed in his temple of Apollo on the Palatine (Pliny *Natural History* 36.25 and Suetonius *Augustus* 29). For the importance of Apollo to Augustus see Liebeschuetz 82-5.

4 It is possible to keep the reading of the archetype: 'bend words to my praises <of you *or* of Messallinus>', but *meas* in this context is tactless, to say the least. Lachmann's *mea* is the simplest correction; original *mea* here would very easily become *meas* because of the frequent rhyming of adjective and noun at middle and end of the pentameter.

6 **ad tua sacra** could also go with *cumulant*; *OLD ad* 32.

8 **sepositam:** 'set apart' for special occasions.

9-10 See notes on 1.3.35 and 49. *memorant* may indicate a particular Greek poetical source, now lost.

11-12 Cf. Paulus Festus p.2 L *Augur ab auibus gerendoque dictus, quia per eum auium gestus edicitur.*

15-16 According to Dionysius of Halicarnassus *Roman Antiquities* 1.55 the Sibyl who prophesied to Aeneas (see 19 below) was the one at Erythrae on Mt Ida; she later migrated to Cumae and sold the original Sibylline Books of oracles in Greek hexameter verse to Tarquin the Proud (see Lactantius *Diuinae Institutiones* 1.6.10 and 13).

The translation of 16 imports a contrast not explicit in the Latin between 'Greek' and 'Romans'. Alternatively, 'in six dactylic feet'.

18 The archetype's 'of whom she sings' is possible, but the Sibyl does not sing of people only; perhaps the scribe's eye glimpsed *raptos* in 20 or *deos* in 22, which caused him to write *quos* for *quid*.

19-22 The Sibyl's prophecy to Aeneas begins at line 39; in between comes a long parenthesis on the early site of Rome, perhaps derived from Varro's *Antiquitates*.

raptos ... Lares: cf. Virgil *Aeneid* 1.378-9 *sum pius Aeneas raptos qui ex hoste Penatis/ classe veho mecum*, where *ex hoste* makes all clear. It is possible that Tibullus heard Virgil reciting parts of the *Aeneid*; it is also possible that both poets were drawing on a common source. For the use of *rapio* in a good sense cf. Livy 27.32.6 *raptus ab suis atque alteri equo iniectus fugit* and Livy 4.28.4.

For discussion of where the Sibyl gave her oracle to Aeneas see Cairns 75-6.

23 **aeternae ... urbis:** the first appearance of this famous phrase; see K.J. Pratt 'Rome as Eternal' *Journal of the History of Ideas* 26 (1965) 25-44 (ref. from Putnam).

formauerat: 'planned' *OLD s.v.* 5c and 'shaped' ibid. 5a.

24 Romulus killed Remus for insulting him by jumping over the wall of his new city (Livy 1.7).

25-26 Cf. Paulus Festus p.245 L *Palatium id est mons Romae, appellatus est quod ibi pecus pascens balare consueuerit, uel quod palare, id est errare, ibi pecudes solerent*. Tibullus seems to be rejecting *balare* but accepting *pascens* and *palare* (the latter by implication from *uagi pastoris* in 29 and perhaps also from the contrast between *pascebant* and *stabant*). He also seems to be connecting Pan and Pales with Palatium. For all this see Cairns 80-1.

27-28 The Greek nature God Pan was identified with the Latin Silvanus, referred to as *siluestri deo* in line 30. For Pales see 1.1.36 note and Cairns 79-80.

lacte madens: cf. 1.1.36.

illic ... ilicis: assonance continues in the pentameter.

29-30 **uotum:** 'as a votive offering'.

garrula: literally 'prattling'.

33-34 The Velabrum lay between Palatine and Tiber

Cf. Varro *De Lingua Latina* 5.156 *quod ibi uehebantur lintribus Velabrum*. So here *uecta* (36) and *linter* (34). See further Cairns 81.

35-36 **placitura:** 'likely to please'; contrast 51 where it means 'destined to please'. For this way of taking it see Merklin 305 n.14. The Latin triangle of girl, true love and rich lover was there before Aeneas arrived.

39 Both Aeneas and Cupid were sons of Venus.

40 The trisyllabic ending could have been avoided: *qui ratibus profugis Troica sacra uehis*.

41-42 Aeneas landed at Laurentum, a few miles below Ostia. It looks as though Tibullus is connecting *Laurentes* with *Lares errantes*.

hospita: literally 'hospitable' and also 'foreign'; *OLD hospita²* 1 and 3.

43-44   The Numicus (modern Rio Torto) runs into the sea between Ostia and Anzio.

Cf. Livy 1.2.6 (of the dead Aeneas) *situs est (quemcumque eum dici ius fasque est) super Numicum flumen: Iouem indigetem appellant.* Dionysius of Halicarnassus *Roman Antiquities* 1.64.5 describes the tomb as a small mound surrounded by rows of trees and worth seeing.

45-46   *super ... uolitat* and *superba* must be intentional word-play; cf. Isidore *Etymologiae* 10.248 *superbus dictus quia super uult uideri quam est.* "When Victory has not decided which side to favour, she flies between the combatants; Ovid *Met.* 8. 13 'inter utrumque uolat *dubiis* Victoria pennis'" Postgate (*Selections*).

47-48   Turnus, chief of the Rutuli, fought Aeneas for the bride Lavinia whom King Latinus, her father, had previously promised to him (Livy 1.2.1).

50   Ascanius *alias* Iulus was Aeneas's son.

52   Ilia was the mother of Romulus and Remus by Mars. The priestesses of Vesta, Roman Goddess of the Hearth, had to be virgins; their duty was to keep the sacred fire in her temple burning.

It has been maintained that lines 39-54 imply knowledge of Virgil's *Aeneid* on the part of Tibullus. This is unlikely for the following reasons: (i) the *Aeneid* does not associate the death and deification of Aeneas with the river Numicus; (ii) there is no mention in the *Aeneid* of a fire in the Rutulian camp; (iii) the story of Ilia is referred to at *Aeneid* 1.273-4 but Tibullus's version has details that derive from another source.

53   **furtim**: cf. 1.3.50 note.

56   **iam**: 'very soon', cf. 1.1.70-71 and 1.9.13 (a usage not noted in *OLD*).

57   **tuum nomen**: 'In Greek it was *Rōmē* = Power' Camps.

Understand *est* with *fatale; terris regendis* is dative, cf. Cicero *Catiline* 3.9 *fatalem hunc annum esse ad interitum huius urbis* (another Sibylline context).

59-60   Literally: 'and where the Orient extends and where in flowing waves/ the River washes down the Sun-God's panting steeds.'

amnis: of Oceanus, the great river thought to circle the earth; cf. Varro *De Lingua Latina* 5.28 *amnis id flumen quod circuit aliquod; nam ab ambitu amnis.*

61   Rome was New Troy.

66   I.e. *et iactauit fusas comas ante caput.*

67-70   The list of Sibyls probably derives from Varro, who is quoted by Lactantius in *Diuinae Institutiones* 1.6. The text here is uncertain and it looks as though something has dropped out between 70 and 71. *Phoebo grata* is unsatisfactory because that would surely be true of all ten Sibyls; and, *pace* Cairns 77, if Tibullus had intended an etymological comment on *Herophile* (= dear to Hera) surely he would have made it clear by writing *Phoebo cara*? For Phoeto (= Gk *Phoito*) as a variant of Phyto, the name of the Samian Sibyl that would not scan here, see Karl Mras *Wiener Studien* 28 (1906) 44 (reference from Cardauns).

71-78 These describe the portents following the murder of Julius Caesar, doing in elegiacs what Virgil had done on a grander scale in hexameters at *Georgics* 1.466-88.

71 **haec:** here feminine, for the more usual *hae*; see K-H 601.

72 **ut:** 'how'.

deplueretque: for the imperfect subjunctive representing the future in past indirect speech, 'was to', see Woodcock §181. There is the usual displacement of *que*; see note on 1.1.40 *composuitque*.

75 **defectum lumine:** 'deserted by his light', *OLD deficio* 2a. The phrase doesn't *have* to mean 'in eclipse'; he could be shining very wanly, obscured by cloud.

79 Surely we need the perfect, not the pluperfect? At 3.11.4 the archetype read *dederant* as here *fuerant*, but *dederant* is demonstrably wrong there. The corruption would be due to a 'knowledgeable' scribe who thought that the third person plural of the aorist must always scan *-ērunt* and who accordingly corrected, or even unconsciously read, *-ĕrunt* as *-ĕrant*. See Housman 1068-9 and 2.3.12 note.

81 The text is doubtful; this would, 1 believe, be the only example of exclamatory *ut* in Roman elegy, though it occurs at Virgil *Eclogue* 8.41 *ut uidi, ut perii, ut me malus abstulit error!* — a rather special imitation of Theocritus. However, it is good Latin, as can be seen from L&S *ut* I.A.2.

82 The archetype read *sacer*, but surely this is pointless repetition after *sacris* in 81? The flames on the altar are always sacred, whether they produce a good or a bad omen. I assume, as Cornelissen must have done, that the scribe with *satur* before him was unconsciously influenced by *sacris* above it and wrote *sacer*; there is virtually only one letter's difference between the two nominatives, *c* and *t* being so frequently confused.

83 **ubi ... dedit:** 'for generalizing clauses in the present, the perfect indicative is the usual tense' Woodcock §217.2(c).

87 For the Palilia see 1.1.36 note, and Ovid *Fasti* 4.721ff.

festa: plural of the noun *festum*.

88 **concinet:** *TLL* compares Horace *Odes* 4.2.41-2 *concines laetosque dies et Vrbis/ publicum ludum.*

89 **leuis:** with *stipulae*, cf. Virgil *Georgics* 1.368 *leuem paleam.*

92 Cf. Plautus *Poenulus* 375 *sine te exorem, sine prehendam auriculis, sine dem sauium* 'let me persuade you, take you by the ears, give you a kiss'. K.F. Smith's note on what he calls 'the jug-kiss' makes entertaining reading.

93 **aduigilare:** literally 'watch over'. A reference to baby-sitting?

94 **balba ... uerba:** there is a tiny example at Persius 3.16-18 *cur non potius .../ ... pappare minutum/ poscis et iratus mammae lallare recusas?* 'Why not rather demand to have your din-din mashed/ And angrily refuse to go bye-byes for mummy?' Strictly speaking, the *balbus* is unable to pronounce certain consonants properly, especially *l* and *r*.

97   Closer: 'or of their clothes stretch canopies ...'.

100   Closer: 'with turf a table and with turf a couch.'

102   Or: 'that later with fervent prayers he may wish annulled' Camps.

103   **suae:** cf. 1.4.75 *pareat ille suae.*

105   **Pace tua:** because Phoebus Apollo was the god of archery; see *Homeric Hymn* 3.131 'let cithara be dear to me and crooked bow'. The common idiom (see *OLD pax* 3) may be meant quite literally here, Apollo's peace being the peace that Actium (where he had a temple) brought in.

110   Leo's *quin* is attractive here. For the confusion see 1.3.14 where all MSS offer *cum* and all editors print *quin*; cf. note on 1.6.21.

112   **iustos:** the adjective is also understood with *uerba* (the so-called apo koinou or 'in common' construction), cf. Propertius 2.20.19 *quodsi nec nomen nec me tua forma teneret* where *tuum* is understood with *nomen*. For more examples see K-S 2.559.

113-14   Cf. Ovid *Amores* 3.9.17 *at sacri uates et diuum cura uocamur.*

115-16   Literally: 'when as prizes of war/ before his chariot he shall carry conquered towns.' Floats representing the towns took part in the triumphal procession.

117-18   Camps takes *ipse* with *miles* in the sense of 'too' (*OLD ipse* 6), thus: 'His troops too bearing bay, with wild bay garlanded.' Probably *agresti* is apo koinou (see note on 112 above). Cf. Paulus Festus p.104 L *Laureati milites sequebantur currum triumphantis ut quasi purgati a caede humana intrarent Vrbem.*

6

The six couplets about Nemesis's dead sister are undoubtedly the finest section of this poem, but their genuinely elegiac tone hardly harmonizes with the jaunty and 'Ovidian' opening (1-14) — at least for modern taste. The praise of Hope is also well done, but again its witty conclusion jars against the sudden seriousness of 29ff. At 44 we are surprised by the intrusion of a *lena*, though the other poems in the Nemesis cycle give the impression that she operates on her own. It is disappointing that Tibullus's distinguished work should end with flawed distinction, but if we think in particular of lines 29-40, Ovid's tribute remains true: *auxisti numeros, culte Tibulle, pios.*

Cairns 185-7 is illuminating on the unexpected changes of direction in the elegy. Murgatroyd (1989) gives a good account of the structure and unity of the poem.

1   This may be the Pompeius Macer to whom Ovid addresses *Amores* 2.6 and *Ex Ponto* 2.10, as Cartault 60 suggested.

quid fiet: strictly 'What will happen to ...', *OLD fio* 12a.

2   **sit ... gerat:** deliberative subjunctive, Woodcock §172.

Postgate (*Selections*) compares Plautus *Trinummus* 595-6 *actumst de collo meo/ gestandus peregre clupeus, galea, sarcina.*

3   **terrae uia:** Camps compares 1.9.8 *terrae opus.*

6   **erronem:** anyone, usually a slave, absent without leave; the military term appears to have been *emansor.*

7   **hic:** probably the adjective, not the adverb, used like *hic homo* in Comedy to refer to the speaker; for the evidence see *TLL* 6.2703.40-66 — *OLD* omits a key passage viz. Cicero *Brutus* 71.

8   **leuem ... aquam:** cf. Horace *Epode* 16.38 *leuis crepante lympha desilit pede.*

10   **et mihi facta tuba est:** the usual expression would be *et mihi facit tuba* 'does for' in the sense of 'suits'; *OLD facio* 29b.

11   He certainly lays it on thick here; one thinks of a character in comedy.

14   **cum bene iuraui:** cf. Ovid *Amores* 3.8.7 *cum bene laudauit, laudato ianua clausa est.*

19-20   Cf. Theocritus 4.41-2 'Cheer up, friend Battus. Perhaps tomorrow will be better. There's hope for the living; only the dead have none.'

The trisyllabic ending could have been avoided by the order *et melius cras fore semper ait.*

23-24   Does this couplet suggest that Hope can be a bad thing? For birds and fish, perhaps, but what Tibullus is saying is that Hope can also be crafty.

ante cibus: 'food in front', cf. 1.3.50 *repente.*

25-26   Slaves were sometimes sent as a punishment to work on the land in chain-gangs, a practice which Pliny in *Natural History* 18.36 deplores.

27-28   Hope and Nemesis are similarly opposed in an anonymous Greek epigram of unknown date (*Anthologia Palatina* 9.146): 'I, Eunous (= Well-wisher), have wrought Elpis (= Hope) and Nemesis beside the altar, the one, that you may hope, the other, that you may get nothing.'

27   **spondet:** also plays with the idea of betrothal; Hope makes Nemesis his *sponsa.*

negat: also 'refuses her favours', *OLD s.v.* 3c.

28   **deam:** Hope had temples in Italy from the time of the First Punic War on (*KP* 5.304).

31   **sancta:** 'vocantur *sancti* piorum manes' Dissen; cf. *OLD s.v.* 3c.

32   Cf. Catullus 101.9 *accipe fraterno multum manantia fletu.*

33-34   'The slave of Love (cp. 17 ...) like other slaves when driven desperate by cruel usage, will take sanctuary and appeal to the higher powers' K.F. Smith.

34   Cf. Catullus 101.4 *et mutam nequiquam alloquerer cinerem*; *cinis* is usually masculine.

35   **suum ... clientem:** 'her dependant'; the dead girl is the poet's *patrona.*

36   'The *ut* here is appropriate because the dead sister has not literally given him this request to communicate; he asks for it to be received "as if" from her' Camps.

For *sis ... ueto* cf. 1.2.26 *nec sinit occurrat.*

37   **neglecti:** Gilmartin sees here a secondary implication that Nemesis has neglected her sister's grave. This is an attractive idea and would give further point to 31-2, but does it square with *dominae luctus acerbi* (41)?

39   **infernos ... lacus:** cf. 1.10.38.

41   **Desino:** for the shortening of final *o* see Platnauer 51-2.

43   **oculos ... loquaces:** K.F. Smith compares Meleager (*Anthologia Palatina* 12.159.3-4): *kai kophoisi laleunta/ ommata* 'eyes that speak even to the deaf', which Tibullus would probably have read.

45   **uetat:** surely it's unnecessary to emend to *necat*?

Phryne is the Greek word for toad

46   *tuncque* looks like an error in cursive script where *it* was read as *tc* (= *tunc*).

47   A's *diro* was probably due to *limine* next door.

49   **nox:** cf. note on 1.9.63 *noctem.*

54   **pars quotacumque:** 'however small a part', 'a fraction'.

BOOK THREE

In the MSS this Book contains twenty poems, all except the first six and the last one connected with Tibullus's patron Messalla. The disconnexion of Poems 1-6 caused fifteenth-century scholars to split the Book in two and refer to Poems 7-20 as Book 4.1-14. This division is unnecessary and the present edition will follow the MSS numbering.

3.1-6, in elegiac couplets addressed to a girl named Neaera, are the work of a poet who calls himself Lygdamus, presumably a pseudonym, though Propertius has a servant of that name. The poet's identity has aroused much scholarly speculation and readers who wish to pursue the question are referred to Harrauer and Dettmer. Whoever he is he writes attractive verse, developing conventional themes in an agreeably personal way — witness the instructions for his funeral in 3.2.

3.7, in 212 dactylic hexameters, is a eulogy of Messalla entitled *Laudes Messallae* or, according to Scaliger who had access to a fragmentary MS now lost, *Panegyricus Messallae*. The poem, dated by Momigliano to 31 BC, the year of Messalla's consulship, and by Schoonhoven to 27 BC, the year of his Triumph *ex Gallia*, is an interesting example of the laudatory verses that prominent Roman public men expected to receive from their dependent poets. It lacks the elegance of Tibullus's authentic celebration of Messalla's Triumph in 1.7 and it is difficult to believe that he wrote it. The author is at his best in the opening paragraph and in lines 106-18.

3.8-18 in elegiac couplets concern the love of Sulpicia, a relative of Messalla (3.14.5-6), and a young man she calls Cerinthus, a name which is also found at Horace *Satires* 1.2.81. At 3.16.4 she refers to herself proudly as 'Servius's daughter' and the general opinion is that this Servius is the son of the famous jurist Servius Sulpicius Rufus, Cicero's friend. Her mother may well have been Valeria (Jerome *Aduersus Iouinianum* 1.46), Messalla's sister, which would make her the great man's niece. It is extraordinary that this aristocratic Roman girl should use her real name while addressing her lover by a pseudonym. In fact she is boldly following the practice of male love poets, who write under their own name but use a pseudonym for the object of their love. Another oddity about these poems is that the five elegies 3.8-12, sometimes known as *Sulpicia's Garland*, are written alternately in the third and the first person. Thus 8, 10 and 12 are spoken by an unnamed poet, whereas 9 and 11 are put into the mouth of Sulpicia herself. The *Garland* is followed by six epigrams written by Sulpicia (3.13-18). These are by far the best poetry in the Book, the work of a highly intelligent, emotional, and independent person. For full discussion and illuminating appreciation one should read Currie and Hinds.

Next comes an elegy of twenty-four lines supposedly written by Tibullus, whose name appears in line 13. The poem is not without charm but some rather clumsy reminiscences of Propertius and Ovid make Tibullan authorship unlikely (see Postgate and Lee).

The Book ends with a four-line epigram of neat construction and effective point, whose author may well be Tibullus.

THE EPITAPH

In the 1570s Scaliger had access to a fragmentary MS, now lost, which began at 3.4.65; in it this epigram was attributed to Domitius Marsus. For the best discussion of what *Vergilio comitem* means here see McGann.
Line 2 refers to 1.3.58.

THE LIFE

Suetonian parallels are as follows: *Nero* 20.3 *insignes ... coma*; *Julius* 45.3 *cultu notabilem*, 50.2 *ante alias dilexit*, 42.1 *contubernalis*; *Augustus* 8.1 *militaribus donis ... donatus est*; *De Grammaticis* 23.1 *principem locum inter grammaticos tenuit*; *Nero* 57.1 *obiit*; *De Grammaticis* 16 *quod etiam uersiculus Domiti Marsi indicat*. For *elegiographos* cf. the parallel formation *mimographos* in *De Grammaticis* 18.

The 'amatory epistles' are usually taken to be poems 8-12 in Book 3, though in fact there is nothing to indicate that these poems are letters; they are short elegies, like 2.2, or epigrams; moreover, echoes of Ovid's *Metamorphoses* and *Fasti* prove that they cannot be the work of Tibullus (Fuchs provides the evidence). It seems more likely that the epistles in question have not survived.

CHRONOLOGICAL GUIDE

BC
?55   Birth of Tibullus. Death of Lucretius.
?54   Death of Catullus.
53   Crassus defeated by the Parthians at Carrhae.
49   Caesar crosses the Rubicon.
48   Caesar defeats Pompey at Pharsalus.
45   Cicero *Tusculan Disputations*.
44   Murder of Caesar. Cicero *De Officiis*.
43   Birth of Ovid. Murder of Cicero.
42   Antony and Octavian defeat Brutus and Cassius at Philippi. Messalla surrenders to Antony.
40   Pollio's consulship. Virgil *Eclogue* 4.
?38   Virgil *Eclogues*. Gallus *Amores* published by this date.
?35   Horace *Satires* 1.
31   Messalla's consulship. Octavian defeats Antony at Actium.
30   Horace *Epodes* and *Satires* 2.
?29   Virgil *Georgics*. Propertius 1.
27   Octavian receives title of Augustus. Messalla's Triumph. Death of Varro.
?26   Tibullus 1. Suicide of Gallus.
?25   Propertius 2.
?23   Horace *Odes* 1-3. ?First edition of Ovid *Amores* 1.
?21   Propertius 3.
20   Settlement with Parthia.
19   Death of Virgil. Horace *Epistles* 1.
?18   Death of Tibullus. Publication of Tibullus 2.

SELECT BIBLIOGRAPHY

ABBREVIATIONS

ANRW   *Aufstieg und Niedergang der römischen Welt* ed. H. Temporini and W. Haase. Berlin 1972—

CIL   *Corpus Inscriptionum Latinarum.* Berlin 1863—

K-H   Kühner R.–Holzweissig F. (1912). *Ausführliche Grammatik der lateinischen Sprache.* Vol. 1 *Wortlehre.* 4th edn Hanover (reprint Darmstadt 1966)

KP   *Der Kleine Pauly: Lexikon der Antike* ed. K. Ziegler. 4 vols. Munich 1964-1975

K-S   Kühner R.–Stegmann C. (1914). *Ausführliche Grammatik der lateinischen Sprache.* Vol. 2 *Satzlehre.* 4th edn Hanover (reprint Darmstadt 1971)

L&S   Lewis C.T. and Short C. (1879). *A Latin Dictionary.* Oxford

OCD   *The Oxford Classical Dictionary* ed. N.G.L. Hammond and H.H. Scullard. 2nd edn Oxford 1970

OLD   *Oxford Latin Dictionary.* 1968—

PCPhS   *Proceedings of the Cambridge Philological Society*

TLL   *Thesaurus Linguae Latinae.* Leipzig, 1900—

Where the works listed below are referred to in the Notes, it is usually by author's name alone or by author's name and date.

André J. (1965). *Tibulle. Elégies, Livre Premier.* Paris

Axelson B. (1945). *Unpoetische Wörter.* Lund

Baehrens E. (1878). *Albii Tibulli elegiarum libri duo.* Leipzig

Barsby J.A. (1974). 'Propertius' polysyllabic pentameters' *Latomus* 33.646-53

Bright D.F. (1978). *Haec mihi fingebam: Tibullus in his world.* Leiden

[Broukhusius J.] (1708). *Albii Tibulli ... quae extant.* Amsterdam

Bulloch A.W. (1973). 'Tibullus and the Alexandrians' *PCPhS* n.s. 19.71-89

Cairns F. (1974). 'Some observations on Propertius 1,1' *Classical Quarterly* 24.94-110

—. (1979) [=Cairns]. *Tibullus, a Hellenistic poet at Rome.* Cambridge

Calonghi F. (1928). *Albii Tibulli aliorumque carminum libri IV.* Paravia, Turin

Campbell C. (1973). 'Tibullus: Elegy I,3' *Yale Classical Studies* 23.145-57

Camps W.A. (1970). *A commentary on Tibullus I and II.* Unpublished typescript with Mr Camps at Pembroke College, Cambridge

Cardauns B. (1961). 'Zu den Sibyllen bei Tibull 2,5' *Hermes* 86.357-66

Cartault A. (1909). *Tibulle et les auteurs du Corpus Tibullianum.* Paris

Copley F.O. (1956). *Exclusus Amator*. Philological Monographs published by the American Philological Association 17

Currie H. MacL. (1983). 'The poems of Sulpicia' *ANRW* II.30.3.1751-64

Delatte L. (1967). 'Key-words and poetic themes in Propertius and Tibullus' *Revue de l'Organisation internationale pour l'étude des langues anciennes par ordinateur*. Liège. N° 3.31-80

Dettmer H. (1983). 'The Corpus Tibullianum (1974-1980)' *ANRW* II.30.3. 1962-75

Dissen L. (1835). *Tibulli carmina*. Göttingen (reprint Hildesheim 1969)

Elder J.P. (1962). 'Tibullus: Tersus atque elegans' in *Critical Essays on Roman Literature: Elegy and Lyric* ed. J.P. Sullivan. London. 65-105

Ernout A.-Meillet A. (1967). *Dictionnaire étymologique de la langue latine*. 6th edn Paris

Fletcher G.B.A. (1965). 'On Tibullus and other poets of the Corpus Tibullianum' *Latomus* 24.45-51

Fuchs H. (1947). Review of L. Alfonsi *Albio Tibullo e gli autori del Corpus Tibullianum, Erasmus* 1.340-3

Gaisser J.H. (1971). 'Structure and tone in Tibullus I,6' *American Journal of Philology* 92.202-16

— (1971). 'Tibullus 1,7: a tribute to Messalla' *Classical Philology* 66.221-9

— (1977). 'Tibullus 2,3 and Vergil's Tenth Eclogue' *Transactions of the American Philological Association* 107.131-46

Gilmartin J.M. (1975). *The structure of the poems in Books I and II of the Corpus Tibullianum*. Typewritten dissertation in Cambridge University Library

Harrauer H. (1971). *A bibliography to the Corpus Tibullianum*. Hildesheim

Heilmann W. (1959). *Die Bedeutung der Venus bei Tibull unter besonderer Berüchtsichtigung von Horaz und Properz*. Typewritten dissertation, Frankfurt am Main

Heyne C.G. (1798). *Albii Tibulli carmina*. 3rd edn Leipzig

Hinds S. (1987). 'The poetess and the reader: further steps towards Sulpicia' *Hermathena* 143.29-46

Housman A.E. *Collected classical papers* ed. J. Diggle and F.R.D. Goodyear. Cambridge 1972

Lee A.G. (1963). 'On Tibullus 3.19' *PCPhS* n.s. 9.4-10

— (1974) [=Lee]. 'Tibulliana' *PCPhS* n.s. 20.53-7

— (1974). 'Otium cum indignitate: Tibullus 1,1' in *Quality and Pleasure in Latin Poetry* ed. A.J. Woodman and D.A. West. Cambridge. 94-114

Lenz F.W. and Galinsky G.K. (1971). *Albii Tibulli aliorumque carminum libri tres*. Leiden

Liebeschuetz J.H.W.G. (1979). *Continuity and change in Roman religion*. Oxford

Littlewood, R.J. (1970). 'The symbolic structure of Tibullus Book I' *Latomus* 29.661-9

Luck G. (1964). *Properz und Tibull: lateinisch und deutsch.* Zurich
— (1969) [=Luck]. *The Latin love elegy.* 2nd edn London

Lyne R.O.A.M. (1980). *The Latin love poets.* Oxford

McGann M.J. (1970). 'The date of Tibullus' death' *Latomus* 29.774-80

Merklin H. (1970). 'Zu Aufbau und Absicht der Messalinus-Elegie Tibulls' in *Festschrift K. Büchner.* Wiesbaden. 301-14

Momigliano A. (1950). 'Panegyricus Messalae and Panegyricus Vespasiani. Two references to Britain' *Journal of Roman Studies* 40.39-41

Murgatroyd P. (1980). *Tibullus I: a commentary.* Pietermaritzburg

Musurillo H. (1975). 'Tibullus II,1 reconsidered' in *Festschrift J.M.-F. Marique.* Worcester, Massachusetts

Naiden J.R. (1938). 'A note on the Panegyricus Messalae 40-44' *Classical Philology* 33.92-6

O'Neil E.N. (1963). *A critical concordance of the Tibullan Corpus.* Ithaca, New York

Palmer R.B. (1977). 'Is there a religion of love in Tibullus?' *Classical Journal* 73.1-10

Passeratius J. (1608). *Commentarii in Catullum, Tibullum et Propertium.* Paris

Pfeiffer R. (1968). *History of Classical Scholarship from the beginnings to the end of the Hellenistic Age.* Oxford

Platnauer M. (1951). *Latin elegiac verse.* Cambridge

Ponchont M. (1967). *Tibulle et les auteurs du Corpus Tibullianum.* Budé, 6th edn Paris

Postgate J.P. (1880). 'On the genuineness of Tib. IV 13' *Journal of Philology* 9.280-6

— (1914). *Tibullus* in *Catullus, Tibullus and Pervigilium Veneris.* Loeb, London and New York

— (1922). *Selections from Tibullus.* 2nd edn revised, London

— (1924). *Tibulli aliorumque carminum libri tres.* 2nd edn corrected, Oxford

Putnam M.C.J. (1973). *Tibullus: a commentary.* Norman, Oklahoma

Rich A. (1884). *A dictionary of Greek and Roman antiquities.* 3rd edn revised and improved, London

Scheid J. (1975). *Les frères Arvales.* Paris

Schoonhoven H. (1983). 'The Panegyricus Messallae. Date and relation with Catalepton 9' *ANRW* II.30.3.1681-1707

Schuster M. (1930). *Tibull-Studien.* Vienna (reprint Hildesheim 1968)

Smith K.F. (1913). *The elegies of Albius Tibullus.* New York (reprint Darmstadt 1964)

Solmsen F. (1961). 'Propertius in his literary relations with Tibullus and Vergil' *Philologus* 105.273-89

Valpy A.J. (1822). *Albii Tibulli opera omnia ex editione I.G. Huschkii.* Delphin and Variorum Classics, London

Voss J.H. (1811). *Tibullus und Lygdamus nach Handschriften berichtiget.* Heidelberg

Vretska K. (1955). 'Tibulls Paraklausithyron' *Wiener Studien* 68.20-46
Whitaker R. (1979). 'The unity of Tibullus 2,3' *Classical Quarterly* 29.131-41
White K.D. (1975). *Farm equipment of the Roman world.* Cambridge
Wilkinson L.P. (1963). *Golden Latin artistry.* Cambridge
Williams G. (1968). *Tradition and originality in Roman poetry.* Oxford
Woodcock E.C. (1959). *A new Latin syntax.* London
Yardley J.C. (1978). 'The elegiac Paraclausithyron' *Eranos* 76.19-34